GETTING BACK to WORK

The Tools for Tough Times project received a grant from the Office of the Secretary of State, Washington State Library as a part of the Renew Washington Project, which is funded by the Bill & Melinda Gates Foundation and the Institute of Museum and Library Services.

SNO-ISLE
LIBRARIES

WHAT READERS ARE SAYING ABOUT THIS BOOK

"Change and the accompanying emotions come unexpectedly. This manual shows readers how to position themselves in the best possible way to effectively manage career change. The examples are some of the best available. If you are in job search or unexpected work transition, you should not be without this manual. I learned a great deal from the author."
~ Dawn Kruchoski, Human Resources Recruiter, U.S. Cellular

"Your book was a godsend to me. I want you to know that it gave me hope when I truly needed it."
~ CK, Customer Services Representative, U.S. Cellular

"The A–Z guide for getting a job or making a career change, this easy-to-follow book will navigate you through endings and on to new beginnings."
~ Brenda Hawes, M.A., LPC, Certified Employee Assistance Provider and Mental Health Counselor

"I didn't know I could negotiate higher salary and benefits. The strategies in this book increased my earning by thousands of dollars, and I negotiated better work conditions."
~ Heather Atlas, Pacific Retirement Services, Marketing and Sales

"A very good and comprehensive piece of work, especially the chapters about the mature worker and the impact of job change on family and relationships."
~ Byron Hansen, Athletic Trainer, NY Giants

"Your book is EXCELLENT! I recommended it to friends and company co-workers."
~ Karlyn D. Henderson, M.A. Organizational Leadership (formerly with Coca Cola)

"*Getting Back to Work* will become indispensable in your job search."
~ Claire Cross, Director, Southern Oregon University

"I am very impressed by Linda's career transition workbook. She provides solid guidance."
~ Deborah Frierson, Director Human Resource Services, Southern Oregon University

GETTING BACK to WORK

*Everything You Need
to Bounce Back and
Get a Job After a Layoff*

LINDA K. ROLIE

New York   Chicago   San Francisco   Lisbon   London   Madrid   Mexico City
Milan   New Delhi   San Juan   Seoul   Singapore   Sydney   Toronto

The McGraw·Hill Companies

Library of Congress Cataloging-in-Publication Data

Rolie, Linda K.
    Getting back to work : everything you need to bounce back and get a job after a
layoff / Linda K. Rolie.
        p.   cm.
    Includes bibliographical references.
    ISBN-13: 978-0-07-163867-8 (alk. paper)
    ISBN-10: 0-07-163867-9
    1. Job hunting.   2.   Job hunting—Psychological
aspects.   3. Career   I. Title.

    HF5382.7.R65   2010
    650.14—dc22   2009019997

1 2 3 4 5 6 7 8 9 10 11 12 13 14 15 16 17 18 19 20 21 22   QPD/QPD   0 9

ISBN   978-0-07-163867-8
MHID   0-07-163867-9

McGraw-Hill books are available at special quantity discounts to use as premiums and
sales promotions or for use in corporate training programs. To contact a representative,
please Email us at bulksales@mcgraw-hill.com.

This book is printed on acid-free paper.

Contents

About the Author

Linda K. Rolie, M.A., has more than 25 of years experience as a career strategist, professional coach, career counselor, and corporate consultant. As the founder and president of Career Services, she has guided thousands of people from diverse backgrounds to successful career solutions and job placement.

Linda received her master's in Counseling Psychology from Lewis and Clark College and bachelor's from University of Oregon. Linda's career history includes outplacement assistance for organizations faced with layoffs, owning a vocational rehabilitation organization employing counselors and job developers, university career counselor, academic advisor, vocational specialist and return-to-work consultant for national insurance companies, expert vocational witness for litigation/employability determinations, patient relations coordinator, mental health counselor, administrator/ human resources director including recruiting physicians, college psychology instructor, and high school health education teacher.

Linda spent 20 years counseling people with limited skills and mental and physical disabilities before transitioning her services to help highly skilled and motivated job seekers. She decided to "repackage" her services and to write this book to expedite the transitional process of job seekers in career transition. Her background provides broad experience in job hunting, interviewing, placement, assessment, and career development/management. Linda advises clients in job transition and those coping with change. She provides career guidance, employment-related resources, and workshops/seminars to individuals who want to expand their professional growth, increase success, and prosper in their pursuits.

Please visit Linda's website at **www.lindarolie.com**. Also, feel free to contact her by telephone or Email her through the website address link linda@lindarolie .com.

Foreword

Imagine you have been handed your pink slip with two weeks' notice stating that you are no longer needed. What are you going to do now?

You decide to go for a mountain hike. You have some shorts, hiking boots, water, and a protein bar in the trunk of your car and you head off for the afternoon. It's a gorgeous day, the sun is shining and there is not a cloud in the sky. At the mountain, you decide to take the mountain loop. There is quite a bit of pep in your step as you think about your hard work and accomplishments. You are thinking this hike is just what you need to decompress and gain fresh perspective.

You are so engrossed, thinking about employment matters and job search that you lose all track of time. You realize you've been hiking for about two hours. It is getting late, so you decide to turn back. But something feels wrong. You look up and see that the sky is starting to get dark and it appears that a storm is brewing. You notice that the temperature has dropped. You continue to walk for about another hour, and all of a sudden you realize you are no longer on the trail and you are LOST. There is this sick feeling in your stomach and then you think…

What is the one thing you wish you had with you right now?

A GPS—that's right, a Global Positioning System—so you can find your way home. Well, this book, *Getting Back to Work*, is **your** GPS as it is for all job seekers in career transition.

You may not have had any control over a job ending, but you do have control over how you react and the decisions you make. You have a choice about the actions you make this day and into your future. Your success is not an accident. Ask yourself, what have I learned from this ending? How am I going to do things differently the next time? Where will I go from here? How will I get there?

When you read *Getting Back to Work*, you are taking an adventure that empowers you to success. There are no shortcuts! Linda Rolie, M.A., Career Strategist, has masterfully outlined a comprehensive, practical approach to landing that next job as quickly as possible, while assisting you in letting go of the emotions associated with job loss and the job search. She will help you to navigate to a new beginning that, if followed, will yield powerful and life-changing results. This book will challenge you to be the very best you can be.

Jennifer O. Frank
Founder of Career Transitions, Beaverton, OR

Introduction

Easy to follow, this book is the A-Z guide for getting a job. *Getting Back to Work* is a self-help manual for job and career change written for the purpose of educating and preparing job seekers for their career transition endeavors. The primary objective of *Getting Back to Work* is to show readers how to implement the most successful methods for finding suitable employment while maneuvering some of the expected emotions that accompany job transition. The corresponding adage—"Give a man a fish and you feed him for a day. Teach him to fish and you feed him for a lifetime"— parallels the purpose of this "job seekers" book.

Getting Back to Work provides the tools and information to gain confidence and for navigating through endings and new beginnings that result in a satisfying job. Competing against equally qualified candidates for a limited number of job openings in today's tough job market, or figuring out a goal, can be challenging; this book provides realistic information and tools to achieve measurable results.

If you feel as though you have been descending in an elevator toward discouragement or depression, but want to get off at the level of *focus, direction, and confidence,* this book will help. Sometimes you have to go down before you can go up.

This how-to manual was developed for individuals who are voluntarily or involuntarily experiencing job change and career transition. The materials are useful for both beginners in the job market and the high functioning career veteran seeking information about *"packaging" oneself,* including skillful job search strategies. Losing a job or looking for one can feel like being in a free-fall. The tools in this book will provide a parasail for smooth gliding.

The rapidly changing world of work continues to create new opportunities to enter or re-enter the workforce. There are millions of men and women looking for work in virtually every industry and professional field. The number of people displaced from jobs due to dissatisfaction, layoffs, a downturn in the economy, corporate mergers, on-the-job injuries, mental health issues, military transition, and other reasons are astounding. Some people are exploring new career goals while others wish to relocate to a more desirable location, perhaps to be nearer family or for better climate. Whatever your circumstances, my hope for you is akin to marking a dartboard on the broadside of a barn, placing a dart in your hand, and helping you aim as close to the bull's-eye as possible.

> *"Begin with the end in mind."*
> **Stephen Covey**

Getting Back to Work contains nitty-gritty information about how to package oneself and get a satisfying job. This book is designed to walk you through the activities required to get in action and stay in action. It includes chapters with timeless and fundamental job search strategies, supplemented by collective personal and professional experience. It provides checklists, self-evaluation materials, sample resumes and cover letters, examples of salary negotiations, interview tips, mock interviews, and more. Readers who want to make use of winning samples and examples can employ the models and implement clear-cut job search methods. The book concludes with an Appendix filled with resources and sites, including job banks, and education, training, and career information.

This handbook provides the opportunity to:

▸ Use the detailed Index to quickly locate a reference or subject matter. If you have not yet done so, review the Index in the back of the book.

▸ Gain practical and valuable information to improve your success.

▸ Participate in structured activities that produce measurable results.

▸ Understand the impact of a career crisis on relationships.

▸ Gain a sense of mastery and control over your goals.

▸ Discover what it is that you really like to do, you are good at, and the world has a need for—therein lies your vocational calling.

▸ Develop a plan of action and marketing strategy.

▸ Locate employers in your desired locale.

▸ Obtain job description vocabulary.

▸ Complete a master job application form.

▸ Receive individual career coaching.

▸ Identify transferable skills, core competencies, knowledge, abilities, and qualifications.

▸ Use current "corporate speak" language. Identify "power" words.

▸ Learn the most effective job finding method: networking.

▸ Create an informative resume and write a unique cover letter that will get an employer's attention.

- Acquire effective interview techniques; answer the questions an employer is guaranteed to ask.

- Negotiate salary and job offers to get the highest benefits you deserve.

- Analyze job offers and corporate culture before accepting a position.

- Gain resources, references, research methods, Internet sites, and job openings.

- Overcome the overqualified objection.

- Successfully transition as a mid-life/mature worker or Veteran.

In this manual, the words *vocation, career, profession, occupation, job*, and *employment* are used interchangeably. Society imposes implied differences to these terms based on education or income levels, but the steps that accompany finding satisfying work are generally the same for anyone undergoing transition.

The words *employer, interviewer*, and *company* are also used interchangeably throughout this handbook and imply an organization for which a job seeker wants to perform work in exchange for income. Other similar terms include *workforce, labor market*, or *industry*.

Getting Back to Work is a compilation of over 25 years' career counseling and vocational consulting experience. To guide you through a smooth career transition and successful landing, take what you want and leave the rest.

> "I am an old man and have known a great many troubles, but most of them never happened."
> **Mark Twain**

CHAPTER 1

Psychology of Job Change

THE WAY THROUGH ENDINGS TO NEW BEGINNINGS

There is a natural order in the process of loss and change. First, there is the ending and letting go, followed by an empty zone filled with confusion and distress. Then, there is a new beginning. Career transition may include a sense of loss, especially if the circumstances around job change are involuntary. There is often a gap in the trail where one experience ends (say college or a former job) and a new direction begins. People often have a strong identity attachment with a job or work environment. Losing a job or being between jobs can feel like a loss of your identity.

Every loss—whether from the death of a loved one, the loss of a job, or having been the victim of theft—tends to set off a natural process of emotions. The late psychiatrist, Elizabeth Kubler-Ross, M.D., identified five normal stages of loss:

1) Denial, with a response such as, *"This can't be true or isn't fair,"* and a sense of emotional numbness or disbelief about your circumstances or (job) loss.

2) Anger (toward a company or co-workers who kept their jobs). Loss of control can foster feelings of anger.

3) Bargaining (*"If I do XYZ, God will rescue me"*) or rationalizing ("I didn't want that job anyway").

4) Depression—missing the routine of work and friendship of co-workers—when the (job) loss hits home even if you were unhappy there.

5) Acceptance—beginning to think about future opportunities—making an action plan, and moving forward.

> *"One thing I do: Forgetting what is behind—I press on toward the goal."*
> *Philippians 3:13*

EMOTIONS ACCOMPANYING JOB CHANGE

Accepting circumstances and emotions surrounding job change can be challenging. Losing a job, changing jobs, or exploring a career path often causes

> *"Being happy doesn't mean everything is perfect, it just means you have decided to see beyond the imperfections."*
> **Anonymous**

anger, shock, denial, fear, confusion, frustration, doubt, skepticism, stress, guilt, anxiety, and/or depression. You may need to take some time to grieve before you jump into job search activities. It may take a year or more for feelings of grief and anger to dissipate. Over time, negative feelings will lessen in intensity and duration.

For your future success, you must deal with your feelings. It is imperative that you move past difficult emotions so as to not bring "emotional baggage" into your future interviews and job. Left to fester, emotional afterburn can sabotage future career opportunities. Studies focusing on tension, distress, anger, and depression reveal that those individuals who write their deepest feelings in a journal (spending twenty minutes a day for five days) have faster success finding jobs with heightened self-awareness and confidence, and lower stress. Writing down your feelings about your circumstances is liberating. Feelings such as grief, fear, and anxiety are normal during job transition. In the case of two equally qualified candidates, when one has dealt with feelings and the other one has not, the latter's unresolved emotions will leak through and reveal resentment toward a former employer, or other negative feelings, even though attempting a positive attitude.

THE COLLABORATION OF CAREER COUNSELING AND THERAPY

There are two aspects to job and career transition—the emotional one and the practical one. Easing the emotional toll of unemployment may require professional help. Creating focus and direction may include deciding whether to use a career counselor and/or therapist. If you want to make the transition faster, then the cost of not getting help may be significant.

> *"Success is not final, failure is not fatal: It is the courage to continue that counts."*
> **Winston Churchill**

There is always some trauma involved in transitioning from one career or job to another. Work gives us a sense of belonging in the world. When we are in career crisis, our sense of self can be filled with doubt and uncertainty. If you are discouraged, fearful, or at a loss about steps to take, or haven't found a career focus, it may be time to invest in yourself. Bringing closure to a job loss or familiar career requires emotional recovery. Successful transition requires practical tools and resources, a new vision, focus, direction, and identified goal. If you are doubtful whether you can identify and acquire work you enjoy and are good at, or question whether an action plan can help you stay the course, a career counselor might be the better choice to help you create your work/life plan.

You must feel safe, secure, and guided through the process of transition whether being helped by either a therapist or career counselor. You may have to deal with your feelings of anger, failure, sadness, and depression. In order to achieve forgiveness for a former employer and also for yourself, you must overcome thoughts such as, "If only I had..." or, "If only he/she had..." Your therapist and/or career counselor should be equipped to move you toward your peak performance—including addressing the chip on your shoulder that is showing up to others (for example, during an interview)—but that you don't see. Bringing emotional baggage into a job interview or new job is sabotage and must be dealt with if you are to regain control of your career. Professional counselors must be able to offer both an emotional and practical side to services. You can't move forward without either a mental or written plan to achieve higher levels of success. This requires focus and implementation.

Career counselors and therapists tend to specialize in niches and it is advantageous to work with one who has skills to meet your specific needs. The following checklist includes services you may want from a career counselor. I request that every client complete and prioritize this "needs assessment" form in order to avoid any assumptions or miscommunication, as well as manage expectations. You should identify the services you want from a potential career counselor and select the right fit for you.

NEEDS CHECKLIST FOR CAREER COUNSELING SERVICES

- ❏ Skills Identification (knowledge, skills, interests, and abilities)
- ❏ Assessment (interests, aptitudes, college major, training, certifications, licenses)
- ❏ Job Search Strategies
- ❏ Create Goals
- ❏ Focus and Direction
- ❏ Job Placement Assistance
- ❏ Personality Type and Job Match
- ❏ Job Application Form Completion (county, corporate, state, non-profit)
- ❏ Values and Work Preferences Identification
- ❏ Professional, Customized Resume
- ❏ Cover Letters
- ❏ Salary Concerns or Salary and Job Benefits Negotiation
- ❏ Plan of Action: Marketing, Networking, and Job Search Strategy
- ❏ Interview Skills

> *"It is our attitude at the beginning of a difficult task which, more than anything else, will affect its successful outcome."*
> *William James, psychologist*

- ❑ Loss/Emotional Issues: Coping Strategies Impacting Unemployment or Career Transition

- ❑ Pre-Retirement or Military Transition

- ❑ Tele-Consulting Service (distance or commute is an obstacle)

- ❑ Resources/Referrals/Networking: Internet sites including job openings, skill sets, wages/salary information, and job descriptions

- ❑ Self-Employment/Business Planning

- ❑ Job Offer Analysis/Proposal Writing

- ❑ Other. Please address services or needs not listed above.

SEASONS OF TRANSITION

"If Winter comes, can Spring be far behind?"
Percy Shelley

Job searches during periods or in areas of high unemployment statistics can seem especially challenging. Remind yourself of a time when your future appeared bright, work was plentiful, and the economy was up—those times will come and go again. Just like seasons change, periods of employment can vary from dormant to plentiful.

The period of transition, whether you are exiting college or the military, new to the workforce, an executive, or a career veteran, can feel like a life crisis, so nurture yourself. Identify and remove any unnecessary stressors. Recognize that these feelings are normal and may come and go. People react to their circumstances and experience change differently and in their own time. Paradoxically, the process of dealing with loss requires change and letting go. Transition requires moving forward and living life on life's terms. Depression may take root when ignoring a part of oneself that wants attention, such as feeling stuck in a job that lacks creative expression. Exploring new options can renew feelings such as hope, creativity, excitement, confidence, and acceptance.

Anger may show up during transition. Anger is actually a secondary feeling following a primary underlying emotion (see Figure 1 on the following page). Consider whether the emotion preceding your anger was (1) loss of pride or self-esteem, (2) fear/uncertainty, (3) pain/hurt feelings, or (4) shock. One reason "anger" occurs is because it is easier to deal with than the root feeling; an angry person feels powerful but a hurt or scared person feels weak or even helpless.

FEEL YOUR FEELINGS AND LET THEM GO

PRIMARY (UNDERLYING) EMOTIONS   SECONDARY EMOTION
▼   ▼

LOSS OF PRIDE ▶
LOSS OF SELF-ESTEEM ▶
FEAR ▶   **ANGER**
UNCERTAINTY ▶
PAIN ▶
HURT FEELINGS ▶
SHOCK ▶

Figure 1 – Depiction of anger as a secondary emotion

A sequence of feelings is also natural and can be expected when you are facing job change (see Figure 2). The feeling of "confusion" can lead to a downward spiral to depression. The solution? Information! Confusion, left unattended, worsens into "frustration." Frustration festers to become "anxiety." Finally, anxiety can plummet you into "depression." In other words, without information, the emotional elevator keeps going down. With information, you can step off the elevator at anytime.

LACK OF INFORMATION

Stagnation:

CONFUSION → FRUSTRATION → ANXIETY → DEPRESSION

Action:

INFORMATION GATHERING → RELIEF

Figure 2 – Example of a chain of emotions

MONITORING NEGATIVE THOUGHTS

Most of us do not monitor our thoughts. Become aware of negative self-talk: *"I'm not good enough," "I'm stupid," "I have nothing to offer,"* and *"I'll never have what I want."* Avoid the type of thinking that consists of "should have, would have, if only, could have." Don't "should" on yourself – *"If only I had or hadn't done that."* Thoughts create emotions that lead to either positive or negative results.

The next step for the confused job seeker is to acquire as much up-to-date and specific information as possible. Choosing the best job goal or career direction

> *"Change your thoughts and change the world."*
> **Norman Vincent Peale**

is like playing a card game; the more cards revealed the more information you have to make good decisions. Then, use that information to take action. Your job is to "suit up" and "show up" every day. Do the footwork and the rest will come. Get into action, stay in action, and keep up the momentum until you are satisfied with the results. Stay in the game.

Paul and Sarah Edwards have written almost 20 books. The common thread in their books is "to enable people to live the life they want to live while doing the work they want to do." For information about their work, free excerpts are available at www.WorkingFromHome.com. In *Finding Your Perfect Work,* they write, "As bad as things may seem, the greatest dreams are often born in periods of the greatest distress. Times like the present make people mad. We get tired of putting up with frustration and disappointment. We grow restless, discontented, dissatisfied, and even desperate. Personal crisis shakes us from our complacency and forces us to find new solutions in order not to give up our dreams. Change presents us with new choices and causes us to seek new options that fire up our dreams."

PUZZLE PIECES

Job searches and career transition are like putting a puzzle together. The more information you get, the more the puzzle comes together. Information can relieve distress. *The more information you have the better decisions you can make for yourself.*

Every person talked with, career book read, Internet resource explored, employer contacted, or skill upgraded adds a piece of the puzzle. In time, the puzzle comes together, creating focus and direction; your career or job is in place, for the time being. There will likely be more change and another puzzle on the horizon. Keep preparing toward the future. Stay flexible, keep learning, and continue adding new tools to your employment toolbox.

The emotional, financial, and physical impact of losing a job or a prolonged job search can be a difficult or even devastating experience. Looking for a job can feel equally uncomfortable. It is important to feel your feelings, then *let them go.* Understandably this is sometimes difficult. Acceptance of your current circumstances (whatever they are), rather than miring yourself in negative thinking or resisting job change altogether, is one solution to making a successful transition. Wayne Dyer said, *"As humans, we are often feeling beings first, who also think."*

"No one can predict to what heights you can soar. Even you will not know until you spread your wings."
Anonymous

"Perseverance is not a long race; it is many short races one after another."
Walter Elliott
British politician

TIME FOR A JOB OR CAREER CHANGE

For today's employees, it is not uncommon to change jobs frequently. For previous generations, it was common to remain in the same profession or even hold the same job throughout one's work life. Today a professional may change jobs about every two years and a blue-collar employee every six months. A college graduate may likely change jobs and careers 12 to 15 times or more.

A fast-changing world of work is today's reality. It requires accepting that you may change jobs or go through career transition every few years. Getting on track and in sync with organizational change requires adaptability, flexibility, and acceptance. It is not uncommon for industries and employees to get hit by new waves of change and downsizing before getting mobilized from the last turnaround. Resistance to the rapidly changing world of work sabotages your potential for new career opportunities.

There are no wasted experiences or mistakes, only lessons, which can often occur through failure. At some point, you will be able to rely on a past experience in your new circumstances. People in career transition, whether voluntarily or involuntarily, are undergoing personal growth pains in order to create future opportunities. Looking for the right job or career direction isn't necessarily just about getting the job but also building your personal character, tenacity, strength, courage, and perseverance.

YOUR FUTURE DOES NOT LIVE IN YOUR PAST

Romanticizing about past employment is characteristic during transition periods. Attempting to resurrect past work experience is not a solution to current circumstances. It is normal to create an idealized account of the past, or to feel regretful, nostalgic, or "homesick" for a previous job, particularly when dealing with present work-related challenges. There is a component of denial when romanticizing about the past that can serve to prevent depression.

Do you recall the story about Moses bringing the people out of slavery in Egypt to a promised land? During the journey, they felt confused and afraid, seemingly

lost in the desert. Some demanded to return—at least they were fed in their prior environment—regardless of their former unhappiness. Career transition and job change can make you feel like you are lost in the wilderness; uncertain whether you will find your way to success. Just like the slaves in Egypt, however, your future does not live in the past.

> "I find the great thing in this world is not where we stand, as in what direction we are moving."
> Oliver Wendell Holmes

You may be very good at the work you have done in the past—just like the slaves in Egypt who were forced to make bricks—but that doesn't mean you want to keep doing the same job. Your future isn't back there. Your future work is ahead of you. You must move forward to reach your goals. You will then reach the promised land.

BURNOUT

The American Psychological Association's website indicates that burnout is emotional exhaustion resulting from overwhelming stress at work. It may be caused by a hostile work environment or fears about job security, but it often results from long hours, stressful deadlines, high expectations, worrying about a project, or taking on more work than you can handle—in other words, working too hard. It can lead to serious conditions, such as depression and heart disease, and you should seek professional help if you are experiencing burnout.

I've been known to plant a garden with my kitchen spoons until they bend like a Houdini magic trick, and use scissors instead of pruning sheers, resulting in gummy blades with broken tips. Similarly, workers who repeatedly perform the same task (whether or not they are good at it or suitably matched for it) become stressed and are at risk for burnout. Symptoms may include anger, irritability, or negativity toward others who make demands; feeling overwhelmed, suspicious, helpless; exhaustion; weight gain or loss; sleeplessness; or headache/ stomachache. Risk-taking, impulsiveness, or excessive spending may color their behavior.

One cause of burnout is failing to stop and pat ourselves on the back with an "attagirl" or "attaboy" to celebrate achievements at intervals. Too often, we rush into another goal before giving due reward to an accomplishment. When will you know you have arrived or attained your goal? What are the specific conditions that must be met? Identify some milestone markers that you expect along the way. What are some easy things you can do to acknowledge your achievements, and how will you remind yourself to do so? Feeling disappointment is caused by unmet expectations. Getting to where you want to go requires flexibility, an open mind, and limiting your attachment to an exact outcome. Stay in the present and head your ship in the direction that matches your interests and is of service to others. Keep a spirit of hope in the present; if you were happy in the past, you can create a happy work environment again.

People going through change must expand like a rubber band. Life forces the job seeker to stretch toward the future. Change can feel uncomfortable and is inevitable. The Buddhist prayer flags are made of gauze that quickly deteriorates, symbolizing the impermanence of all things. You have likely faced challenges in your life that have since passed. Our greatest challenges are usually the means that give way to significant personal development. Breakdown is the first step to break through, but it can feel very uncomfortable. Don't quit. Keep walking forward. Your future is ahead of you, one day at a time.

You can create and develop a satisfying job and your career goals will come into focus. You will arrive at your destination on time. Do the footwork, and each step will bring success into clearer vision.

"I know of no more encouraging fact than the ability of man to elevate his life by conscious endeavor."
Henry David Thoreau

DISCUSSION QUESTIONS/EXERCISES

1. Describe three ways in which you are creative when you are not at work. How much time do you want to spend in these activities?

2. Where do you see yourself five years from now? What does it look like? What are you doing?

3. What is your dream job? How do you expect to get there? What is it going to take to achieve it? What is preventing you from taking the steps to accomplish it?

4. When did you feel most or least grateful... productive... engaged... energized... inspired...generous... expansive... fearful?

5. What are the pros and cons of making a job change?

Moving Through the Stages

PREPARING A PLAN OF ACTION

> "The secret of getting ahead is getting started. The secret of getting started is breaking our complex overwhelming tasks into small tasks, and then starting on the first one."
> **Mark Twain**

When you are ready to get on with your job search, it is time to create a plan of action. This will require you to write an outline that includes each activity you need to do including deadlines for completion. This will help you to feel success and not set yourself up for failure. Be practical and realistic when designing activities to perform. Read your plan of action often, especially on days when you are feeling a little blue, in order to remind yourself how much you have achieved. Pat yourself on the back after you accomplish goals. Design daily, weekly, and monthly goals, including time frames for completion. Get a mentor (friend, coach, career counselor) to keep you accountable. Develop a support system that includes friends, colleagues, and local employment resources.

WORK/LIFE BALANCE

Keep a realistic and practical approach to your dream job or career goal. Assess what you are good at and enjoy doing and whether there is a market for your skills. Match what you most want to do with opportunities that people will pay for.

The process of merging your desires and resources, or finding a way to turn your goals and opportunities into marketable work, is not accomplished over-night. Some people have to narrow down choices from too many options, and others must broaden their work search alternatives because they perceive too few opportunities.

The best work builds self-esteem through accomplishments, instills confidence, keeps motivation high, and earns a good living. In addition, the best work is that which provides for balance in other life activities. Today's traditional job hunting isn't just about finding work; it's about creating a life in practical terms that will support one's goals, including balance in lifestyle. Francis Gilbert, PhD, Clinical Psychologist for Veterans writes, "Consider how you can make your life a little less full so that it will be a bit more satisfying."

WHERE DO YOU SEE YOURSELF THREE YEARS FROM NOW?

What do you want your life to look like? A good exercise is to ask, *"Where do I see myself three years from now? Where do I see myself five or seven years from now?"* Get in a quiet place and spend some time thinking about this. What images do you see? What are your surroundings and environment like? Write out your vision and keep it nearby. Keep your career goals to the next three to seven years rather than a lifetime.

In considering what you want in your next job, ask yourself the question, "When were you really motivated and satisfied?" Next, make a list of what tasks or functions you performed. Identify what, specifically, was stimulating or gratifying for you. Clearly analyze what motivates and fulfills you. Write your responses. This exercise may help give you answers to find future work. Consider whether you are motivated enough to want to perform more of these responsibilities in your next job.

"If a man knows not what harbor he seeks, any wind is the right wind."
Seneca

GOALS

Goal setting is a skill that many people have difficulty with. This section provides information about the mechanics of setting and achieving goals. Although this book is about analyzing your career path, your career goals need to be in accord with the other parts of your life. Consider your vision for your family and home, finances, spiritual and ethical life, continuing education, health, and social and civic life. When you begin to refine your career goals, you will want to make sure that they don't conflict with goals in these other areas. Balance in your day-to-day life prevents burnout and supports general happiness and greater physical and mental health.

It may be time to examine your goals or lack of goals. A sense of satisfaction often occurs when you are either making progress toward or have reached a goal. Happiness is based on the word "happens." Happiness may occur from external conditions, such as starting a new job, beginning a new relationship, marrying, buying a new car, or experiencing a sunny day. You can't make the sun shine but you can identify and acquire a job you are happy in. Conversely, unhappiness can occur if you are not making progress toward a goal, have no goal, or are pursuing an undesirable/unrealistic goal.

To become happier, you must identify and make progress toward your goals. Begin now by planning out a week, month, or year ahead. The key is to identify measurable actions you must perform to make progress toward your goal. Get a friend, colleague, career counselor, or other individual to help you and hold you accountable.

Keep paper and pen handy so you can jot your goals down anytime, even when awake ruminating in the middle of the night. After a few days or weeks, re-visit your list and cross off everything except the goals you really want. If you had unlimited resources, what would you do? What would your goals be if you *knew* you would succeed?

SETTING GOALS

The word "goal" can be intimidating. It is imbued with the notion of success and failure, probably from its close association with athletics. Like every concept, goal setting can be reframed in a manner conducive to your perceptions. Goals can also be described as "the big picture," dreams, wishes, and vision.

The concept of SMART goals was developed by Paul J. Meyer, who writes, "Objectives are described as being very precise, time-based, and measurable actions that support the completion of a goal." Objectives must: 1) Relate directly to the goal; 2) Be clear, concise, and understandable; 3) Be stated in terms of results; 4) Begin with an action verb; 5) Specify a date for accomplishment; and 6) Be measurable.

You can formulate goals in different ways. If you are an auditory learner, you will want to express your vision verbally with a career counselor or trusted friend. Similar to brainstorming sessions in the business world, it is important to list ideas initially without judgment. For visual learners you may want to paint a picture or create a collage to represent your destination. For kinestic learners, you may want to write about your feelings or verbally express your feelings about your goals.

Fran Tarkenton, in his book *How to Motivate People*, recounts an example of goal setting. As the quarterback for the Minnesota Vikings, he knew the team owners were intent on getting into the Super Bowl. At the beginning of the season, he asked his offensive coaches how that vision could become a reality. The Vikings were good defensively, but their offense was lacking.

Tarkenton analyzed the record books of playoff teams from the previous years and uncovered the critical variables to win. The specific objectives included the number of average yards per rush, and blocking the right person on the opposing team.

Whenever you make a decision about your activities and resources, ask yourself if it takes you closer to, or farther from your goal. If you answer "closer to," then you've made the right decision. If you answer "farther from," you know that you will need to tailor your decision-making more accurately in the future. The steps to achieve goals are not only about attitude; instead, they require the right behaviors that move you in the right direction.

> "The best way to predict the future is to invent it."
> Alan Kay
> computer scientist

> "Each one of us has a fire in our heart for something. It's our goal in life to find it and keep it lit."
> Mary Lou Retton,
> Olympic gold medal winner

ACHIEVING GOALS

Your "big picture" is your beacon and guiding star in your journey to successful life/work. You should re-visit your journal, or collage, or mission statement regularly to fire up your enthusiasm.

Analyze your goal and break it down into manageable components. Answering the following questions will help you create a plan of action:

~ ***Can you measure your goal accurately?*** Can you describe the behaviors and outcomes necessary to achieve your goal? For example, you may say, *"I want a job."* You must define the activities that will land you the job. Break it down by "targeted due dates" and set deadlines. To accomplish your goal, you may need to: analyze your transferable skills, assess your strengths and capabilities, write your work history with a PAR format (see PAR in Chapter 6), review various resume samples, select a preferred style, write your resume, perform X number of employer calls per week, make X number of networking contacts, and so forth.

~ ***Is it realistic?*** Do you have the skills, information, and knowledge necessary to reach your goal? Do you need help from others? Do you have the physical and financial resources to support your work toward your goal?

~ ***Is it meaningful?*** One method of increasing the meaningfulness of tasks is to define the intrinsic and extrinsic value to you. Can you arrange to receive recognition from others for completing a task? Will you feel the intrinsic satisfaction of a job well done? Are there any pleasurable or adverse consequences attached to completing or not completing the task? Do you require an immediate reward upon completing the task or are you willing to wait?

~ ***Is your goal easily understood?*** Describe your target simply (e.g., *"I want a job"*). If your goal consists of more than one objective (e.g., *"I want a job with the criteria of [insert salary, commute distance, title, etc)] . . ."*), delineate each objective separately and also rank their importance in your overall plan.

~ ***Do you "own" it?*** Arnold Schwarzenegger describes the "confidence cycle" as achieving interim goals that provides a sense of confidence and attaches to your next leg of the journey. Your mental commitment to your goal is one of the most important factors in achieving it.

On a daily or weekly basis, identify the objectives and break down the specific tasks that are required to accomplish your goals. Use a calendar to schedule dates to perform the activities and mark due dates for meeting deadlines. This

> *"Life is a great big canvas; throw all the paint on it you can."*
> *Danny Kaye*

method will help you accomplish the objectives toward achieving your goal. Allow time to evaluate your progress and reward yourself.

Remember that while you can have goals remain flexible in your attachment to the outcome. The results may not yield what you planned. Conditions outside your control may confound your efforts or your priorities may change. Life happens...and your goals may require new definitions.

Identify barriers when setting goals. What obstacles can you remove? Ask for help with creative brainstorming. Set time frames for what you have to do. My question to you is **"What is preventing you from accomplishing your goal?"** Possible responses may include *"I don't really have the skills, ability or knowledge"* or *"I'm afraid I might fail"* or *"I don't want it badly enough to really work for it"* or *"I'm afraid what others might think"* or *"The goal is too difficult to accomplish."* What are some negative things that might happen if you reach your goal? What are some positive things that might happen if you reach your goal?

Ask yourself, *"What could I do so these things don't prevent me from reaching my goal?"* and *"Who can help me?"*

MISSION STATEMENT

Corporations and small businesses often post a mission statement. It describes complex long-range planning and helps focus the decision-making of the company's employees on specific outcomes. You can create a mission statement to help you visualize and guide your career path and direct your life. It outlines what you intend to achieve and what inspires you. It brings focus to your sense of purpose. It can help to simplify the complex, and ease decision-making. Your mission statement should reflect what you intend to achieve and what inspires you. It is what guides your ambition, goal, or intent.

Although this book is about analyzing your career path, don't overlook your personal life as part of the equation for being healthy, balanced, and productive. Consider your schedule and how much time you want to spend with family/activities/work. Balance in work/life prevents burnout and supports general happiness and greater physical and mental health.

Write and verbalize your mission statement and refine it with a career counselor or trusted friend. Keep it visible, such as near your computer or on your refrigerator door. Read it frequently to remind you of your goals and to re-direct you if you get off track.

There is no one formula for articulating your ideas into a mission statement. What is the problem or need you are trying to address? What makes you unique? Who are the beneficiaries of your work?

Franklin Covey identifies a mission as *an inner urging to pursue an activity or perform a service. A calling. What one intends to do or achieve.* What is your aim, goal, dream, intent, objective, or target? What guides and inspires you? What gets you out of bed in the morning? It doesn't have to be huge to be worthy. It must be big enough to create change in your life and future. You choose what you value, dream of, hope for, and become. Below are some **headings** to help you outline your mission statement.

~ **Purpose and/or Mission:**

~ **Cores Values:**

~ **Beliefs:**

~ **Vision:**

~ **Guiding Principles:**

~ **Activities:**

~ **Benefits:**

EXERCISE: CREATE YOUR LIFE/WORK

For a final exploration on this topic, perform one or more of the following creative project assignments that answers the question, *"What do I want my life to look like?"*

Collage: Gather an assortment of magazines or other printed material and prepare a collage as a project. On a large poster board, cut and paste pictures that answer the question, *"What do I want my life to look like?"* Next, cut and paste pictures that answer the question, *"What do I want my work/career to look like?"* Is there a pattern?

Journal: Purchase a journal or writing pad. Write in a journal as a project. Answer the question, *"What do I want my life to look like?"* Next, answer the question, *"What do I want my work/career to look like?"* Is there a pattern?

Painting: Paint a picture as a project. Gather art materials and products. Answer the question, *"What do I want my life to look like?"* and *"What do I want my work/career to look like?"* What colors, size, shapes, and textures would it have? What mood is created? What environment reveals it best?

As your project develops, consider how it reflects the values and preferences you explored in the previous sections. What additional values or preferences does it suggest? Place your work piece in a setting where you can view it daily. Seeing it every day will help keep you on track as you pursue your goals.

"Dream big dreams; then put on your overalls and go make the dreams come true."
Fred Van Amburg

"Don't ever confuse having a career with having a life."
Chinese proverb

HOW MUCH TIME AND ENERGY ARE YOU WILLING TO PUT FORTH?

To acquire satisfying employment, you may have to accommodate a multitude of job tasks, spend money on new training, commit to a high learning curve, make some demanding changes, relocate, and experience a host of emotions. Can your financial circumstances afford a career transition? What impact does your desire to undergo a job transition have on your family and other relationships?

Establish how much time and how many resources you are willing to put forth to make your dream job come true. Just like building a house, it may take longer and cost more than you thought it would, or it might happen sooner than you think and you may not feel ready to accept a change. For best results, keep investing your energy toward your goal and stay the course. You can create and design the work you want. But, know if and when you have to cut your losses, when you have given it your best, and when you may need to change directions. If you need a dramatic job change, what career attracts you that would provide a remarkable difference?

DISCUSSION QUESTIONS/EXERCISES

1. What do you hope to acquire from this book?

2. Do you need to repackage yourself or re-invent yourself? How would that look?

3. What is your ideal job? Describe your perfect workday.

4. What are you willing to take on in order to achieve your dream? What are you prepared to let go of?

5. Outline your professional mission statement. Develop your mission statement with a journal, collage, or painting.

6. Identify two goals that you would like to achieve. Write your objectives using the SMART model.

The Effect on Your Personal Relationships

COMMUNICATION WITH OTHERS

We all need support and encouragement to flourish. The job seeker's emotional state may be more fragile than usual during this difficult time when feelings of self-esteem, identity, and security are under attack.

People in job change situations may feel added stress, which can bring out the worst characteristics. Some typical reactions that stressed job seekers may experience include an increase in pessimism, hypersensitivity, emotional overreaction, hostility toward self or others, depression, illogical thinking, avoidance of normal activities, rigid attitude, obsession with details, closed mindedness, inability to consider alternatives, dependency on others, and verbal criticism toward self and others. In addition, some people cope by overindulgence or denial of reality through TV, shopping, sleeping, self-absorption, overeating, exercise, computer games, or other addictions. A loss of normal interests, distancing of friendships, and withdrawal or isolation may also occur when the job seeker is feeling overwhelmed.

People closest to us may resist our job change the most, whereas acquaintances support us more. The people close to us experience many of the same feelings we do when first coming to grips with our career crisis. This includes shame, fear, anger, upset, worry, and relief. Hopefully, these significant people will lift your spirits, provide support, offer love, give encouragement, and even think of suggestions. They may even infuse you with faith and assure you that whatever course you take will lead to success. The job seeker's relationships with family, friends, neighbors, career counselor/coach, job-related contacts, and other community members are invaluable resources during job change endeavors.

There are some things you need to know about communicating with the significant people in your life about matters related to your job search or career change. Spouses and friends provide the always-handy "coach" for most people, and, while that can be beneficial, it also may have a downside when expectations are unmet.

"If one advances in the direction of his dreams, one will meet success unexpected in common hours."
Henry David Thoreau

TALK TO YOUR FAMILY AND FRIENDS

Talk to your family and friends about your job transition circumstances. Be honest and tell them what is going on. Keep them informed.

Due to pride, many times people don't want anyone to know they have lost their job, but the more people looking for you the better the chances of finding a good job. Keep in mind that the emotions you are feeling, at some level, your family and friends are probably feeling. Recognize that things may be challenging for a while and everyone gets through hard times. Most families and friendships are stronger as a result of going through difficult times together.

A spouse is usually the first person to hear the news that an individual has been fired or laid off, or wants to change jobs. Job transition may improve, add stress to, or have little effect on the relationship.

In some marriages, a layoff or job change may create new stress or a "rub" in the flow of the relationship. This usually occurs when one partner has a different idea about how the unemployed partner should get a new job or meet fiscal obligations. In spite of their loving kindness and suggestions (which are probably meant to be helpful), their best advice may not work for you. It is important to balance common goals for the marriage and the goals of each person finding his or her respective career path.

In a marriage, both partners must experience joy in their day-to-day work (whether outside the home or as a homemaker) in order to bring joy into the relationship. When one person is unhappy in an unsuitable job, it can bring turmoil to the relationship. Job dissatisfaction or a period of unemployment may create havoc that can drag down the relationship.

Dual career couples cite increased income and more career freedom as primary benefits. Most couples want flexible work hours in order to attend to personal responsibilities, as well as benefit plans that match their needs, including cafeteria plans/health insurance, vacation time, retirement plans, tuition assistance, child/elder care, spouse relocation assistance, and telecommuting.

There is no doubt that having a job can eliminate strain in relationships that results from how to pay the bills or how to spend a day. Active employment can also thwart increasing alcohol and drug consumption during a period of unemployment. Try to remember that your circumstances are temporary and keep communication open with your spouse, children, parents, and friends.

Your job change may "trigger" loved ones

Family, friends, and acquaintances can project their own fears, attitudes about work, and job insecurities onto you. They may have all sorts of ideas and advice that opposes your goals. Your job change circumstances may trigger their employment and money issues. They may, for example, suggest that you get any job in order to bring immediate resolution to the situation, regardless of whether it will bring you dissatisfaction. They may feel embarrassed that you are not currently working, that the situation reflects on them. Avoid the temptation to satisfy other people and be true to yourself in your search for satisfying work. More than anything, though, know that loved ones' suggestions are usually well-intended.

Meanwhile, the friends and family in your life have their own challenges to deal with, so be careful not to overly tax the relationships. A little forewarning is that these same people only have so much to give you during your career transition journey. They simply will not be able to "be there" for you all the time, even when you really want to be fortified. The confusing part about acquiring comfort and support from those closest to you is that you never know for sure when it might be forthcoming.

Perhaps Monday mornings (when you are accustomed to starting your work week) are a trigger time when you are most apt to feel desperate for reassurance and seek emotional relief from fear and insecurity. Your parent or wife/honey or friend may not be able to infuse you with strength and courage. Just like you, they don't own a crystal ball to advise you or give insight on where to go in your work endeavors. Be thankful for the support they provide when they can. Your loved ones probably want to help you as much as possible, but may nevertheless fall short as trained career counselors or psychotherapists.

The point is, we never know whether we will feel reassured or deflated after talking to our close family members about our employment circumstances. They want to be there for us, are well meaning, and offer support through this trying time, but realistically they have limited resources to provide. It is important not to overly deplete relationships and to develop many different resources for direction and guidance during a work transition.

Discussion questions/exercises

1. Identify some of your typical stress reactions and behaviors.

2. What coping strategies would help you manage your stress constructively?

3. What resources can you use, in addition to family and friends, for direction and guidance during work transition?

> *"To keep your faces toward change, and behave like free spirits in the presence of fate, is strength undefeated."*
> *Helen Keller*

4. What career do your friends, parents, or spouse/partner think you should pursue?

5 What career would you pursue if you didn't care what your friends and family thought?

CHAPTER 4

Career and Job Change

EXPLORING CAREER GOALS

The most difficult job transition is one in which you completely change job titles and industries. For example, a chef does not usually decide to become an engineer. In order to give yourself a promotion and a smooth career transition, you may wish to *"Stay in the same ocean, but land on a different shore."*

When exploring career options, how much change do you want in your work environment? Do you want to stay in the same ocean but land on a different shore? Do you want to switch from a lake to river or swim the current stream?

Usually, the quickest job placement involves seeking the same job title in the same industry. Other types of job change include seeking the same job title in a different industry or a different job title in the same industry. In between these degrees is the job searcher who seeks a similar job title in a similar industry.

Consider the table below. Can you identify some applicable job titles and industries for your job search? What information would help you decide if you want a new career or a new job in your same industry? What is required to make your current job satisfactory?

	Same Industry	Similar Industry	Different Industry
Same Title			
Similar Title			
Different Title			

In the sections to come, we'll explore a variety of issues and strategies, some of which will help you assess your risk tolerance while you move toward your goals.

> *"Those who wish to sing, always find a song."*
> **Swedish proverb**

"And the trouble is, if you don't risk anything, you risk even more."
Erica Jong

INITIAL CONSIDERATIONS TO THINK ABOUT

Consider the following: If you want to perform a different type of work, what are the circumstances driving your need for change? What will fulfill your vision, values, and work preferences? Look for a common thread in your work history. Are there any patterns of behavior that you need to break? Before you move ahead, reflect on your past choices.

Feelings of aversion with a job situation cause some people to make a fast get-away and jump into the first job that comes open. You learn soon enough that you landed in a new work location but in the same distasteful predicament.

It may be time to give yourself a promotion and dump the dead weight of work tasks you no longer enjoy, in exchange for ones you do enjoy. When you come home at the end of the day, you want to say, *"My day went quickly and I felt useful, productive, and of service to others."* This requires you to identify three or four tasks you most enjoy performing and figure out which position would allow you to do those during the workday.

When your particular industry is on a down-turn, you might find it necessary to change career directions because competition for positions is so high. Some people outgrow their present work circumstances and seek a more challenging and fulfilling career endeavor. People who are willing to take on the challenges of changing jobs or exploring a new career do so because they simply will not feel fulfilled if they don't do it. In the book, *Cool Careers for Dummies*, Marty Nemko and Paul and Sarah Edward pose the question, "What would your twin tell you to do?"

The ideal job will be different at different phases of our lives. Gratification from work is different during each stage of adult development. Those work values and preferences that influence the Generation Xers are typically different from those of the Baby Boomers and mature workers.

EMOTIONAL CHALLENGES IN CHANGING CAREERS

When we undergo changing jobs or careers, there are consequences. The challenges come with highs and lows. One day you may be deliriously happy and the next doubting your decision. Faith and fear do not make good roommates. Faith dispels fear and fear dispels faith. One day freedom and financial satisfaction appears within your grasp and the next day you fear financial insecurity.

Fear is often masked as reasonable caution and careful planning when in truth one is stalling to avoid facing unpredictability. Perpetual formulating prevents any real progress. Get away from your need to cover every contingency or search for perfection. Free yourself to take the risks and actions necessary for success.

Even if changing careers or seeking a new job is the right choice for you, it will likely be difficult at times to achieve. Those things we work hardest for we appreciate the most. Such a change will require a great deal of perseverance, tenacity, networking, facing obstacles, upgrading of skills, and dealing with an emotional roller coaster. You may experience rejection, financial cost, hard work, and feelings of discouragement mixed with excitement. But if you have a vision for fulfillment and satisfaction in your work, the struggle will be worth the success in the end!

THE IMPORTANCE OF SELF-ASSESSMENT AND REPACKAGING YOURSELF

If you determine that you are ready to undergo a job or career transition, you probably have a desire to transfer your skills to work that is satisfying and will give you a sense of usefulness and purpose. First, make a plan of action for yourself. Conduct a thorough self-assessment of your qualifications, education, and abilities that will transfer to a different work experience. List all education, work history, unpaid work experiences, internships, hobbies, and volunteer opportunities. Consider how to repackage yourself using your strengths and values while limiting weaknesses. Answering the following questions can help in your self-assessment. *What are the differences between your former or current job description(s) and ideal job description? What do you like best and least of the tasks? In which jobs were you most and least content? Where was there the most energy and gratitude? Who wants what you have to give? How are your preferred skills transferable to another field?*

EDUCATION—DO YOU NEED MORE?

Evaluate whether more education is truly applicable to your goal. Merely putting more education on your resume is not necessarily the solution. Watch out for any inclination to go back to school simply because it is safe, is familiar, and may provide a temporary solution to career confusion. Determine if you want more education for stimulation or to enhance your specific goals.

When you are assessing a job goal, consider what you need to be competitive. Would more education, training, or accreditation help? You may not need an expensive new graduate degree. Rather, consider a different approach. For

> *"The best way to predict your future is to invent it."*
> **Frank Maquire, founder of Fed Ex**

example, if you want to work in human resources, determine whether your work experience and education is sufficient to qualify for the examinations/certifications administered through the related professional organization, namely, the Society for Human Resource Management.

You can earn advanced professional recognition and credentials unique to various professional fields without earning another degree. Professional journals, organizations, and online websites can help you access this type of information. Call and speak with a representative or someone performing the job you aspire to and ask questions. How would you acquire relevant credentials to make you more competitive? Tell a prospective employer that you are willing to participate in this type of education and skills upgrading.

If you target jobs that would prefer a particular degree or certification, enroll in at least one course that is part of an accredited program or curriculum. Then, include the course name, school, or online college program on your resume. In your cover letter and during an interview, reveal that you are currently involved in a study program leading to a degree. Showing this type of intention is a statement that you are staying current in your field and is often sufficient to get a job. You are not misleading prospective employers since you may decide to complete the accredited program for a degree.

Two sites for researching college or graduate school programs include: www.Petersons.com and www.GMAC.com/GMAC (Graduate Admissions Council).

When my friend Brenda suggested we enroll in a graduate level Introduction to Counseling class, I did not plan to earn a master's degree but ended up doing so. The employer I was working for agreed to pay for half of the tuition since the training directly related to the work I performed for the company as an internal consultant.

CHOOSING A NEW CAREER OR JOB

If you don't know which career you want to pursue, list five jobs you are interested in. Gather as much information about each job option as possible. Talk to people who work in the career you are considering and ask them questions. See the "Information Interview" section in this chapter for more information about how to do this. There is no pressure on either party during an information interview. It may lead to a job, but the goal is simply to get information. In addition to getting valuable information, you are building your network of personal relationships. Ask what kind of education, certification, or licensure the job requires. Ask about the pros and cons and the day-to-day job routine.

Get information on personal earning capacity and opportunities for growth, as well as labor market and employment outlook projections.

You will find many website resources in this book related to your specific needs and interest. For employer contacts and labor market, perform a Google search by entering "labor market information" and/or "labor market information in [insert state]."

You may learn that you need to upgrade your current skills or acquire new skills. Learn all you can about the new career. Explore the Internet. Join a couple of professional associations and/or read professional journals. Attend conferences and training and talk to as many people in the field as possible.

You want to make yourself knowledgeable and skilled in the shortest amount of time and expense. Think about your short-term and long-term goals. Apply your education and training investments to get where you want to be in the long term.

INFORMATION INTERVIEW

• *Decide what specific job you want information about*

Deciding what job you are working toward may be the toughest and most time-consuming part of career transition. Once you have chosen a specific career area, it is best to talk with someone in that field. Talk with someone in the geographic area where you would like to be working, or if you are concerned about the perception of a competitive threat, call someone in a different geographic area, which may prevent that discomfort.

• *Finding names of people to contact*

Identify the people or organizations with which you are familiar and that appeal to you in order to gain information. Keep in mind that the reason you want to talk to these people is not to get a job from them; rather, they are a source of information and may refer you to talk to somebody who can also help you. Make the purpose of your call clear early in the conversation. Connections can be made through friends, relatives, neighbors, professional associates, former co-workers, colleagues and supervisors, religious or social affiliates, the Chamber of Commerce, college counselors, career counselors, and employment department representatives. Consider your lawyer, insurance agent, homebuilder, accountant, or other vendors/suppliers you know, as well as former competitors, clients, or customers.

> *"In order that people may be happy in their work, these three things are needed: They must be fit for it. They must not do too much of it. And they must have a sense of success in it."*
> **John Ruskin**

> *"We'll either find a way, or make one."*
> **Hannibal**

Ask them for a suggestion of someone for you to interview. Say something like, *"Do you know of anyone who works as a [insert job title]?"* or, *"Do you know of anyone who works in the [insert industry title] field?"* Most people are pleased to be asked and want to be helpful. Ask if you can use their name as a reference or for a referral letter and then follow up on their recommendation.

Explore Internet websites or company telephone directories for the names of employees who have the job title or work in the department you are interested in. Company research can be found at www.WetFeet.com and www.Hoovers.com. You can target a specific company, give them a call, and ask! Once you have a name, use the suggestions below, and call the person to set up a 20-minute information interview.

- **Before you call**

Research the company and know a little about the business. Think about how this occupation might fit with your interests, skills, values, and long- and short-term goals.

- **What do you say when you call?**

"Hello, my name is _____. I am a(n) (College Student, Alumni, former employee for . . .) and I am very interested in learning more about a career in [insert title]. Would you have 10–20 minutes some time in the next week when I could meet with you to ask a few questions and get some advice?" (Make it clear that you are not asking for a job right now.)

"Hello, my name is_____. I am considering becoming a [insert job title]. I've read a lot about the field but would like to talk with someone who is actually in that career. I wonder if I could ask you a few questions about your experience."

If you are having trouble getting past the gatekeeper (e.g., the receptionist), you might try this one:

"Hello, my name is _____. This may be one of the stranger [trust me, that word works] calls you've received today, but I really need your help. I'm still trying to figure out what I want to be when I grow up. I think I may want to be a(n) [insert career], but I'm not sure yet. I've read about the career, but feel I should talk with someone in the field. Can I ask you to see if your boss might be willing to answer just a few questions about what it is like to work as a [insert job title]?"

- **Before you go to an information interview**

  ✓ Write out the questions you are going to ask.

> **"Only those who dare to fail greatly ever achieve greatly."**
> **Robert F. Kennedy**

✓ Dress as if you were going to a job interview.

✓ Be on time.

✓ Have your personal business cards available.

(See Chapter 14 about preparing and distributing your personal business cards.)

• **_Suggested questions to ask_**

Ask any questions to further your understanding of the career area. A list of questions is provided below. These are meant only as a guide to help you clarify what is truly important to you in a job. Make the questions applicable and specific to the person you are interviewing.

❑ How did you get into this career/job?

❑ Please walk me through a typical day . . . (on this job, in this career, in this company . . . whatever is relevant).

❑ What do you find to be the best and worst things about your career?

❑ What are the skills most important to succeeding in your career?

❑ What do you know now that you wish you'd known when you were deciding to enter this field?

❑ Can you think of anything I should know about this field that is unlikely to find its way into print?

❑ Please tell me about your background and interests.

❑ What advice do you have about the smartest way to prepare for this career?

❑ What jobs in this field provide particularly good learning experiences?

❑ Where are good job openings listed?

❑ What kind of salary can I expect upon entry into this field?

❑ Are there any particularly interesting specialties within your field?

❑ How is the field changing?

❑ Why might someone leave this field?

❑ Who else do you think I should talk with or what else should I read before deciding whether to pursue this career? Any event I should attend? Any organization I should join?

❑ What other advice would you give someone entering this field?

> **_"Out of clutter, find simplicity."_**
> **_Albert Einstein_**

❑ How did you prepare for the job you have?

❑ What training would you recommend for someone interested in this field? What experience or skills are required to be competitive?

❑ What do you like most about what you do?

❑ What do you like least or find the most challenging about what you do?

❑ Are there special problem areas in your job (or in this company) such as dangerous conditions, high stress, or boring and repetitive tasks?

❑ What kinds of jobs can one consider when training in this field?

❑ How many years of education are required for this particular job?

❑ What are some related or similar jobs to what you do? What is the typical entry-level position?

❑ What do you spend most of your time doing at work?

❑ What do you see in the future for this line of work? What is the industry outlook?

❑ What is your work environment like?

❑ What is important for advancement in this field?

❑ What is the competition like for a job in this field?

"Life is change. Growth is optional. Choose wisely."
Karen Kaiser Clark

ADDITIONAL SUGGESTIONS

Be conscious of the 10-20 minute time limit. If you want to talk longer, that is fine, as long as you are not stretching the interview longer than the person would like. Ask permission to continue. You will be surprised by their agreement to continue.

Be sure to bring paper and pens with you to jot down ideas and information.

You can leave them with a copy of your resume or a personal business card, but only if they ask or it appears appropriate to do so. Remember this is not a job interview and you have told them that. So honor your word.

Follow-up with a handwritten note thanking them for their time and information, as well as to remind them of you (refer to Chapter 20 and the section about "thank-you" letters). Be sure your address and phone number are on the note and include something specific that you appreciated.

Self-employment and layoffs

The good news about layoffs in your work industry is that they create more opportunities to become self-employed. You may be able to perform the same or similar work as an independent contractor.

After layoffs are completed, hiring freezes typically occur. Organizations still have a need to get things done, but have fewer employees to do them. This creates opportunities for small businesses and independent contractors to acquire short-term and possibly long-term projects. Gradually increasing your customer base to include multiple sources of income is wise when venturing into self-employment. One drop in the bucket at a time will eventually fill the bucket. For those who possess particular in-demand skills or knowledge, temporary or permanent self-employment may be a viable option. For more information on this topic, read about self-employment and developing a business plan.

Transitional Job

Many people changing careers go through a transitional job (or two or three) before settling into their niche. If you need a job immediately to pay the bills, consider one that will keep the wolf at the door from getting inside. This approach to career change offers a temporary bridge while you explore alternatives. Gaining a sense of personal power can be accomplished by taking even small steps. If you don't have a job or are dissatisfied with your current job—but don't know what you want to do and whether you need to completely re-invent or just repackage yourself—a transitional job may help relieve some pressure. Whenever possible, of course, it is helpful if this transitional job has some connection to the career path you wish to follow in the future.

Two part-time jobs

You may want to consider working one or two part-time jobs. You never know where a part-time job may lead or the opportunities it may present. A part-time job may also provide you the opportunity to pursue an independent venture. You may want to use your practical skills in one job and use other skills, or fulfill your own passion, in another job or in self-employment. Or, you may not be able to find a full-time position in your industry quickly enough to meet your financial needs, but you can find two such part-time jobs. You can work those part-time jobs while you take your time to find an appropriate full-time position.

In this chapter, we've talked about a variety of strategies to consider in increasing your tolerance for the risk and challenges posed by the desire to change. Now take a moment to reflect on these ideas with the discussion questions or exercises on the following page.

> *"Knowledge of what is possible is the beginning of happiness."*
> **George Santayana**

DISCUSSION QUESTIONS/EXERCISES

1. Based on your past experiences, evaluate your risk tolerance for changing jobs based on a scale of 1 to 10 (1 being low and 10 being high).

2. Think about your future. What would you like your career path to be? What incremental steps can you take to accomplish your goal?

3. Identify three or more tasks that you want to perform in your next job.

4. What have you been dissatisfied with in your current or former jobs?

5. What do you want instead?

6. What is driving your need for change? If you want a more satisfying work experience, identify what circumstances need to occur and/or what values need to change.

7. Are you able to identify any common themes in the questions above? Are there patterns reflected in your work history, volunteer experience, homemaking, school projects, research tasks, or hobbies?

8. Evaluate your preferences, values, and skills on a scale of 1 to 10 with 1 as least important and 10 as most important.

9. Are there any deal breakers?

10. What additional skills do you need to add to your employment toolbox? Where can you acquire these skills?

11. What are five jobs most interesting to you and where can you get more information (family, friends, current job holders, Internet)? List alternatives and be specific.

12. List five questions you would like to ask in an information interview.

13. Identify five people doing the kind of work you want to perform.

14. What do you need to add to your life?

15. What do you need to do differently to realize your goal?

16. What resources could assist you when writing a business plan for self-employment or sub-contracting?

Finances: Resources and Budgets

FEELING PRESSURE AND STAYING AFLOAT

People who are going through career changes have a significant amount of pressure. In addition to confusion about future goals, the number one concern is resources. When looking for work during a period of job transition, the job seeker must be 100 percent committed to the job hunt and pay the bills at the same time.

The loss of a job usually means that the primary source of funding has dropped. In addition, the job seeker will likely incur new expenses he or she didn't have while employed or in college. When the source of funding for monthly bills, and for job search-related expenses, are no longer accessible, it can feel like a crisis.

You may have heard the common recommendation to keep six months of living expenses in an accessible savings account for such an emergency, but the reality is that few people are able to do this. In order to look for work without income, you may have to be extra cautious in managing cash, resources, and savings.

If you are worried about having enough money for this transition, be encouraged that with some careful planning, and temporary adjustments, feelings of insecurity and fear can change to feelings of abundance and fulfillment. Money, like seasons, comes and goes. By using some caution, common sense, and the suggestions to follow, you can weather this financial challenge.

Losing a job or looking for a job can feel like a free-fall. Often there was nothing you could have done that would have prevented the current circumstances. But this adversity contains the seeds for new opportunity; your job is to cultivate those seeds. It is always darkest before the dawn and may even go pitch black, but this too shall pass.

The following are some suggestions for managing finances, resources, and budgets during this challenging period.

> *"Growth demands a temporary surrender of security. If we don't change, we don't grow."*
> *Gail Sheehy*

TIPS / RESOURCES

Think about what expenses to cut back.

Prepare in advance for items that are going to be drains on money. What things are there that you typically spend money on each day, week, or month that are truly necessities, and what could you do without for even a little while? For example, do you realize that if you are used to spending three to five dollars a day on specialty coffee that you are paying upwards of $75-$100 *a month* just for that? Sometimes just a little awareness of what we spend without thinking can help us reign in some much-needed money here and there.

Review the benefits provided by your former employer.

Assess whether your employer offers a severance package (financial support following termination), or if you can acquire the cash value of unused vacation or sick leave. Some employers provide an Employee Assistance Program (EAP) that can be used at no charge for personal and confidential counseling services. Take advantage of an EAP opportunity if available and seek out a qualified therapist or career counselor who can help you figure out what you want to do.

Apply for unemployment benefits.

If eligible, apply for unemployment benefits and then stretch out the money. Some people overlook applying for unemployment out of pride or not understanding the process. In some states, you can work part-time and earn up to a particular percentage of the weekly gross unemployment benefits without a penalty. Also, ask a benefits representative (or community college counselor) about dislocated workers programs, what they offer, and where they are.

Consider other resources.

If absolutely necessary, consider other resources, such as a retirement plan. Obviously, it is best to avoid using retirement funds, but such an option may be better than incurring new debt. If you have a company retirement plan, consider borrowing from the plan if it allows you to pay it back over time. A company retirement plan may not be taxable and distributions not penalized. These plans may have loan provisions, so check with the plan's administrator before making decisions about withdrawing resources. You should also consider consulting with a tax professional before making this decision.

Keep your credit in good order.

Contact your creditors (your credit card companies, banks from which you have loans, etc.) and talk with their accounts receivable representative. *Briefly* tell them about your new circumstances. Tell them you are unexpectedly and temporarily unemployed, but that you value your credit rating and certainly want to avoid collection. Remember, the organization to which you owe money does not want to enlist the services of a collection agency because such agencies retain half the money they receive as their fees. It makes sense for both you and the creditor to cooperate with each other and reach an acceptable agreement. Ask that you be allowed to make lower payments temporarily and agree to a monthly payment date. Then do everything reasonably possible to fulfill that agreement. This creates a win-win situation for both parties and eliminates the need for a collection agency. Finally, keep your creditors informed as your circumstances change.

A regular payment, say $10 a month, will prevent the credit card company's system from going into a "red flag" mode necessitating an unwelcome telephone call. Speak with the company bookkeeper and ask that a note explaining the agreement be placed in your file. If any changes are made in the payment plan, be sure to notify the bookkeeper in writing or by telephone. If you must, explain that you are not able to make your minimum payment but intend to do so once you are employed and regain a source of income.

Communicate with people and follow these suggestions to keep your credit in good order. If your finances are not in order, now is not the time to burden your circumstances further. Consider going to a consumer credit counseling service (which you can find in your local yellow pages) to get help managing your debt. These services are there for just this reason and are a valuable resource during a period of unemployment.

Look into health insurance coverage and related costs.

Health insurance coverage and related costs during unemployment may be a consideration in the event you are not covered by a plan. Know your rights under COBRA. If you had health insurance with your former employer, COBRA offers the terminating employee the opportunity to continue the same policy coverage under the group rate during the eligibility time period (about 18 months). You, instead of the former employer, must pay the premium, but the policy is under the group plan so the cost is less than an individual policy. If someone has a pre-existing illness, coverage cannot be denied. For people meeting the income eligibility requirements, a state health plan may be available for children.

If you are able to consider yourself self-employed, even on a very part-time basis, you might want to explore the affordable health insurance offered by the National Association for the Self-Employed. Because of their very large membership base, they are able to negotiate very reasonable rates on health and other forms of support.

> "There is only one way by which you can achieve prosperity. It is to take charge of your mind."
> **Eric Butterworth**

> "We can only be said to be alive in those moments when our hearts are conscious of our treasures."
> **Thornton Wilder**

Research other financial resources.

Small business associations sometimes have training programs that offer small business loans. Colleges and universities can provide information about scholarships to help with tuition for upgrading your skills, education toward a degree, or vocational training. Some local job programs provide assistance to individuals who meet low-income requirements. Your local Goodwill chapter offers job placement and training assistance. Accessing these programs may open a back door to companies because employers are afforded tax credits and subsidized wages for hiring certain preferential candidates through these programs.

If you have a disability.

If you have a disability, your State Department of Human Resources and the Vocational Rehabilitation Division may help you with retraining, skills classes, the purchase of business clothing, or other job–related services. Workers' compensation benefits (as a result of an on-the-job injury) or long-term disability insurance carriers may provide training, job placement assistance, and adaptive work site modifications, as well as a financial settlement to close a claim (similar to auto or other personal injury claims). For more information about Veterans and employment or disability, see Chapter 12.

UNEXPECTED EXPENSES

Expect to incur some new expenses for your search for work. Look at your clothes and determine if you need to budget for dry-cleaning costs, new suits, shirts/blouses, shoes, and so forth for interviews. *It is wise to dress for a job interview one step above what you would normally wear to the job on a daily basis.*

Some prospective employers or recruiting companies may reimburse travel expenses for a job interview. Be sure to negotiate in advance the costs covered and reimbursement agreements associated with these types of interviews.

Anticipate some costs associated with your work search activities, such as paper products (stationery, envelopes), stamps, and long-distance telephone charges. Keep in mind that colleges, public libraries, job centers, and the county employment departments often provide job search services and computer access at no charge. And, even if you're avoiding that four-dollar cup of coffee, many coffee shops do also offer free Internet access.

Keep an itemized list and receipts for all of your job search activities and related expenses. The cost associated with job hunting and moving or relocation for a job may be deductible on your tax returns. Job search expenses can be tax deductible if itemized as job search, but may not be if itemized as resume writing or career counseling.

> "Remember this –
> that very little is
> needed to make a
> happy life."
> **Marcus Aurelius**

Assess your discretionary expenses, such as entertainment, Internet fees (as entertainment or for job research), dining out, gifts, magazines, and newspapers. The library is a good resource for daily newspapers (including wants ads), magazines, and professional journals that list job opportunities. Money is a reflection of time and energy. Do the footwork and the money will follow.

BUDGETING

There are only so many expenses you can reduce when assessing finance and budget concerns during a period of unemployment. Consider what are fixed expenses (the required, basic costs of living) and what are optional expenses that can be reduced (like beer and cable TV). Write them down. Too many people try to manage their financial lives from memory! Especially during financially challenging times such as this, having a written budget can fend off disaster.

Now that there is not a steady paycheck coming, first think about what not to do. Don't dig yourself into a hole of financial debt that will be brutal to climb out of. Think about which expenses you will completely eliminate and where you will simply cut back.

Basic budget worksheet for the displaced worker

Complete the following Basic Budget Worksheet in order to assess your finances.

BASIC BUDGET WORKSHEET *for the Displaced Worker*

CATEGORY	BUDGETED MONTHLY	AMOUNT SPENT MONTHLY	DIFFERENCE
INCOME:			
Severance//Vacation Pay			
Unemployment Benefits			
Other Sources of Income			
TOTAL INCOME:			
EXPENSES:			
Housing: Mortgage or Rent			
Home Owner's/Renter's Insurance			
Utilities (gas, water, electricity, trash)			
Telephone			
Home Repairs/Maintenance			
Groceries			
Health Insurance (medical, dental, vision, etc.)			
Prescriptions/Co-payments			
Clothing/Dry Cleaning			
Child Care			
Job Search			
Computer, Internet			
Auto Loan			
Auto Insurance			
Gasoline/Oil			
Auto Repairs			
Other Transportation (tolls, bus, subway, taxis)			
Debt (list minimum monthly payments from each creditor)			
Discretionary Expenses			
Entertainment/Recreation			
Dining Out			
Hobbies			
Magazines/Newspapers			
Pets			
Other Miscellaneous Expenses			
TOTAL EXPENSES:			
NET INCOME (INCOME LESS EXPENSES):			

CONCLUSION

In this chapter, we've taken a look at how to survive some of the common financial challenges associated with the period between a layoff, or other decision to terminate employment, and the attainment of a new position. As you can see, while this is certainly a period of uncertainty and worry for some, one need not despair – with some concentrated effort, accessing the right resources, and using available tools, one can survive this period largely unscathed.

Now is the time to begin the process of exploring one's potential for new opportunities. For that, we'll begin with an exploration of your transferable skills. But first, take a moment to reflect on the points in this chapter as they apply to your life, by completing the discussion questions.

DISCUSSION QUESTIONS/EXERCISES

1. Why is it important to budget expenses when you are between jobs or careers?

2. Identify your necessities and luxuries. Which are critical to maintain?

3. What discretionary items can you give up?

4. What are your financial resources?

5. Is an employer willing to pay for all or a portion of career transition services? What is preventing you from asking?

6. How can you manage your resources until you get a job you really want?

7. What financial changes are required for you and your family during this period of transition?

Identify Your Transferable Skills

Transferable skills are akin to tools in a toolbox. Your employment toolbox contains the tools of your trade. The personal characteristics you use to get work done are behavior competencies, personal skills, and traits and are separate from job skills and knowledge.

Transferable skills are defined in forensic application as *knowledge, skills, and abilities to successfully perform job functions essential to business operations demonstrated from either past training (education) or employment (paid or unpaid work experience) that makes a person employable and may include aptitudes (potential abilities) and interests.*

Transferable skills are adaptable ("portable" if you will) abilities required to perform a specific task or function to a variety of work settings or jobs. Some examples include: *writing, editing, composing, teaching, applying artistic knowledge, using logic to solve problems, interpreting information, planning/organizing, diagnosing, following technical instructions, making decisions, negotiating contracts, keeping financial and production records, managing databases, using equipment skillfully, applying reasoning and judgment, rendering designs and layout, directing work of others, inspecting products, observing regulations and policies, maintaining records, estimating costs, understanding specifications, supervising others, understanding computer operations, verifying accuracy, delegating, communicating effectively, instructing, planning long-range or future projects, estimating value of property, preparing budgets,* and so on.

Also included in this category are some general physical abilities that people often overlook, such as *finger dexterity and eye-hand coordination.* In addition, *self-management* skills include discipline (e.g., controlling emotions with difficult co-workers or customers), time management (e.g., beginning your job search at the same time each day or arriving to work on time), and reliability (e.g., getting a project completed or consistently performing competently in job-related activities).

CORE COMPETENCIES

Core competencies are capabilities and include your knowledge and key functions that contribute to business results. Keeping up-to-date with corporate speak includes assessing what you know and the expertise that you can deliver using current buzz or power word language. For example, executive positions refer to job duties as "accountabilities" and "deliverables." Terms include TQM (Top Quality Management), knowledge management, process reengineering, Best Practices of [insert industry], BKM (Best Known Methods), Advanced [insert industry] Knowledge, distance learning, design and management of [insert industry], diagnosing, framing, and improving aspects of [insert industry], and so forth.

"Competencies," as defined by Kenneth H. Pritchard, *"are the knowledge (bodies of information, such as engineering), skills (such as problem solving), abilities (capacities to perform), personal characteristics (such as decisiveness), and other person-based factors that help distinguish superior performance from average performance under specified circumstances."* For example, the functions for an HR competency-based approach are: 1) selection and placement, 2) training and development, and 3) performance management and compensation. Internet sites to help you develop core competency vocabulary are listed in the Job Description section of this chapter. For example, use Google.com and enter "[e.g., engineer] core competencies." A good site for core competencies with skill levels is www.train.org.

YOU ARE QUALIFIED FOR A VARIETY OF JOBS

One of the most challenging yet important job search activities is **identifying your transferable skills.** When you are questioning if you are skilled enough, instead ask all the ways you are skilled! Tap into your gifted areas—how you are skilled—and subsequently you tap into your spirit.

There is a difference between *soft skills* and *hard skills*, but both are valued in the workplace. Soft skills are about social or people skills: interpersonal communication, leadership, consensus building, appearance/posture, and so on. Hard skills refer to those job-specific skills that are required by your current occupation (e.g., engineering, software development, financial reports, etc.). *Career success depends on a combination of these two categories of skills. In other words,* **both** *are* **important!**

To best represent these important skills when selling yourself to a prospective employer, a list of one-word action verbs, or what I refer to as skill "buzz" words, is useful to consider when writing a resume and cover letter, or to effectively communicate in an interview. Below are examples of some buzz (power words) and qualification phrases. Select those that best describe the skills you enjoy doing and perform well.

> *"Independent of others and in concert with others, your main task in life is to do what you can best do and become what you can potentially be."*
> *Eric Fromm*

For a complete list of action verbs, see the list in this chapter. For a complete list of qualification phrases, see Chapter 7.

EXAMPLES OF SKILL "BUZZ" WORDS AND DESCRIPTORS

~ *Analyze* (ability to examine in detail)

~ *Evaluate* (assess the value, need, or worth)

~ *Restore/Renovate* (able to renew and repair)

~ *Perform* (adept in exhibiting a skill)

~ *Consult* (provide expertise in recommending a solution and plan)

~ *Repair/Troubleshoot* (diagnose and correct)

USE QUALIFICATION PHRASES TO DESCRIBE YOUR SKILLS

~ *Excellent* speaking and presentation abilities

~ *Knowledgeable* in computer technology

~ *Proficient* in detailed data analysis

~ *Able to* plan programs and organize events

~ *Capable* of selling materials and influencing people

~ *Strong* computer repair skills

~ *Excellent* communication skills, both verbal and written

~ *Adept at* project management and building contracts

~ *Competent* leadership skills

~ *Ability to* manage people

~ *Strengths in* overseeing programs and projects

~ *Skillful in* financial planning and implementing budgets

It takes time, thoughtful consideration, and careful selection of words to identify your skills and write your resume. The words you select are powerful tools that best describe your specific transferable skills. The result is an eye-catching resume, a sharp cover letter, and an improved ability to speak about your qualifications.

"If we all did the things we are capable of doing, we would literally astound ourselves."
Thomas Edison

THE PAR TECHNIQUE: PROBLEM, ACTION, RESULTS

The PAR technique is a method of sharing your transferable skills in story form that can be used during a job interview. You may likely participate in what is termed a "behavior-based interview" during which you will be asked to share "real-life" experiences in which you have exhibited competencies similar to those required by your prospective employer. The PAR technique will help you prepare for this increasingly common method of interviewing that starts with the question, "Tell me about a time when. . . ."

The PAR technique requires you to *describe three of your greatest achievements or accomplishments that are work-related.* The intention is for your responses or stories to reveal how your skills can provide value to the employer and uniquely correspond to the job for which you are applying. This approach will set you apart as unique from the other candidates.

Problem: In most cases, a problem (or situation) that you have addressed or solved for a current or former employer forms the basis of your story. It may be perceived as an opportunity. Briefly explain the circumstances, with some specific details so the interviewer can "see" the problem as you saw it.

Actions: What actions did you take to arrive at a solution? (Use action verbs and qualifying phrases.)

Results: What were the results, both tangible and intangible? (Quantify, if possible, the sales increases, improvements, productivity, or whatever relevant outcomes resulted from your efforts.)

How will this assignment help you in an interview? It can reduce feelings of intimidation or uncertainty of some interviews by adding confidence. Employers like actual examples from past experiences as indicators of future performance. Instead of simply stating that you "foster team building," specific examples about overcoming group conflicts, improved results, or leadership style are more effective. Employers want hard performance evidence. You must be able to articulate brief, specific stories that reveal your core competencies.

• *An example of a PAR Story*

Problem: A resident in a crowded tourist town discovered information about commercial property development plans that would eliminate parking for the neighborhood (problem or situation).

Action: He got *creative, pro-active,* and *solution-oriented* by placing phony parking tickets on neighbors' cars in order to apprise the tenants to expect real tickets in the future. He *coordinated* and *organized* the homeowners, *performed research* about ordinances and statutes, *sched-*

> *"Do not let what you cannot do interfere with what you can do."*
> *John Wooden*

uled meetings with the city council, and used *good time management* to insure participation.

Result: By implementing *negotiation* skills, the matter was satisfactorily resolved. Adequate parking was retained for the residents and commercial property, creating a *win-win solution*.

This example demonstrates transferable skills such as *pro-active* and creative *problem solving, coordination of people and projects, research,* and *interpersonal communication* requiring *conflict management*. When you tell a story you know and trust, enthusiasm wells up naturally and the interviewer is engaged. **The PAR story is about skills you know you can perform.** You have a proven track record of performance, based on your story of accomplishment, so you can talk about abilities such as analyzing and project completion skills with measurable and quantifiable results. The PAR can become part of an "Accomplishment Profile" for additional marketing documentation to include with your resume. Chapter 16 about Resumes highlights this topic in the section, Portfolio/Biography/Accomplishment Profile.

Assignment: Think of a problem or situation (opportunity), what you addressed, how you did it, and the results. Be especially specific about what "actions" were required because these are examples of your abilities. What follows is a detailed list of action (buzz) words to consider as you create your story. Or, for another handy tool (when you're having trouble thinking of "just the right word"), create an Internet shortcut on your computer desktop or Favorites folder for www.thesaurus.com

> "First say to yourself what you would be; and then do what you have to do."
> **Epictetus**

ACTION VERBS (AND OTHER "POWER" WORDS)

A	Appraised	B	Clarified
Accelerated	Appreciative	Balanced	Classified
Accomplished	Approved	Brainstormed	Coached
Accurate	Arbitrated	Budgeted	Collaborated
Achieved	Arranged	Built	Collected
Achiever	Articulate		Communicated
Acted	Artistic	C	Competent
Adaptable	Ascertained	Calculated	Compiled
Addressed	Assembled	Calm	Completed
Adept	Assertive	Caring	Composed
Administered	Assessed	Cataloged	Computed
Adventuresome	Assigned	Categorized	Conceived
Advised	Assisted	Cautious	Conceptualized
Advocated	Astute	Centralized	Condensed
Alert	Attained	Chaired	Conducted
Allocated	Audited	Charismatic	Configured
Analyzed	Authored	Charted	Conserved
Anticipated	Authoritative	Checked	Consistent

Consolidated
Constructed
Consulted
Contracted
Controlled
Converted
Convinced
Cooperative
Coordinated
Copied
Corresponded
Counseled
Created
Creative
Critiqued
Customized
Cut

D

Debated
Decisive
Defined
Delegated
Deliberate
Delivered
Demonstrated
Dependable
Designed
Detailed
Detected
Determined
Developed
Devised
Diagnosed
Diligent
Diplomatic
Directed
Directive
Disapproved
Discovered
Discreet
Discussed
Dispensed
Displayed
Dissected
Distributed
Doubled
Drafted
Dramatized
Drew
Drove
Dug
Dynamic

E

Earned
Economical
Edited
Educated
Effective
Eliminated
Empathized
Enabled
Encouraged
Energetic
Enforced
Engineered
Enlisted
Enthusiastic
Envisioned
Established
Estimated
Evaluated
Examined
Exceptional
Executed
Exhaustive
Expanded
Expedited
Experienced
Experimented
Expert
Explained
Expressed
Extracted

F

Fabricated
Facilitated
Fashioned
Filed
Financed
Firm
Fixed
Flexible
Followed
Forecast
Formulated
Founded

G

Gathered
Gave
Generated
Guided

H

Handled
Headed
Helped
Hired
Hypothesized

I

Identified
Illustrated
Imagined
Implemented
Improved
Improvised
Increased
Independent
Influenced
Informed
Ingenious
Initiative
Innovative
Insightful
Inspected
Inspired
Installed
Instituted
Instructed
Integrated
Interacted
Interpreted
Interviewed
Introduced
Intuited
Invented
Inventive
Inventoried
Investigated

J

Judged

K

Kept
Knowledgeable

L

Launched
Lead
Learned
Lectured
Led
Lifted
Listened

Logged
Loyal

M

Made
Maintained
Managed
Manipulated
Marketed
Mediated
Memorized
Mentored
Methodical
Modeled
Moderated
Modernized
Modified
Monitored
Motivated
Motivator

N

Navigated
Negotiated

O

Objective
Observed
Obtained
Offered
Opened
Operated
Ordered
Organized
Originated
Overhauled
Oversaw

P

Painted
Perceived
Perceptive
Performed
Persuaded
Persuasive
Persevering
Persistent
Photographed
Pioneering
Piloted
Pioneered
Planned
Played

> "We are told that talent creates its own opportunities. But it sometimes seems that intense desire creates its own opportunities."
> *Eric Hofer*

"From a little spark may burst a mighty flame."
Dante

Pleasant
Practical
Predicted
Prepared
Prescribed
Presented
Printed
Prioritized
Problem-solved
Processed
Produced
Programmed
Projected
Promoted
Proofread
Proposed
Protected
Proved
Provided
Publicized
Published
Punctual
Purchased

Q
Questioned
Quick
Quick-learner

R
Raised
Rational
Read
Realistic
Realized
Reasoned
Received
Recognized
Recommended
Reconciled
Reconstructed
Recorded
Recruited
Redesigned
Reduced

Referred
Refined
Rehabilitated
Related
Reliable
Remembered
Remodeled
Rendered
Renovated
Reorganized
Repaired
Reported
Represented
Researched
Responsible
Responsive
Resolved
Resourceful
Restored
Restructured
Retrieved
Reviewed
Revised
Revitalized
Risk-taker

S
Scheduled
Screened
Selected
Self-motivated
Self-reliant
Sensed
Sensitive
Separated
Served
Serviced
Set Goals
Set Up
Sewed
Shaped
Shared
Showed
Simplified
Sketched

Sold
Solved
Sophisticated
Sorted
Sparked
Spearheaded
Specified
Spoke
Staffed
Standardized
Started
Stimulated
Streamlined
Strengthened
Stressed
Stretched
Strong
Structured
Studied
Succeeded
Summarized
Sung
Superseded
Supervised
Supplied
Supportive
Surveyed
Symbolized
Synthesized
Systematized

T
Tabulated
Tactful
Talked
Taught
Team-built
Tended
Terminated
Tested
Thorough
Tough
Traced
Tracked
Traded

Trained
Transcribed
Transferred
Transformed
Translated
Traveled
Treated
Trimmed
Tripled
Trouble Shot
Tutored
Typed

U
Umpired
Uncovered
Understood
Understudied
Undertook
Unified
Unique
United
Unraveled
Unusual
Updated
Upgraded
Used
Utilized

V
Vacated
Verbalized
Verified
Versatile
Vigorous
Visualized

W
Washed
Weighed
Widened
Withdrew
Won
Worked
Wrote

JOB DESCRIPTIONS: HELP TO IDENTIFY YOUR SKILL SETS

How do you identify your skill sets, find power words, and locate other buzz speak in order to prepare for a job interview? It helps to have the written job description that describes duties and responsibilities for a job opening. Access to job descriptions help you write a good resume designed toward one or more positions. They also help prepare you to speak knowledgeably during an interview. Job descriptions can also be useful to explore whether or not you want to pursue the job title as a career goal, or what skills you may need to upgrade.

Most people have not analyzed the jobs they have performed on a day-to-day basis, nor have they clearly defined the duties associated with those jobs. You would be amazed and encouraged about how much you have done in work tasks, and the skills you possess, if you analyze your job duties and translate them into a targeted vocabulary before beginning to write your resume or going to your interview. This will set you apart from the competition!

An informative resume and job interview requires explicit use of pertinent words that describe your knowledge, transferable skills, abilities, accomplishments, and qualifications. Learn about the job title or general work industry in which you are interested. Write a comparative list of all the power and skill buzz words associated with that industry and position. This method is the beginning of writing a great resume and cover letter, as well as crafting your introduction in a job interview.

"If you have the belief that I can do it, I shall surely acquire the capacity to do it even if I may not have it at the beginning."
Mahatma Gandhi

HOW TO ACQUIRE JOB DESCRIPTION VOCABULARY

One particularly good resource is the *Occupational Information Network* (or O•NET), which can be most easily accessed at http://online.onetcenter.org For some, this site may be a "ticket to ride" when writing a resume or accessing job description responsibilities and related information. *There is a hard copy book* also accessible at most public and college libraries. This resource provides a comprehensive database of job titles and occupation descriptions, worker attributes, alternative job titles, and job characteristics so you don't have to "re-invent the wheel" creating your skills set of vocabulary.

Much of what you need in order to write your resume and unearth the vocabulary for job duties may be found in the O•Net site. Used in combination with the "qualification phrases" listed in Chapter 7, you can select which "soft skills" and "hard skills" you want to emphasize. *Soft skills* are those that every employer seeks in a candidate such as grooming, time-management, interpersonal relationship skills, etc. *Hard skills* refer to your technical knowledge, abilities, and industry applications.

Other useful Internet sites to help you develop a job description vocabulary include *America's Career InfoNet* (www.acinet.org), the *Wall Street Journal's* career-related site (www.careerjournal.com), and of course, the general website search engines such as www.google.com or www.webcrawler.com (a meta-search engine that simultaneously searches other search engines such as Google, Yahoo!, Ask Jeeves, etc.).

For example, enter "Accountant job description" (or any preferred job title) in Google search engine and see free job description information and job openings posted. In addition, www.iseek.org can provide good job description information. Other valuable sites are found in Chapter 13 about Job Search and Career Exploration Internet Sites.

If you are saying something like, *"That's the point. If I knew the title of a job my skills transfer to, I would be pursuing it,"* then the O•Net (http://online.onetcenter.org) and "IMatch" site (www.qualityinfo.org) sites should be most useful. You can conduct a search that links skills with occupations and perform exercises to uncover work interests and values that link to career possibilities. The site also provides an Ability Profiler (an aptitude test) and wage/salary and employment data. If you have a disability, you can identify essential functions of a job and determine if a reasonable accommodation will overcome a barrier.

Career One Stop (www.onestopcoach.org) provides an interactive process and includes a function called "Create Customized Job Description" as well as an Occupation Search option in order to obtain lists of knowledge required and tasks performed for respective job titles.

> *"Life isn't about finding yourself; it's about creating yourself."*
> *F. W. Wilcox*

Other information resources include major Internet job search banks such as www.monster.com, www.hotjobs.com, and others. Here you can research your work industry and job title interests. Some job opening descriptions are more detailed than others but still provide job duties and skill set vocabulary that can be helpful. ***Remember, however, that when using these job search banks to look for a job, less than 10 percent of job openings are filled through the entire job banks combined.*** It is better to spend the majority of your time networking for the good jobs than depending on Internet job applications without a referral.

Some folks prefer doing their research the "old-fashioned way." Your local public library and librarian can help you select reference books and access to database resources that define occupational or job descriptions. With a library card, you may also be able to access databases and publications or articles from your personal computer, unless restricted by your local library. You can likely find your local public library's website at www.libdex.com, which has links to over 18,000 libraries.

Bringing your transferable skills and new vocabulary together

What follows are sample stories about individuals involved in career transition who applied these techniques to their career transition efforts.

• Example one: accounting, financial planning

John disliked his former job in the banking industry dealing with customers in debt. He wanted to use his knowledge and transferable skills in financial services, but instead of managing debts, he wanted to help build people's financial assets. In other words, he wanted to "repackage" his career and day-to-day work routine with a promotion. This way he could help people avoid getting into debt in the first place and increase their financial worth. He developed his resume using skill "buzz" words from his employment experience to support his goal of becoming an investment planner. He dumped the dead weight of work he no longer wished to perform, and focused on the job tasks he most enjoyed. By the way, using this method, John got the job and loves his work!

This is the job description that John *no longer* wanted to perform:

The Dictionary of Occupational Titles (DOT) and *O•NET* books describe a Credit Counselor as someone who "provides financial counseling to individuals in debt. Confers with client to ascertain available monthly income after living expenses to meet credit obligations. Calculates amount of debt and funds available, method of payoff and estimate for debt liquidation. Contacts creditors to explain client's financial situation and to arrange for payment adjustments so that payments are feasible for client and agreeable to creditors. Establishes payment priorities to reduce client's overall costs by liquidating high-interest, short-term loans or contracts first. Opens account for client and disburses funds from account. Keeps records of account activity. May counsel client on personal and family financial problems, such as excessive spending. May be required to be licensed." (*DOT* 160.207–010)

John had also worked as a *Bank Teller*, described in *The Dictionary of Occupational Titles* as someone who "receives and pays out money and keeps records of money and negotiable instruments involved in financial transactions. Makes deposits, verifies amounts, and examines checks for endorsements. Pays out money, enters transactions, into computer to record and issues receipts. Places holds on accounts for uncollected funds. Orders supply of cash and counts incoming cash. Balances currency, using calculator and computerized accounting. Reconciles data. Opens new accounts and promotes or sells products such as travelers checks, savings, bonds, money orders and cashier checks. Prepares financial documents." (*DOT* 211.362–018)

Notice the required abilities and tasks associated with accounting and finance occupations like those in which John has expressed an interest:

> ❏ **Bookkeeping**
> ❏ **Computerized accounting**
> ❏ **Computer systems & applications**
> ❏ **Auditing data processing**
> ❏ **Pricing and inventory control**
> ❏ **Cash flow management**
> ❏ **Report writing**
> ❏ **Record management**
> ❏ **Credit analysis**

> ❏ **General & cost accounting**
> ❏ **Planning & analysis**
> ❏ **Actuarial & underwriting analysis**
> ❏ **Foreign exchange**
> ❏ **Information systems/spreadsheets**
> ❏ **Capital budgeting**
> ❏ **Stop loss & internal controls**
> ❏ **Financial planning**
> ❏ **Strategic development**

> *"Whether you think you can or think you can't—you are right."*
> **Henry Ford**

> **"If you can dream it, you can do it."**
> **Walt Disney**

Perhaps you can now see how John's new work as a *Financial Planner and Investment Consultant* has allowed him to use his transferable skills from his work experience. In addition, he *upgraded* his education by enrolling in a self-study program and passing certification requirements. John *repackaged* himself so he could change his career from *negative* work that required debt consolidation to *positive* work that involved financial asset management.

• *Example two: sales, marketing, & public relations*

Mary has been employed as an *Administrative Assistant* to an insurance agent for more than 15 years. She performs many of the administrative and insurance sales tasks for her boss, keeping much of the business in good working order, and provides customer service. Mary wants to upgrade her work endeavors in order to earn more money and gain more freedom in her time management. Mary interviewed for a job with another insurance company and accepted employment as an agent contingent upon her passing her licensing examination. She repackaged herself as an *Insurance Agent*.

The Dictionary of Occupational Titles defines a *Sales Agent of Insurance* (alternative title: *Insurance Agent*) as one who "sells insurance to new and current clients. Compiles lists of prospective clients and explains leads for additional business. Contacts prospective clients and explains features and merits of policies offered, recommending amount  and type of coverage based on analysis, using persuasive sales techniques. Calculates and quotes premium rates for recommended policies, using calculator, rate books, and computerized cost programs. Calls on policyholders to deliver and explain policy, to suggest additions or changes. May collect premium from policyholders and keep record of payments. Must hold license issued by state." (*DOT* 250.257–010)

Insurance Agent occupations are described as requiring the following skills and tasks:

☐ **Writing business contracts**	☐ **Contract negotiations**
☐ **Market development**	☐ **Promotional writing & correspondence**
☐ **Presentations & communications**	
☐ **Promotional strategies & implementation**	☐ **Influencing & persuading**
☐ **Public relations**	☐ **Advertising & new business development**
☐ **Customer service/needs assessment**	☐ **Purchasing & comparative analysis**
	☐ **Strategic planning**
☐ **Sales development**	☐ **Cost analysis**

This time, on your own, imagine which of the knowledge, skills, and abilities in this list align with the work experience Mary already had as an administrative assistant. These are the transferable skills we've been discussing thus far.

• Example three: administrative assistant

Shannon likes performing administrative tasks and wants to get a better job as an administrative assistant with a different company. She read the job description in *The Dictionary of Occupational Titles* and *O•Net* and selected pertinent action skill buzz words relevant to her abilities. This information gave her a base from which to begin writing a great resume. The Dictionary of Occupational Titles describes an administrative assistant as a person who "aids executive in staff capacity coordinating office services, such as personnel, budget preparation; records control and special management studies. Keeps practices efficient, including reporting procedures, unit operating practices, record keeping systems, forms control, office layout, suggestion system, budgetary requirements and performance standards. May revise established procedures for improvement. Coordinates collection and preparation of operating reports, such as time-attendance records, terminations, new hires, transfers, budget expenditures, and statistical records of performance data. Prepares reports, including conclusions and recommendations for solution of administrative problems. Issues and interprets operating policies. Reviews and answers correspondence. May assist in budget needs and annual reports of organization. May interview job applicants, conduct orientation of new employees and plan training programs. May direct services, such as maintenance, repair, supplies, mail, and files. May compile, store, and retrieve management data, using computer." (*DOT* 169.167-014)

With this example, see if you can pull out the critical buzz words that Shannon would want to emphasize in her resume and interview preparation.

• Example four: interior design

Jan was bored as a furniture sales representative, and she was not earning the income she desired. She didn't like her limited workspace and the incentive plan didn't seem fair based on individual motivation. When questioned, Jan stated she really wanted to perform work that involved setting up interior design displays. Jan researched the job responsibilities and companies that employed interior design representatives. She wrote a unique resume utilizing her transferable skills in merchandise and customer service, and practiced interview skills. Jan got the job and negotiated an increase in salary. Her work conditions are more suited to her lifestyle, and she is enjoying her new work!

You can "repackage" yourself to design and create the job and work environment better suited to you. Your priorities change as you mature. You outgrow jobs—and like a rubber band—must stretch yourself into new and better job opportunities.

Would it be helpful if you analyzed your transferable skills? Do you need help to repackage yourself? Find a professional who can help unearth your transferable skills.

WHAT ARE YOUR PERSONAL STRENGTHS?

Which of the following words best describes you on the job and in your personal life?

Creative	Strategic	Analytic thinker	Strategist	Counselor
Agreeable	Accurate	Straightforward	Tactful	Curious
Organized	Flexible	Individualistic	Loyal	Artistic
Risk-Taker	Cautious	Understanding	Humorous	Assertive
Practical	Patient	Tolerant	Generous	Friendly
Visual	Auditory	Kinestic	Kind	Persistent
Accepting	Competitive	Social	Helpful	Honest
Supportive	Attentive	Spontaneous	Cooperative	Responsible
Realistic	Idealistic	Punctual	Reliable	Quiet
Self-Directed	Verbal	Listener	Controlling	Materialistic
Mechanical	Dependable	Passive	Conscientious	Logical
Independent	Imaginative	Stable	Outgoing	Sensitive
Conservative	Logical	Persuasive	Decisive	Athletic
Ambitious	Critical	Scholarly	Economical	Involved
Optimistic	Individualistic	Strong	Adventurous	Conventional

Can you identify personal strengths that make you feel strong that are not listed? Ask your family and friends to identify words that best describe you. Who can you ask about your strengths? Do others see you as you see yourself?

Marcus Buckingham states, *"people grow most in areas of natural performance, satisfaction, and creativity."* To take his free career workshop, visit www.oprah.com/money/career/marcus/course/marcus_course_main.jhtml.

The goal is to build on your strengths and manage your weaknesses. Focus on your strengths and you will discover your uniqueness, personal power, and passion. What is it about your strengths that are important to you? Identify what specific activities strengthen you. Identify the action verbs listed in this chapter and then shake the tree to explore how that action verb strengthens you.

A satisfying workday should consist of 80 percent playing to your strengths. Answer the questions, *"What invigorates you?"* And, *"What depletes you?"* How can you use your personal power well and channel your strengths productively? How can you expand your career to perform more of your strengths? If your boat has landed on the wrong shore, identify what activities you are performing that leave you feeling wrung out and stop doing them.

> *"High achievement always takes place in the framework of high expectations."*
> **Charles Kettering**

Although this section is about assessing your personal strengths and performing more of these characteristics in your work setting, consider *what weakens you—not what are your weaknesses.* What activities specifically do you abhor? Akin to doing more of what you enjoy, the goal is to minimize the tasks that leave you drained and depleted. A pharmaceutical sales representative candidate summed this up by stating, "Assembly kind of jobs make me feel depleted. I hate that kind of work." This client feels energized by traveling to medical groups, building relationships, and providing needs assessments for managing customer expectations and excellent service. Naturally he would feel frustrated performing assembly tasks that oppose acting on his strengths.

It is challenging to take a leap and set your sights on locating work using the strengths you enjoy and are good at. But you will be happier and productive when you do this. Good fortune to you!

CHARACTERIZING YOUR CAPABILITIES

How are you effective in terms of what you know, how you perform, and how you get along with people? Ron Venckus, behavioral consultant, breaks down some competencies that are common for success in most work environments. These include problem solving, decision-making, interpersonal communication, leadership, teamwork, and customer service. If asked by an employer what are your contributions to an organization, you will want to be able to answer specifically. Consider the following.

Problem solving requires a needs assessment to clarify the situation. Effective questioning techniques and listening skills are valuable to determine the cause and what happened in a problematic situation. Problem solving requires the ability to consider alternative solutions and consequent impacts to evaluate the best outcome or result.

Decision making is a cognitive reasoning process that leads to selecting an action and may involve selecting from a list of alternatives. Good decision making may require dealing with emotions, maintaining objectivity, considering the impact on others, use of analysis and review, understanding issues and topics, and judgment ability.

Interpersonal communication involves relating with people. It requires listening and understanding the thoughts, feelings, and concerns of others and the ability to connect with a wide variety of personality types. The ability to work with others often requires communication skills, both oral and written, and is an important factor for managers. It may require the ability to influence relationships, as well as establish and build rapport. Other components involve genuine interest in people, empathy, positive attitude, and ethics.

> "The future belongs to those who believe in the beauty of their dreams."
> **Eleanor Roosevelt**

Leadership includes the ability to build trust and confidence. Other components involve vision, influencing, persuading, and listening. It extends beyond job duties and knowledge because it includes the personal side that is used to get work accomplished. It may require questioning, articulate communication, courage, sharing beliefs and values, and character.

Teamwork has components such as applying patience, coping with conflict, motivating, communicating, listening, presenting, contributing ideas, providing feedback, and sharing values. It usually involves a number of people working on a common project toward accomplishing a goal. And, it likely involves diverse temperament types. It requires an answer to the question, "What do I bring to the success of a group?" Consider your ability to demonstrate the following: fairness, respect, credibility, conflict resolution, motivation, contributing to setting goals, communication skills, concern for others, delegating, assessing priorities, identifying strengths and weaknesses, coaching skills, and collaboration.

Customer relationship management is upscaled Customer Service in corporate speak or excellent customer experience satisfaction. It includes extending this competency to internal customers (those you report to and those who report to you), as well as external customers. It requires a needs assessment to be able to understand, meet, and exceed the requirements and expectations of a customer. Breaking down the components, it is your ability to communicate, listen, think creatively, generate ideas, and serve in order to create favorable impressions. What differentiates you from others from the first point of contact, during, and after the interaction? Factors may include empathy; ability to persuade and influence, effectively diffuse disagreements, acknowledge error, or miscommunication; analytical thinking; solution-focused results; flexibility; diplomacy; tact; and open-mindedness.

The purpose of this effort, that is to say, distinguishing your personal skills, traits, and behavior competencies from job skills and knowledge is to help you with ideas on how to develop vocabulary in your resume and job interviews. Identifying your competencies and power words in your job title will increase your confidence and effectiveness. For information about applying your competencies/capabilities in a job interview, see Chapter 20.

Wendy Enelow writes about "showcasing your critical accomplishments to make your resume shine" in an article on her website (www.WendyEnelow .com) and includes the following.

> Bottom line ... the more accomplishment-driven your resume, the more effective by reason of the interest it will generate, and the more inter-

views you will get. Always remember that resume writing is sales and that you are the product. Showcase the product's distinctive features and you are bound to make a sale!

Focus your resume on what you have performed to improve operations, increase revenues, expand market share, strengthen profits, reduce operating costs, enhance business processes, upgrade technologies, deliver projects on-time and within budget, launch new products, build a strong workforce, and more. The challenge, however, is to identify those specific achievements.

To help identify accomplishments and achievements, a list of 13 professional profiles follows. Use this information as a guideline to help you dig deep into your career and identify what makes you such a good hire. In other words, what can you bring to a new position?

ACCOUNTING AND FINANCE—It's all about the money!

- Improvements in revenues, profits, ROI, EBITDA, and other financial measurements

- Design/implementation of cost controls and quantifiable results

- Negotiation of contracts, including dollar amounts, profits, cost savings, and more

- Implementation of automated programs, tools, and technologies to optimize business performance

- Partner relationships with investors, pension plan administrators, board of directors, auditors, and others

- Merger, acquisition, joint venture, and divestiture experience

ADMINISTRATION AND OFFICE MANAGEMENT—It's all about organization and efficiency!

- Design/implementation of streamlined work procedures and processes

- Introduction of automated tools, programs, and systems to enhance efficiency

- Internal and external communications responsibilities

- Contributions to improved operations, cost reductions, and overall performance improvements

- Personnel training and development experience, and the success of those employees

- VIP and executive responsibilities and relationships

CUSTOMER SERVICE—It's all about customers, clients, patrons, and others!

- Improvements in customer service and customer satisfaction scores

- Top industry rankings for quality of customer service organization

- Contributions to sales growth

- Key account management responsibilities and results

- Introduction of automated customer service technologies and tools

- Reductions in customer service operating and overhead costs

ENGINEERING—It's all about development and improvement!

- Engineer/design of new products and their positive financial impact on the organization

- Engineer/design of new processes and their positive financial impact

- Redesign of existing products and their resulting financial/market/ customer impact

- Patents awarded and/or pending

- Integration of advanced technologies to expedite engineering and expand capabilities

- Project planning, management, staffing, leadership, and financial success

EXECUTIVE AND GENERAL MANAGEMENT—It's all about bottom-line performance!

- Measurable increases in revenues, profits, EBITDA, ROI, and other financial indices

- Leadership of/contributions to strategic planning and long-term business development

- Leadership of/contributions to mergers, acquisitions, joint ventures, and business-building initiatives

- Success in expanding into new markets, new geographic regions, new countries, and more

- Improvements in organizational performance, infrastructure, productivity, yield, and more

- Recruitment and leadership of successful management teams (and their contributions)

Discussion questions/exercises

1. What skills are you good at in your current or a previous job that you would like to emphasize in seeking a new job?

2. Analyze all jobs, volunteer experience, sports coaching, and work-related experience during the past 5 years, 7 years, and 10 years.

3. Go to www.online.onecenter.org and at least two other sites to acquire information about job descriptions. Pay specific attention to your self-management (e.g., time management, motivation, etc.) and transferable skills.

4. What methods would you use to determine if your skills are current?

5. In what ways do your transferable skills line up against potential jobs or careers?

6. If you do not know, how can you identify a career counselor you can work with?

7. List as many transferable skills as you can that you might focus on in your next resume revision and/or interview preparation.

8. List action verbs you can use in your resume and cover letter.

9. List your core competencies.

10. List your personal strengths. Identify tasks that enliven you.

Job Related   *Self-Management*

"What is your purpose—what is your calling? What I know for sure is if you ask the question, the answer will come. What I know for sure is you have to be willing to listen for the answer. You will have to get still enough to learn it and hear it and pay attention, to be fully conscious enough to see not just with your eyes but through them to the truth of who you are and what you can be."

Oprah Winfrey

Qualifications That Get Results

QUALIFYING PHRASES THAT BEST DESCRIBE YOUR SKILLS

The following are examples of qualification phrases and general strengths relevant to job performance. These statements are about "capabilities" that support competency areas and are what make your resume unique. They include capacities in *communication, organization and coordination, problem solving, analytical/critical thinking, time management, accountabilities and deliverables (productivity), leadership and supervision, quantifiable results,* and other qualifying phrases.

Examples below introduce the sentence with effective lead-ins (i.e., *Excellent, Ability to, Adept in, Outstanding,* etc.). The statements applicable to you should be selected so the reader understands how you are uniquely capable. This method allows your resume to float to the top of the stack. If a phrase appears too "fluffy," edit it to fit your communication style. Don't be concerned if a phrase seems to overlap into different categories. Mix and match words to your liking. The phrases are designed for use in a variety of work settings.

COMMUNICATION

❑ Excellent communication skills; able to get along with a variety of personality types.

❑ Demonstrated ability with interpersonal communication skills; adept at establishing and maintaining relationships with peers and supervisors.

❑ Adept in cross-functional teams and integrative communication skills.

❑ Able to work independently as well as collaborate with co-workers.

❑ Effective communication skills by planning, providing direction, and assigning responsibilities.

❑ Adept at meeting people's personal needs and instilling a feeling of importance.

- ❑ Persuasive communication skills while incorporating a positive team environment.

- ❑ Adept at compelling negotiation, mediation, and diplomacy skills.

- ❑ Bring an exuberant approach to work; add enthusiasm, energy, and positive spirit to the workplace.

- ❑ Well-developed conflict management skills; ability to instill practical harmony.

- ❑ Able to effectively use diplomacy and tact in communications; skillful at gentle persuasion.

- ❑ Instill team building and enthusiasm toward corporate goals.

- ❑ Possess calm temperament and adaptability for working with a variety of personality types; maintain considerate and cooperative work style.

- ❑ Capacity for communicating expectations and parameters for goal accomplishment.

- ❑ Exceptional communication skills; experienced facilitator.

- ❑ Ability to encourage the cooperation and contribution of others.

- ❑ Strong sense of commitment and loyalty to people and organizations.

- ❑ Outstanding diplomacy that produces win–win results for all participants.

- ❑ Consistently excel at inspiring team to meet goals.

ORGANIZATION AND COORDINATION

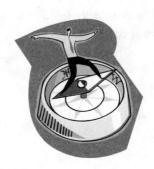

- ❑ Proven ability in strong organizational and coordination skills.

- ❑ Excel at multi-tasking, evaluating, and prioritizing workload.

- ❑ Keen sense of detail in organizational and data management.

- ❑ Demonstrated ability to coordinate people, information, and resources.

- ❑ Ability to clarify processes, build consensus, and instill cooperation to meet goals.

- ❑ Excellent skills in data and records management, including software applications.

❑ Expert organizational skills.

❑ Enlist collaborative efforts to achieve plans.

❑ Pro-active problem solving and barrier removal.

❑ Able to create, develop, and implement projects and cost-effective measures.

PROBLEM-SOLVING

❑ Adept at straightforward, direct, and logical problem solving.

❑ Talent for creative problem solving, including removing obstacles and barriers.

❑ Provide clear focus, action, momentum, and pro-active approach for meeting goals.

❑ Capacity for understanding how individuals, processes, and systems interrelate.

❑ Strong problem solving skills at a functional level, including the ability to act with decisiveness.

❑ Strengths in the use of logical thinking and diplomatic communication skills.

ANALYTICAL THINKING

❑ Capacity for developing new systems, concepts, and paradigms; use of independent thinking to meet future needs.

❑ Strong ability to influence through analytic and intellectual capacities.

❑ Strength for bringing clarity to complex issues. Incorporate analytic systems thinking.

❑ Skillful at determining the long-term impact of plans or strategies.

❑ Demonstrated ability to bring understanding to principles and underlying problems.

❑ Excellent analysis for design, planning, and problem solving.

❑ Prefer concrete, realistic, and pragmatic action in work methods; logical and structured thinking style.

❑ Able to synthesize and organize information yielding strategic and systemic results.

"You can only fail if you stop too soon."
Dr. Jonas Salk

❑ Ability to develop compelling models and theories while providing logical analysis to traditional or new thoughts and systems.

❑ Maintain structure and pragmatism when acting on plans; strength in analysis and methodical implementation.

TIME MANAGEMENT

❑ Capacity for detailed follow-through; task- and results-oriented.

❑ Proven self-starter; autonomous and effective program development and project completion abilities.

❑ Excel at evaluating and prioritizing work tasks.

❑ Proven history of dependability, timeliness, and efficiency.

> "We can go through our whole lives worrying about our future happiness and totally miss where true peace lives—right here, right now."
> Peter Russell

ACCOUNTABILITIES AND DELIVERABLES

❑ Proven history in . . . resulting in 20 percent recovery of customer base, with 70 percent increase in revenues.

❑ Apply concentrated efforts toward defined goals and roles, leading to results.

❑ Talent for implementing and delivering innovative service models.

❑ Consistently exceed and surpass production goals.

❑ Able to provide direction and focus for project completion.

❑ Adept at overcoming obstacles with creative problem solving.

❑ Masterful in finding practical, and concrete solutions for difficult problems.

❑ Talent for producing results; enterprising and resourceful.

❑ Able to instill a clear, precise, structured, and efficient plan of action; focus on targeted outcomes.

❑ Enjoy seeking out challenges and improving methods of operations.

LEADERSHIP AND SUPERVISORY CAPACITY

❑ Strengths in training, supervising, and managing personnel while instilling positive attitudes for goal achievement.

❑ Effective leadership skills by planning, providing direction, and assigning responsibilities; persuasive communication skills.

> "Success is the progressive realization of a worthy ideal."
> Earl Nightengale

❑ Established supervisory skills, including encouraging the cooperation and contributions of others.

❑ Lead by encouraging others, setting priorities, and communicating accurate information.

❑ Influence by imparting commitment, cooperation, and consideration while overseeing details.

❑ General strength for initiating and promoting professional growth and potential.

❑ Ability to clarify processes, build consensus, and instill cooperation to meet goals.

QUANTIFIABLE RESULTS

❑ Propelled a $3+ million cutting-edge service provider to Fortune 500s.

❑ Reversed company from loss to profit in less than 90 days.

❑ Positioned a startup for $2 million sales year one and $10 million sales year three.

❑ Reduced supply chain costs $2+ million.

❑ Turned around $7 million operation; reduced cost 5 percent and modernized operations.

❑ Led major benchmarking analysis and assessment; projected to reduce operating costs $8+ million.

❑ Negotiated with providers to reduce costs while maintaining vendor service levels.

❑ Rescued $29K lost revenue through auditing system and analysis of detail.

❑ Developed database that eliminated errors and improved turnaround time 85 percent.

❑ Reduced operational costs 30 percent annually through strategic procedures, including bringing key projects in-house.

❑ Created profitable alliances with Microsoft, IBM, Intel, Edge Wireless, and others.

❑ Grew Asian service revenue from zero to $1 million by reengineering European operation.

❑ Negotiated acquisition that added $2.5 million funding for organization in highly competitive market.

❑ Spearheaded $2 million capital project ensuring data security.

❑ Added technical infrastructure systems and processes resulting in efficiency models for account purchases.

❑ Penetrated new markets through developing partnerships with Fortune 500 companies.

❑ Created product offerings, including software yielding over $1 million annual sales.

❑ Raised $7 million in funds for non-profit organization, through public/private sectors.

❑ Built alliances with international firms resulting in revenues increase from $1.5 million to $6 million.

OTHER QUALIFYING PHRASES

❑ Excellent skills in interdepartmental integration.

❑ Proficient at computer technology skills, including knowledge of. . . .

❑ Extensive background in business correspondence, writing, and editing; proficient in spelling, grammar, and punctuation.

❑ Proficient with network administration skills, including technical knowledge and expertise.

❑ Consistently responsive, compassionate, and appropriate in caregiving; sensitive attention to the needs of others.

❑ Adept at crisis management; deal effectively using incisive analysis and appropriate action.

❑ Fast learner; quickly able to develop competence and expertise.

❑ Effective at fostering a service-oriented work environment.

❑ Excel when creating a warm, supportive environment focused on promoting harmony and understanding; facilitate individual and group development.

❑ Able to execute logistics and implement effective operations.

❑ Passion for new challenges; highly motivated by work opportunities.

> *"Determine that the thing can and shall be done, and then we shall find the way."*
> **Abraham Lincoln**

> *"The world is full of people that have stopped listening to themselves or have listened only to their neighbors to learn what they ought to do, how they ought to behave, and what the values are they should be living for."*
> **Joseph Campbell**

> *"Treat people as if they were what they ought to be, and you help them to become what they are capable of being."*
> *Johann Wolfgang von Goethe*

❑ Thorough investigative skills; attention to pertinent fact gathering and extensive report writing.

❑ Well-developed personal assistance abilities with a focus on customer service.

Other lead-ins include: ***Cut costs, Grew . . . , Played key role in . . . , Introduced (cost-saving systems...), Spearheaded . . . , Revitalized . . . , Improved . . . , Recognized for . . . , Designed . . . , Won . . . , Resolved . . . , Consolidated . . . ,*** and review the list in Chapter 16, Style/Format-Lead In Tips.

DISCUSSION QUESTIONS/EXERCISES

1. Select 20 qualification phrases that best fit you. Narrow down your 20 selections to your top 10 qualification phrases. Prioritize your top 10 qualifications.

2. Rephrase the selected qualifications to fit your unique capabilities, as needed.

3. Which of the qualification phrases would you most like to perform in your next job?

4. Which of the qualification phrases do you want to develop further—beyond your current capabilities? How can you upgrade your employment toolbox to accomplish this?

Awareness of Your Work Values and Preferences

KEY INGREDIENTS FOR JOB SATISFACTION

In order to find happiness in work, it is important to identify your work values and work preferences. The chances for greater happiness increase when your preferences and values are aligned with your work.

Work values are tendencies or inclinations that are intrinsic aspects of your work environment or requirements that are inherently important to you (e.g., autonomy, opportunities for leadership, an environmentally conscious company, etc.). Work preferences are what you experience as satisfying work conditions, and include preferred external factors or conditions in the physical environment of your work setting (e.g., a window in your office, personal temperature control, availability of personal technology, etc.).

For example, Sue liked being her own boss in an environment that allowed her to use her motivation within her own time frame developing and implementing creative projects, and earning a satisfactory income. She listed her dislikes about her past jobs and then wrote the opposite words to discover what she values. She created and designed her future work based on her work values.

The exercises below will help identify your work values and work preferences. In order to discover five work values that are important to you, list five things you disliked or found unpleasant in past job(s). Next, for each task, list the opposite word for the thing you disliked or found unpleasant. Therein lie your work values. For example:

> "You never know what is enough unless you know what is more than enough."
> William Blake

Dislike	Opposite/Value
Punching a time clock	Flexible time management
Bosses and layers of management	Being own boss
Boredom	Developing and implementing creative projects
Arbitrary salary increases	Income based on self-motivation and accomplishment
Micro-management	Independent, professional respect
Pressure to rush job completion	Reasonable time frames

EXAMPLES OF WORK VALUES

Check off your important work values:

- ❑ Accomplishment
- ❑ Aesthetics
- ❑ Affiliation
- ❑ Authority
- ❑ Autonomous
- ❑ Balance
- ❑ Challenging
- ❑ Collaboration
- ❑ Colleagues
- ❑ Commitment
- ❑ Company culture
- ❑ Competence
- ❑ Competitive
- ❑ Consistency
- ❑ Contributions
- ❑ Control
- ❑ Cooperation
- ❑ Creativity

- ❑ Discipline
- ❑ Diversity
- ❑ Earnings
- ❑ Enjoyment
- ❑ Excitement
- ❑ Expression
- ❑ Fairness
- ❑ Faith-based
- ❑ Flexibility
- ❑ Flexible time-management
- ❑ Honesty
- ❑ Income
- ❑ Independence
- ❑ Influencing
- ❑ Integrity
- ❑ Interesting
- ❑ Knowledgeable

- ❑ Leadership
- ❑ Learning
- ❑ Management
- ❑ Outdoors
- ❑ Predictability
- ❑ Respect
- ❑ Responsible
- ❑ Risk-taking
- ❑ Salary
- ❑ Service
- ❑ Simplicity
- ❑ Stability
- ❑ Status
- ❑ Structure
- ❑ Team effort
- ❑ Time freedom
- ❑ Trust
- ❑ Variety

EXAMPLES OF WORK PREFERENCES

1   *Benefits:* Medical insurance, 401K pension or retirement plan, stock options, life insurance, vacation, personal days, sick leave accrued or paid, child care provision, and health/exercise facility.

2. *Job title/position:* The job has the title one wants, for example, administrator, director, chief of operations, executive secretary, general manager, administrative assistant, computer technician, and so on.

3. *Compensation:* Salary/hourly, profit sharing, bonus, commission, production, travel, cell phone, company car, paid personal days, holiday pay, percentage of growth, partnership, flex time, home office (telephone/equipment), expense package.

4. *Promotion potential:* Basis of determination, merit, time frame for evaluation review, tenure status, conditions and criteria for meeting.

5. *Location:* Physical locale of job tasks, commute distance, travel required, fieldwork, home/office options, telecommute options, and equipment provision.

6. *Policies and procedures:* Written in an employee manual or open-ended; issues of confidentiality established; Human Resources Department.

7. *Work setting:* Supportive staff, industry, and environment; team-oriented or independent; flexible time management or set hours including time clock, scheduled breaks and lunch; size of organization; layers of management; local or national company; lunchroom on/off campus.

"There are two primary choices in life: to accept conditions as they exist, or accept the responsibility for changing them."
Dennis Waitley

JOB SATISFACTION FACTORS

Among the results of the *2004 Job Satisfaction Survey,* conducted by SHRM and CNNfn, were these job-satisfaction factors listed as "very important" by the employees that responded to the survey in rank as follows: 1) Benefits, 2) Compensation/pay, 3) Feeling safe in the work environment, 4) Job security, 5) Flexibility to balance work/life issues, 6) Communication, 7) Relationship with immediate supervisor, 8) Management recognition of employee job performance, 9) Opportunities to use skills/abilities, 10) The work itself, 11) Overall corporate culture, 12) Autonomy and independence, 13) Career development opportunities, 14) Meaningfulness of job, 15) Variety of work, 16) Career advancement opportunities, 17) Contribution of work to organization's business goals, 18) Job-specific training, 20) Relationship with co-workers, and 21) Networking.

> *"The important criteria for job satisfaction are to do more of what you like and less of what you don't."*
> **Eric Allenbaugh**

DISCUSSION QUESTIONS/EXERCISES

1. List five work values that you want reflected in your next occupation.

2. List five work preferences that you want in your next occupation. (Be specific. Define and clarify these preferences.)

3. Rank the job-satisfaction factors in order of importance to you.

More Self-Discovery: Assessment Instruments

INDIVIDUAL DIFFERENCES, PERSONALITY, AND CAREER INTERESTS

Individuals differ from one another in their work preferences and values. These individual differences seem to arise as part of our natural birthright. Personality and temperament impact job choices and performance. Many of our personal characteristics and our strengths and weaknesses are pre-programmed. Psychologists have written volumes about how people are highly formed at birth, with fundamentally different predispositions (in essence, the starting "program" you're given). Some of these predispositions (e.g., eye color, height, preference for social contact, intellectual ability) are relatively stable and unchangeable. Others (e.g., specific skills, values, interests, and knowledge) are more changeable.

Certain personality traits are better suited for particular occupations. For example, how you primarily perceive the world may come from intuition rather than the five senses; how you make decisions using thinking or feelings (i.e., with your head or heart); when managing expectations, whether you make decisions quickly or are slow to gather information before making a decision.

We are innately predisposed as Introverted or Extraverted (or equally balanced). An introverted personality may be forced to develop extraverted characteristics growing up in a culture which values assertiveness, or conversely, the extravert may get censored.

Of course, "types" are not black and white. If you want more information about how your personality type matches career strengths and weaknesses, complete the assessment on my website for a detailed, individualized report that includes an interpretive session.

> **"Your work is to discover your work and then with all your heart to give yourself to it."**
> **Buddha**

Exercise: Does your personality match up with a job?

Take this assessment by Jane Boucher, author of *How to Love the Job You Hate* (www.janeboucher.org) and learn how some aspects of your personality match job traits.

First: Circle all the words that apply to you most often. If you circle a word in one column that also appears in other columns, circle it as many times as it appears. Be spontaneous. Try not to think too long about your choices. Then fill in the totals under each column. Your highest score is your primary personality; your second highest score, or tie score, indicates your secondary or combination personality.

People Person	Detail Person	Command Person	Support Person
Convincing	Analytical	Adventurous	Conforming
Cooperative	Cautious	Ambitious	Conscientious
Friendly	Critical	Center of attention	Meticulous
Generous	Curious	Dominant	Structured
Helpful	Independent	Energetic	Conservative
Intuitive	Inventive	Impulsive	Obedient
Insightful	Intellectual	Optimistic	Orderly
Kind	Introverted	Pleasure-seeking	Persistent
Popular	Methodical	Self-confident	Practical
Sociable	Precise	Sociable	Self-controlled
Tactful	Rational	Enterprising	Unimaginative
Understanding	Reserved	Leader	Efficient
Open-minded	Theoretical	Persuasive	Patient
Service-oriented	Experimental	Action-oriented	Thrifty
Imaginative	Perfectionist	Frank	Humble
Impractical	Idealistic	Practical	Modest
Colorful	Complicated	Concrete	Stable
Expressive	Persistent	Innovative	Down-to-earth
Total_____	Total_____	Total_____	Total_____

Next: Is your job "you"?

After calculating your scores, read the following descriptions of each of the personality types. You'll find that no single profile describes you exactly, but you are probably a unique combination of types as indicated by your scores. If you find you are in the kind of work that best matches your personality, any problems you are having may be due to specific situations, policies, or people. If you find your job doesn't match your personality, you may want to consider changing jobs, or even careers.

People Person—You like people and people naturally like you. You are happiest when you work with people to make their lives better. You probably find that people come to you with their problems and you find it difficult to say no to anyone in need. Your greatest satisfaction comes from people-oriented professions such as teaching, counseling, sales, public relations, acting, the ministry, social work, nursing, and health care. Paperwork and organizational procedures tend to frustrate you, as you would rather deal with people. You need to feel appreciated, and a pat on the back often means more to you than high pay. The key for you is to feel you are helping people.

Detail Person—You may spend your whole life asking, "Why?" You are the one who loves to analyze and interpret. You want to understand why things work the way they do. You enjoy research, information analysis, abstract ideas, theory, and science. You may be a teacher (especially college), physicist, engineer, doctor, economist, lab technician, or computer systems analyst or designer. You may also choose a less technical profession such as writing, commercial art, or architecture, but you will usually choose one that allows you to invent new meanings and methods or improve existing methods and systems. You work best with minimal supervision and get frustrated with bureaucracy and imperfect quality. The key for you is the freedom and time to analyze and perfect things or ideas.

Command Person—You are the mover, shaker, leader, decision-maker, organizer, manager, entrepreneur, and go-getter! You're a bottom line, results-oriented person, and you usually do what you set out to accomplish. Obstacles are simply a challenge you enjoy overcoming. Failure isn't even in your vocabulary. Even if a project doesn't work out as you planned, you just move on to the next one. You'll never be called a quitter. However, you may be called aggressive, domineering, or bossy. You prefer being in charge, but you need to be more encouraging and less demanding of your co-workers. You can be a great motivator and inspiring leader. The key for you is to work hard, play hard, and accomplish your goals.

Support Person—You may sometimes feel invisible or taken for granted, but you prefer behind-the-scenes work. You are the support that holds the organization up. You do the work that requires patience and thoroughness. You like established procedures, regulations, and routines. You probably enjoy fields such as computers, bookkeeping/accounting, statistics, engineering/training, and skilled mechanical work. Because of your patient, diplomatic nature, you are probably also good at teaching or counseling. Though you tend to be a reluctant leader, you are usually a good mediator between people and keep things flowing smoothly. The key for you is to be part of an established routine that works and to keep things orderly and predictable. (Reprinted by permission from Jane Boucher.)

> *"Our job in this lifetime is not to shape ourselves into some ideal we imagine we ought to be, but to find out who we already are and become it."*
> *Steven Presfield*

> *"There is no need to reach high for the stars. They are already within you—just reach deep into yourself."*
> **The Quote Garden**

DISCUSSION QUESTIONS/EXERCISES

1. Based on the self-test, how does your current and/or previous job(s) match your personality? How does your personality conflict with the job(s)?

2. What specific expertise do you want to use in your career? What general skills or abilities do you want to use in your career?

Do You Have a Calling?

SPIRITUALITY AND YOUR VOCATIONAL CALLING

"Vocation" comes from the Latin word *vocare,* which means "to call." A "calling" is defined in *Webster's New World Dictionary* as "an inner urging toward some profession or activity; vocation." Certain people seem to have life callings for certain vocations.

Matching personality types to career satisfaction is one method that may be useful for discovering your "vocational calling." Remember the words of Henry David Thoreau *"If a man does not keep pace with his companions, perhaps it is because he hears a different drummer. Let him step to the music which he hears, however measured or far away."*

Each person is responsible for the nature of his or her own work. Traditional perceptions such as, "a man's job is to provide" and "a woman's work is heart of the home" are appropriate for some, but not suitable for everyone. A man totally supporting a woman financially, or vice versa, may not even be healthy for some couples. In a work setting, we want to be authentic and acceptable. It can drain our sense of identity when we compartmentalize aspects of our personality— acting one way on the job and differently elsewhere. Integrity is unimpaired wholeness—doing work that reveals our authenticity.

Scriptures of various religions reference the word "work" numerous times. Work was meant as a gift and intended for joy. In the beginning, Adam was a dutiful landscape designer, gardener, and botanist who went about naming things. Eve performed her work in daily rounds. Abel was a veterinarian, and Cain was a farmer, including the job of "husbandry" (the act or practice of cultivating crops and breeding and raising livestock; agriculture). When it comes to over-working and keeping balance in work/life, one of my favorite sayings is, *"God likes it when we work, but He loves it when we dance."*

Often, contemplative discussions about career or job change include a desire for "love" or "heart" in the workplace. Your right livelihood is a matter of reso-nance—doing work you enjoy that enables you to reveal the love you are—so that work is an expression of love, not just being "in service" to others. One doesn't so much "find" love in one's work, but "brings" love to it. The work we enjoy the most is the work where our love will be revealed.

Spirituality in career development is about quality of life and making a contribution. Much of what gives us meaning and fulfillment is being of service to others. Where your skills serve people's needs, a likely income source awaits. Incorporating the skills you find most enjoyable and interesting will result in satisfying work. We tend to do better at what we're attracted to.

We tend to attach worth to what a person does for work. During periods of unemployment or job dissatisfaction, our self-worth is challenged. Sometimes the greatest teacher is failure. Proverbs 24:16 reads, *"For a righteous man may fall seven times and rise again."* Sometimes we have to pick ourselves up by our bootstraps more than once.

We are often sidetracked by difficulties and expect to see barriers removed before we even try to pass through them. Keep moving ahead in faith for the path to open.

You have to do the footwork and steadily continue performing focused action to accomplish results. Aspirations and possibilities alone are not enough.

Ask yourself these questions: ***"What goals would I set for myself today if I knew I could not fail?"*** and ***"What announcements would I make if I knew I could succeed?"*** Make your decisions based on the good that can be accomplished if you succeed rather than on the possibility of failure. Success happens to those who take the risk. In the book, *Simple Abundance*, Sarah Ban Breathnach writes, *"The world needs dreamers and the world needs doers. But above all, the world needs dreamers who do."*

Too often, people who lack passion and challenge continue working in jobs in which the spirit suffers, torn between playing it safe with a proven track record and fear of taking a risk into the unknown. Especially in mid-life, people may believe that age precludes a successful career transition.

If you are experiencing career transition in your 40s, 50s, or 60s, you are exactly where you should be! You are just now becoming mature and most useful and qualified to grow into new, challenging and purposeful work that is of greater service and contribution to others. You have paid your dues and it is time for a promotion.

THE IMPORTANCE OF ATTITUDE

The topic of money usually enters conversations about job search and career transition. For the most part, everybody wants more money. In some ways, money has a unique capacity to affect peace of mind. Yet, how hard we work does not necessarily equate to the size of our cash cow.

> *"Dreams come true; without that possibility, nature would not incite us to have them."*
> *John Updike*

John D. Rockefeller believed he had a gift from God in his power to make money, as referenced in the book, *The Purpose Driven Life*. In a different vein, for others not to have too much is a very real gift, lest it corrupt. Do a self-check examination. Ask yourself honestly whether you have the "more is better" disease. Peace of mind can come from simply living with less. In the Buddhist tradition, living plainly is summarized as "less is more."

Marsha Sinetar writes, *"Do what you love and the money will follow"*—and in many cases your passion can pay cash. There are those who have successfully turned their recreation or leisure passion into a positive cash flow.

Most of us spend a considerable amount of our lives focusing on our income. That is, until we're running out of time, then we begin to concentrate on our effect. A sense of security from a paycheck can be abruptly derailed in today's work-turnaround. A frequently mentioned fear is about "security" and getting a job.

For many people, money is the greatest test of trust and faith. The dollar bill reads, "IN GOD WE TRUST." Trust the Creator, not the money.

Don't overlook spiritual compensation found in work settings. When an employer is unable to raise your net income to an anticipated level to satisfy you, consider non-cash benefits referred to as "psychological values." Among psychologically fulfilling job factors are that you

- enjoy your boss and co-workers;

- are given recognition, promotions, and respect;

- share trust and integrity; and

- are able to have family time, challenge, autonomy, and variety, to name a few.

Charles Swindoll writes, "The longer I live, the more I realize the impact of attitude on life. Attitude, to me, is more important than the past, than education, than money, than circumstances, than failures, than successes, than what other people think or say or do. It is more important than appearance, giftedness or skill. It will make or break a company . . . a church . . . a home. The remarkable thing is we have a choice every day regarding the attitude we will embrace for that day. We cannot change our past . . . we cannot change the fact that people will act in a certain way. We cannot change the inevitable. The only thing we can do is play on the one string we have, and that is our attitude. I am convinced that life is 10 percent what happens to me and 90 percent how I react to it. And so it is with you . . . we are in charge of our Attitudes."

Finding your right occupation may require perseverance and patience. Hold on and don't give up. Walt Disney went bankrupt three times before he achieved

> *"It is good to dream, but it is better to dream and work. Faith is mighty, but action with faith is mightier."*
> **Thomas Robert Gaines**

> *"The U.S. Constitution doesn't guarantee happiness, only the pursuit of it. You have to catch up with it yourself."*
> **Benjamin Franklin**

financial prosperity. Abraham Lincoln had less than three years of formal education and met defeat and failure from 1831 until 1860—and he became perhaps the greatest political leader in American history. Ultimately, you, too, can succeed.

DISCUSSION QUESTIONS/EXERCISES

1. What contribution do you want to make, if any, with your life's work?

2. To what extent do you believe the following statement? "Much of what gives some people meaning and fulfillment is being of service to others. Where one's skills serve people's needs, a likely income source awaits." Support your answer with specific information. What impact will your belief have on your career or job search?

3. Take a moment to pay attention to your inner feelings and urges regarding your career path. What inner urgings are you noticing or experiencing? How does this translate to a job choice? Take as long as you need to sit quietly and contemplate this.

4. Have you discovered an unmet passion through your career exploration thus far? Can that translate into a job or career?

5. Answer the questions, "What goals would I set for myself today if I knew I could not fail?" and "What announcements would I make if I knew I could succeed?"

6. Where does money rank among your top five-job priorities?

7. How do you know when you are making "enough" money?

8. What is your definition of success?

9. What is your definition of fulfillment?

10. What forms of remuneration other than money would be of value to you (psychological or spiritual values)? List five and rank in order of preference.

For I know the plans I have for you," declares the Lord, "plans to prosper you and not harm you, plans to give you hope and a future."
Jeremiah 29:11

The Mature (Older) Worker

AGE-RELATED BIASES

Many of my clients, more often than not, include their age when they introduce themselves to me (such as "I am 54 years old and . . ."). A fear exists in many people approaching or over age 50 that age precludes a successful job search. Various opinions exist about whether age-related biases negatively impact older workers' employability.

Many mature workers, referred to as *"mid-lifers,"* feel they are discriminated against due to their age, but many employers do express a willingness to hire mature adults, especially for their work ethic, expertise, self-management, and supervisory skills, as well as reliability that younger workers may lack. Some employers are disillusioned with younger workers' attitudes and inexperience.

One of the fastest growing segments of the workforce comprises people aged 55 to 68. The rising labor force participation rate of the 55+ age group is receiving an array of publicity. Aging Baby Boomers are active in today's job market. You haven't earned the "mature" worker distinction until you reach at least 58 years of age. Instead of retiring, people enter their second, third, and fourth careers. Age is not the significant factor in career decision-making that it once was. We live much longer and are expected to work years past previous retirement age. Some people prefer to work well into their 80s and 90s, because they enjoy the work they do. And, unfortunately, due to the recent economic downturn, which has left a lot of retirement funds in poor shape, more and more mature workers have been either keeping their jobs or re-entering the workforce out of necessity.

Many of the Baby Boomer generation are biologically, attitudinally, and mentally 10 or more years younger than their parents were at the same age, and their lifestyles reflect this. If you are functionally or attitudinally younger than your biological age, then this is reflected in the way you tend to live your life—and people notice! If you are 50 years old, but attitudinally or functionally older, then you are for all practical purposes acting old (and people notice). The point is: Stop perceiving your age as an obstacle. Ask yourself what occupation you

> "The second half of life represents the first real chance we've had to define ourselves and to live in a manner of our own choosing."
> **Leider and Shapiro**

would like if you were younger, such as in your 30s. Don't limit your career choices based on your age.

Pre-retirement transition gives way to thoughtful consideration to ways to be creative and productive, to identify work that gives meaning, to implement strategies to repackage oneself, and to gain greater control over money. More older workers are saying "no" to retirement and continuing to work full-time, or choosing semi-retirement phases. Phased or transitional retirement means gradually working fewer hours or not ending full-time employment. Many of these individuals are transitioning because of some kind of personal or organizational change, merger, acquisition, or reorganization. A smaller percentage is dismissed from jobs due to performance. Some are returning to the workforce after a period of retirement, homemaking, or letting go of a business. Others are looking for work after divorce or death of a spouse. Some seek relocation, a better opportunity, or semi-retirement.

The demand for older workers is expected to increase in the future. Older employees are more likely to remain in their positions whereas younger workers tend to change jobs more frequently. The first wave of Baby Boomers (born between 1946–1964) will reach age 65 in 2011. The United States Bureau of Labor Statistics reveals that of the 4,864,000 people who are over 65 and willing and able to work, 96 percent of them are working at the time of this writing. Of this number, just over 50 percent work full-time and the rest are working part-time (less than 35 hours a week). Breaking down the statistics even further, there are 2,705,000 people in the labor pool (working or seeking work) in the 65-69 age range, with 97 percent working. Of the workforce in the 70-74 age range, 96 percent in the labor pool are employed. There are 888,000 in the 75 and over labor pool and approximately 53 percent work full-time and 47 percent work part-time. Of this group, there are 319,000 in the 80+ age range workforce, with 97 percent of them working.

I like the saying that "40 is the old age of youth and 50 is the youth of old age."

Organizations need skilled older workers who possess good work ethics. The employee who performs as a good generalist but also contributes sub-specialty skills may become indispensable and exempt from layoffs. The question, *"What is preventing you from upgrading your skills?"* is pertinent for any job seeker to answer. For example, if you are a surveyor or information specialist and have not updated your skills for a while, learn CAD or computer troubleshooting skills in order to add value beyond your day-to-day job description. If you do enroll in such a program, it is important to convey to an employer during an interview that you are currently involved in some type of a skills upgrading effort. This indicates that you have professional goals and makes you more competitive versus an equally qualified candidate who is not enrolled in a value-added course of study. If you need to improve your data entry (typing) speed and accuracy, download software at www.typingmaster.com. To upgrade Internet learning, go to www.pcwebopedia.com or www.Whatis.com

Factors that contribute to the selection of more mature workers include technical skills, confident first impressions, well-prepared resumes, loyalty, and productivity. Other keys for success include talking about yourself and skills as meaningful to the employer. See Chapter 20 (Job Interviews) and Chapter 6 (The PAR Technique) as methods to connect with an employer during an interview. It may feel uncomfortable looking for work as an older worker but getting a job is far from impossible. The emphasis is about putting your best years of knowledge and experience to work.

Older workers must get past real or perceived age bias and focus their efforts on promoting their goals and positive attributes. Each demographic group faces particular stereotypes and biases. For example, some men think they were not selected for positions filled by women, while some women think they are disadvantaged because it is still a man's employment market. Women are concerned about child-care activities and issues unique to women. Some workers think they are discriminated against due to their sexual preference or lack of a college degree. Some people think a disability is an advantage or that affirmative action precludes them. And you know what? In some cases, the people who perceive these things might be right. But in many cases they are wrongly assuming that some hurdle exists and therefore shooting themselves in the foot by not going forward with pursuing their goals. You'll never know until you try.

GENERATIONAL MIX

The generational mix includes the "Veterans," born before 1945, the "Baby Boomers," born between 1945-1964, "Generation X," those born 1965-1980, and the "Nexters," born 1980-2000. A very general portrayal of generational strengths indicates that Veteran workers are perceived as steadfast, loyal, and persistent in getting the job done. Baby Boomers are eager and hardworking. They may make good consultants after retiring from full-time work. Generation X workers are flexible where work conditions are vague. However, they do tend to value autonomy and put a high premium on "fairness" in the workplace. Thus, they prefer flatter organizational structures and may more often find themselves in conflict with authority figures. Finally, they tend to put a high premium on "entertainment" or have a higher need for changing stimulation in their work environments. The Nexters' identity is still evolving and shares some traits with Generation X.

The X-Generation wishes the mature workers would retire to make room for them. Or, they believe they lack the skills that mature workers possess, while mature workers may think youth is more desirable to employers. The future trend, influenced by an anticipated shortage of younger workers, is that it may become more common for four generations (people between the ages of 18-82) to work side by side in organizations. As the Baby Boom generation postpones retirement, younger workers may be competing against their grandparents in the labor force.

> **"Guilt not the past. Fear not the future. Waste not the present."**
> **Anonymous**

The advantages usually outweigh the disadvantages of an intergenerational workforce, but conflicts occur regarding acceptable work hours, work ethic, respect, organizational hierarchy, acceptable dress, dealing with change, and technology issues. In an interview, consider asking about whether the company has a range of generations in the work setting and whether that has been perceived as positive or negative in general. This shows you are current on the topic and the challenges that human resource departments face. Be prepared to address how you can overcome any potential problems. Express that you can work effectively with a generational mix and that you appreciate learning from others.

AGING IMAGE AND APPEARANCE

Don't try to look younger than you are but consider investing in an image consultant, make-up session, or new hairstyle and cut in order to appear your best. You don't want your appearance to look outdated and old-fashioned. Fitness may add a competitive edge over an equally qualified candidate. Here are a couple of tips: One's fitness overrides others' attitudes about aging. Also, ***the single most cost-effective method to enhance the mature worker's appearance is a teeth-whitening process.***

A frequently asked question about age and job search is *"Should I dye my hair to cover the gray?"* Consider what image you want to project that matches the job. A mature executive, whose appearance matches the traditional role, may have the advantage over a younger worker for a highly skilled management position. Conversely, the "younger worker-look" may better match the part for the snow skiing and skateboard shop job. I have a mature client who decided to shave his gray mustache after wearing it for 25 years. We were amazed over his more youthful appearance, and his employment offer!

NEGOTIATING A SATISFACTORY SALARY FOR THE MATURE WORKER

Merely landing a job is not necessarily the challenge for all mature workers; rather, the difficulty is in negotiating a satisfactory salary in light of their experience. Mature workers are more likely than their younger colleagues to have held positions in management that pay higher salaries. Competition for highly desirable upper management jobs can be stiff. Learn to implement the best interview strategies.

As individuals age, their salary prospects tend to go up in light of experience, until the position's earning capacity plateaus, and then salary may decline for a variety of reasons. The older job seeker is more likely to transition to self-employment, consulting, part-time employment, community/volunteer service, semi-retirement, or a combination of options.

An employer can be convinced to pay more than the original salary "range" to a mature worker who uses good salary negotiation skills. *Salary determination should be based on three criteria: your experience and education, the job responsibilities, and going-rate* for a comparable position within or outside a given locale. For more complete coverage about negotiating salary and job offers, read Chapter 21. Never reveal your salary history or salary requirements in correspondence, job applications, resume, or similar documents. Chapter 19 (Job Application Form) provides more information about this subject. More often than not, disclosing this information before a job offer is made will decrease a starting salary.

Mature workers may take longer to find a job, especially one that meets their requirements. The length of time for the older worker to secure employment can be discouraging, since the longer the time since the last employment, the lower the success rate. However, the mature worker can acquire work quickly and receive earnings commensurate with their abilities. At the time of this writing, the average job search lasts 18 weeks. (Bureau of Labor Statistics) In 2007, the most recent number published by the Bureau of Labor Statistics, the average wage per job in the U.S. (covered employment) was $44,458. For the link to this information, go to www.bls.gov/cew/home.htm.

THE VALUE OF CAREER COUNSELING AND PROFESSIONAL ASSISTANCE

Older workers may require career counseling to better market themselves. Older workers tend not to accept help in resume development, cover letter writing, and interview strategies, erroneously thinking that job search methods used in the past will land them a job again. They may not want to spend the money to invest in career counseling, but it is important for older workers to learn new

> *"There are no limits. There are only plateaus, and you must not stay there, you must go beyond them."*
> *Bruce Lee*

techniques in job search skills. Mature workers should practice interviews in a role-play or mock interview setting with a competent career coach.

Job search strategies for mature workers include defining the job seeker as multi-dimensional. Drawing from a background of diverse skills and the ability to perform multi-tasking roles offers added value to an employer. Career counselors can provide job leads as well as assess suitable goals. Suitability is a key component of job selection. An older worker may not be a good match in a loud music store designed to attract the Generation X or younger listeners, but may be a good match for a customer service position in another type of company. Customizing cover letters and resumes to present the mature worker in the best light improves chances for acquiring an interview.

RESOURCES

Executive job search sites include www.careerjournal.com, www.sixfigurejobs.com, and www.execunet.com.

www.2young2retire.com—advocates renewal and regeneration in the post-50 time of life, including meaningful work, community service, life-long learning, better health and relationships. It offers resources including True Story profiles, links, Getting Started tips, columnists, a subscriber newsletter, and book, *Too Young to Retire: 101 Ways to Start the Rest of Your Life.* The popular chapter "101 Opportunities for the Open Minded" lists career choices uniquely relevant to the age group.

www.2ndhalfstrategies.com—is designed to help facilitate your vision, set aside stereotypes of aging, and create a new personal legacy with the inherent opportunities that aging creatively offers. Articles, workshops, tele-classes, newsletter, links, and other resources are available to assist with inspiration and renewed purpose.

www.boomercareer.com—is the publication for sophisticated, active Baby Boomers who want their careers to be vital components in fulfilled and challenging lives.

www.notyetretired.com—Not Yet Retired. A new breed of seniors and the Baby Boom generation is revolutionizing retirement by discovering creative retirement alternatives.

www.thirdage.com/money/career—offers a variety of articles and timely reports on subject matters related to finding successful work opportunities.

www.myprimetime.com/work—provides featured articles with topics related to family, money, health, and work.

www.monster.com—aging issues expert Linda Weiner posts her articles.

> "People travel to wonder at the height of mountains, at the huge waves of the sea, at the long courses of rivers, at the vast compass of the ocean, at the circular motion of the stars; and they pass by themselves without wondering."
> **St. Augustine**

> "We turn older with the years, but newer every day."
> **Emily Dickinson**

• Starting your own business after 50

BOOKS

- *The Best Home Businesses for People 50+* by Paul and Sarah Edwards

- *Don't Retire, REWIRE!* by Jeri Sedlar and Rick Miners

- *Second Acts: Creating the Life You Really Want, Building the Career You Truly Desire* by Steven M. Pollan and Mark Levine

- *It's Never Too Late to Plant a Tree*, by Mel and Morrie Helitzer

DISCUSSION QUESTIONS/EXERCISES

1. If you are young, what could you imagine learning or appreciating about an older worker?

2. Conversely, if you are an older worker, what could you imagine learning or appreciating about a younger worker?

3. What biases do you have about working with someone not your age? Explain what you could do to bridge the gap.

4. What image, if any, do you want to project on the job? What changes might you need to make to accomplish this image?

5. If you have a disability, what accommodations would you recommend to an employer to enable you to perform the essential functions of the job? If you don't know, where can you find this information?

6. What is the minimum salary you require to meet your monthly expenses?

7. What is a satisfactory salary for work you want to perform? Is the amount realistic based on the labor market in your community? If you do not know, where can you obtain salary/survey information?

Disability and Employment

OVERCOMING OBSTACLES

> **"Do what you can, with what you have, where you are."**
> **Theodore Roosevelt**

A frequently asked question is *"During a job interview, do I discuss my disability or not?"* You do not have to reveal your disability (defined as limitation of a major life activity) to a potential employer unless it directly affects your ability to perform the essential functions of the job. It is helpful if the "essential functions" are spelled out, but many companies have yet to include this as a category on a job description. If you have a disability, communicate effectively about how your abilities and qualifications match the position's description. If your disability does not preclude your performing the job's essential functions, you may choose not to mention it.

An employer cannot ask, *"Do you have a disability?"* Rather, an acceptable question is *"Can you perform the duties of the job you are applying for?"* You can tell a potential employer about your disability during an interview, on the job application form, after you have been offered the job, or when beginning the job. It is probably best not to disclose it on the job application form to avoid any premature misconceptions.

If your disability requires some worksite modifications, such as an ergonomic workstation or adaptive equipment, discuss what accommodations are required. Many employers have never been educated about accommodating a disability, and it is up to you to address up-front any potential barriers. It is usually lack of information and subjective judgments—not objective or firsthand experience—that determine an employer's opinion toward workers with disabilities. Go the extra step and discuss how to bring solutions to overcome obstacles to employment. Having the solution to or an alternative for an employer's misperception of a problem demonstrates your forthright approach to handling potentially sensitive matters. How you handle yourself in the interview is an example about how you can be expected to come across in other work situations. Present yourself as confident, proactive, and knowledgeable.

If an employer is not informed about a disability during an interview, misunderstandings due to lack of communication may occur. For example, the employer who interviews a hearing-impaired candidate may look away while asking a question—and feel put off by a lack of response—because the candidate did not hear the question posed. A lack of information may cost a disabled candidate an otherwise perfectly suitable job. In this circumstance, tell an interviewer if you have a hearing impairment. Say, *"I have a hearing disability in both ears and it is helpful if you speak up and look directly at me. Otherwise, my hearing impairment does not affect my work abilities."* This straightforward approach demonstrates to the employer your communication and problem-solving skills.

If you decide to discuss your disability, avoid playing the "ADA card" or "victim" in any way as an attempt to force your hiring. Better to put your cards on the table about your strengths, skills, and knowledge that is useful for the employer. Larger companies are more likely to hire people with disabilities having more familiarity with such practices.

> *"A pessimist is one who makes difficulties of their opportunities and an optimist is one who makes opportunities of their difficulties."*
> *Harry Truman*

DISABILITY ACCOMMODATIONS

There are a lot of misconceptions about the cost of disability accommodations. The average cost of modifying a workstation is around $500 or less. For a large company (Microsoft, for example) this amount is insignificant for a good employee, but $500 may not be regarded as a "reasonable accommodation" for a small start-up business. Access Technologies, Inc., telephone number 1-800-677-7512, can assist with assistive technology information. For information about job accommodations, call the Job Accommodation Network at 1-800-526-7234.

If you have any barrier or impediment to employment, call your local state Vocational Rehabilitation Division and ask for an eligibility evaluation to determine whether you are eligible for services. The Workers' Compensation Division may be able to provide assistance for some eligible injured workers. Extensive websites, information, and resources are available about Adaptive and Assistive Technology and Job Accommodations, Americans with Disabilities Act (ADA), Employment for the Disabled, Brain Injury, Career Exploration, Education and Training, Employment Information, Job Search/Placement, Mental Illness, Rehabilitation Agencies, Spinal Cord Injury, and General Health. Explore www.aapd-dc.org, and www.rehabchicago.org.

VETERANS

The U.S. Department of Veterans provides training and employment placement assistance for eligible veterans with disabilities. Contact your State Veterans Employment Service, a department for the State Employment Services, listed under state government agencies in the telephone directory. The U.S. Department of Labor (DOL) has a Veterans Employment Training Service (VETS) to assist with locating employment opportunities. The Disabled Veteran Outreach Personnel (DVOPs) matches employers with qualified candidates who are veterans. Special consideration is given to veterans who are entitled under

> "It is never too late to be what you might have been."
> George Eliot

the Vietnam Era Veterans' Readjustment Assistance Act (VEVRAA). The largest military-related job board on the Internet, www.VetJobs.com, has helped thousands of vets find jobs.

SOCIAL SECURITY, DISABILITY BENEFITS, AND EARNED INCOME

You can work and get Social Security at the same time. While you are working, your earnings will reduce your benefit amount only when you reach your full retirement age. If you are not already receiving benefits, be sure to contact Social Security at the beginning of the year you reach full retirement age. Even if you are still working, you may be able to receive some or all of your benefits for the months before you reach full retirement age. For a full treatment of this subject and the formula to determine how much your benefit will be reduced, visit www.ssa.gov/retire2/whileworking.htm.

If you are interested in earning income but don't want to lose Social Security disability benefits, special rules make it possible to still receive monthly payments. For a thorough examination of this topic, go online to www.ssa/gov/disability and visit the "The ticket to work/work incentives" site. You can also order a brochure titled, "Social Security: Working While Disabled? How We Can Help," which describes incentives at a glance, how your earnings affect your Social Security benefits or payments, special rules for workers who are blind, how long Medicaid will continue, and special deductions for work expenses.

THE FAMILY AND MEDICAL LEAVE ACT

This act allows employees who have met minimum service requirements (12 months employed by the company with 1,250 hours of service in the preceding 12 months) to take up to 12 weeks of unpaid leave (in one block of time or intermittent use) for: (1) a serious health condition, (2) caring for a family member with a serious health condition, (3) the birth of a child, or (4) the placement of a child for adoption or foster care. When the employee is ready to return from leave, they must be restored to an equivalent position with equivalent pay, benefits, and conditions.

Women affected by pregnancy or related conditions must be treated in the same manner as other applicants with similar abilities or limitations. An applicant is not required to apprise a prospective employer during an interview if she is pregnant, and she must be permitted to work as long as she is able to perform the job. An employer must hold a job open for a pregnancy-related absence the same length of time as for employees on sick or disability leave. For more information, go online to www.eeoc.gov/facts/fs-preg.html.

CHAPTER 13

The Labor Market and Methods for Obtaining Work

HOW IS YOUR JOB-FINDING IQ?

True, false, or maybe?

1) Technical experts who specialize in one specific skill are more employable than individuals with broad experience in several areas.

False: Many employers want candidates with broad experiences and background skills. Value is added when a candidate can operate in diverse settings and function with multiple projects.

2) When applying for a job, it is most effective to first go through the human resources department and take the procedural steps.

False: It's been said that *"human resources' function is not to hire you, it's to screen you out."* Some of the best jobs are obtained by scheduling a face-to-face meeting with the person who makes the hiring decisions. A candidate can meet with the human resources personnel at a later time when mutual interest in the position has been established.

3) Most job openings are found in the "Help Wanted" section of the newspaper.

False: The "hidden job market" accounts for about 80 percent of job openings. That is four out of every five jobs! This is the reason that *networking and personal contacts are the most successful methods for locating job openings.* Often, people hire people they know regardless of exact experience or skills for the job.

4) Be sure and ask family and friends to help you in your job exploration.

True: Tell family and friends about your job search and ask them to help you in your networking efforts by passing along any information they may have now or hear later.

> *"Most people see what is, and never see what can be."*
> **Albert Einstein**

> "Life is what we make it. Always has been, always will be."
> Grandma Moses

5) Mass mailings of your resume and cover letter are an effective way to find prospective employers with job openings.

False: Mass mailings (the shot gun approach) are considered one of the most ineffective, costly, and time-wasting efforts for your job search endeavor. Unsolicited resumes and cover letters usually get ignored by companies, which may receive volumes of such correspondence daily. If you use mailings, target an appropriate company and a specific individual within the company.

6) Most job openings are filled by executive search firms and recruiting companies.

False: A small percentage of job openings are filled through executive search firms and recruiting companies. These types of recruiting firms are looking for candidates, usually executives or physicians, who meet very selective criteria to match a specific employer's need. These firms charge the employer a substantial fee for the placement.

7) Employers tend to read resumes thoroughly when selecting candidates for an opening.

False: Employers tend to scan a resume within two to six seconds looking for specific skills and phrases that are key to the job's responsibilities.

8) People tend to stay in good jobs for a long time.

False: Research about turnover rates varies. The fact is that people now tend to change jobs frequently compared to previous decades. It has been estimated that workers change jobs as frequently as every six months and professionals change jobs every two years on average. This means more turnover and job openings for you!

9) The state employment division/administration services will find a job for me.

False: The state employment division/administration is a source of unemployment benefits and limited job openings. The department may provide access to computers and state and local employment statistics, wage data, and select job openings. This is only one resource, a limited one, to incorporate in your job search networking database. Local colleges also have career placement centers that provide job postings and use of facility resources.

10) A private employment agency will get a job for me.

Maybe: There are different types of contingency firms that work for clients and companies. An employment agency will make you sign a contract that you agree to pay a percentage of your income to that agency if you take a position they locate for you.

11) Professional journals' employment sections are a good resource for job openings.

Maybe, but probably not: Ads in national newspapers (such as the *Wall Street Journal* and the *New York Times*), magazines (the *National Business Weekly* or the *National Ad Search*), and professional journals do announce job openings. Each ad results in thousands of applications that increases competition and reduces the odds for you securing an interview. Unless your qualifications and resume specifically match the job, don't expect a job placement.

12) Internet sites, such as Monster.com and Hotjobs.com are a good resource for job openings and placement.

Maybe: These sites are a limited resource. Less than 10 percent of jobs are filled through all of these types of websites combined, and of those 10 percent more than 67 percent did so on company websites. This is only one job search resource and correspondingly perhaps worth less than 10 percent of your effort. Your chances increase if you explore openings specifically posted on the employer's website.

13) The holiday season is a slow time for hiring in the job market.

False: The holiday season (Thanksgiving through New Year) is seeing a new trend as a time of good hiring prospects. Employers and hiring managers are in good spirits and the time is opportune for job search activities. There tends to be less competition during this time because applicants get busy with other life activities, or are of the mistaken notion that hiring does not take place during the last six weeks of the year. Take advantage of this time and the decrease in applicants, including the socialization that comes with the season. Use the telephone to call employers directly and send your cover letter and resume. New company budgets with new positions are created during this period. Attend holiday social events where you can meet new people and let them know you are job-hunting in order to get referrals. If the employer is waiting until after the new year to finalize a new hire, your proactive approach could ensure you the position.

14) It is good strategy to get feedback from friends and family about your resume.

False: Opinions abound about what your resume should or should not look like, but asking for advice from anyone other than a professional or someone employed in your field is a mistake. You should ponder feedback and recommendations from recruiters, human resource management, resume writers, or those who specialize in your industry. However, even professional ideas and biases about what will be the most effective will vary. Ultimately, you must be able to defend your resume content and format.

> *"Only use your energy to focus on what you want."*
> **Anonymous**

> "Do not follow where the path may lead. Go instead where there is no path and leave a trail."
>
> **Ralph Waldo Emerson**

15) To get a job sooner, you should apply at large corporations.

False: Seventy percent of job openings are now created by small businesses, not large corporations. Since the negative economic impact of 9/11, overseas outsourcing, downsizing, and recession, job losses have been recovering through new jobs with start-up businesses and small to mid-size companies. If you are good at something, getting a job with a smaller business is usually quicker. If you are a "projects queen" or "projects king," small companies often go through a business development phase and hire independent consultants to perform work on a short-term or long-term basis. If you are good at one project, the company may give you two or three or more and it can lead into full-time employment. You may decide that working as an independent consultant for multiple small companies is your ideal job.

16) It is good strategy to get another college degree.

Maybe: Often job hunters question whether a degree will help secure a job. Putting more education or another degree on your resume is not necessarily a fix. In assessing if a degree is important, ask yourself some questions. *"Am I going back to school because it is a familiar environment that provides the pretence of career development?" "Am I considering school because I don't know what my options are otherwise?" "Am I afraid, and therefore delaying my job search?"* Are you thinking, *"A college degree worked well for me once so maybe it will again?"*

People who have bachelor's, master's, and doctorate degrees may earn more money or be more likely to get the job, but only if the degree is specifically pertinent to the job or field. But don't hide out in an academic program you are not excited about, thinking it is real career action.

17) It is a waste of time to apply for a position without a job opening posted.

False: An employer wants to know how you will make or save money, or save time for the company, regardless of whether a current opening exists. You may be able to create a new position or fill a potential opening. Employers often wait for the "right" candidate to come along. Many employers do not post these unique and really good positions.

18) A good resume is imperative to perform a job search.

False: The first rule of job search is to talk with as many people as possible anywhere and anytime. A resume is a valuable document in your job search, but it will not replace your need to communicate to people about your job interests.

RELOCATION, UNEMPLOYMENT RATE, AND THE LABOR MARKET

Relocation, within or outside the United States, requires information and planning. Your decision about whether to relocate often includes factors such as the quality of life an area provides, schools, unemployment rate, job growth rates by occupation, and cost of living. You may want to research how many people in your occupation reside in the area of interest. What are the expected future demands, and how many job openings over the next 10 years are projected in terms of growth and replacement? Are openings due to retirement, death, or job transition? What are areas of saturation versus demand for your field? Which areas have a population growth that equates to a need for jobs and services?

The employment rate is the ratio of job seekers to the working population. When the employment rate is low, few people are unemployed. I live in the state of Oregon, which has held one of the very highest unemployment rates of all 50 states for ages. The adjacent state, Washington, frequently competes with Oregon for this status, as does Alaska. Conversely, inland neighbors such as Idaho and Nevada have had unemployment rates lower than the national average. Does this mean you should move to Idaho or Nevada to look for work? Not necessarily.

"Job growth" is a factor that should be considered in addition to a state's unemployment rate. During recent periods of high unemployment, Oregon has had one of the highest percentage increases in job growth; people continue to move to Oregon and acquire work in spite of a high unemployment rate. Also, the unemployment rate within each county may exceed or lag behind a state's average.

If you are looking for a job in a state that has an unemployment rate lower than the national average, which is nearly 10 percent according to the most recent data from the Bureau of Labor Statistics, Anthony Balderrama, CareerBuilder writer, writes in a 2008 article, "Best and Worst States for Jobs." The following are the top three ranked by unemployment rate.

South Dakota: Unemployment rate: 3 percent; Population: 796,214; Mean annual wage: $30,460; Top industry: Trade, transportation, and utilities (20.2 percent)

Idaho: Unemployment rate: 3 percent; Population: 1,499,402; Mean annual wage: $34,290; Top industry: Government (23 percent)

Wyoming: Unemployment rate: 3.1 percent; Population: 522,830; Mean annual wage: $34,290; Top industry: Government (23 percent)

> *"The gift of fantasy has meant more to me than my talent for absorbing knowledge."*
> **Albert Einstein**

> *"You must be aware of shifting intention to what you do want— and away from what you don't want."*
> *Wayne Dyer*

Conversely . . .

Michigan: Unemployment rate: 7.6 percent; Population: 10,071,822; Mean annual wage: $41,230; Top industry: Trade, transportation, and utilities (18.4 percent)

Mississippi: Unemployment rate: 6.8 percent; Population: 2,918,785: Mean annual wage: $30,460; Top industry: Government (21.2 percent)

South Carolina: Unemployment rate: 6.8 percent; Population: 4,407,709; Mean annual wage: $33,400; Top industry: Trade, transportation, and utilities.

The analysis does not always take into account the unexpected or unforeseeable, but each state has a state employment securities or department/division/administration that compiles reports about occupational staffing patterns. For a summary of 12 districts or coverage by region, go to www.federalreserve.gov/FOMC/BeigeBook that highlights various economic data.

If you want information about what state, city, or county would improve your chances for job placement, the following may help. Go to the Internet site, www.acinet.org. Click on the link entitled "State Information." Each state is linked separately with supply and demand analysis and expected job growth/projection demands.

To post your resume for job openings by city and job title, type in the name of the city, plus "jobs.com" It doesn't work every time but can be worth your effort if it serves you.

GLOBAL EMPLOYMENT

Countries' work permits and visa regulations vary. Information can be obtained through the embassies in the United States. Your chances for success improve if there is a demand for your transferable skills or your employer transfers you to another country. A reverse-chronological or functional resume may be used with more detail about education/courses and credentials that otherwise are unfamiliar to readers in other countries. You should have a language/cultural interpreter review your documentation for foreign language correctness. The American Translators Association provides a list of individuals who are accredited. An accredited translator will translate resumes and ensure that the format matches a country's common business practices. For example, American and British spell English words differently (e.g., counselor and counsellor, analyze and analyse, acknowledgement and acknowledgment, learnt and learned, spelt and spelled), so you want to use the spelling applicable to the country to which you are applying. Standard paper size also varies (e.g., Europe uses "A-4" whereas America uses 8½ by 11 inches) so adjust your computer "page setup" function to format accordingly.

Europe tends to emphasize teamwork rather than individual achievement. Work experience is better listed in reverse chronology rather than a functional format. It is not uncommon for European companies to ask for a handwritten resume that will be judged on neatness, language competence, and handwriting analysis. A photo and more personal information are often included as well.

You would be wise to check with the country's embassy or consulate to learn what requirements exist to work overseas. Some European countries and New Zealand may require that you start a business and present a plan, financing, relevant experience, and the economic benefit including creating jobs. Explore international job search resources in www.overseasjobs.com.

CLASSIFIED ADS, EMPLOYMENT AGENCIES, AND OTHER METHODS

Blind ads are job advertisements that do not provide the name or address of the company. These ads are used by companies who need to advertise a job opening but want to limit the number of applicants dropping by the place of business or telephoning for more information. Blind ads allow the company to keep the job opening and business identity private. These ads allow the hiring manager to review the candidate resumes at his or her convenience.

Executive search firms vary in cost and services, but seek degreed candidates or areas of unique expertise such as physicians, hospital administrators, business managers, trainers, and so forth. They either charge you, the job seeker, or the organization a fee if you are selected for the job. A retained search fee can be upward of $35,000 for a physician. Read the fine print when signing any contracts. Some search firms split their fees between you and the company that hires you. Other executive search firms may provide you with a resume, executive coaching sessions, and an employer database for your targeted locale. The fee can be upward of $10,000 depending on the package purchased. The idea is that for every 1,000 resumes mailed, you will get five employers to contact you for a possible interview. My personal opinion is that most job seekers can acquire employment by using the techniques in this book without the expense of an executive search firm. The Internet and library provide access to an employer database.

The staffing industry (also referred to as contract firms, employee leasing companies, or temporary agencies) assists companies that are seeking ways to reduce the cost of overhead and employee benefits. Some of the largest employers in today's workforce are in the staffing industry, one of the fastest growing businesses in America. The staffing company is technically the employer, providing you the job interview, paycheck, tax withholding, insurance, and other require-

"You control the way you feel by acting the way you want to feel." Anonymous

> *"Nothing happens until something moves."*
> **Albert Einstein**

ments by law, but your job duties are performed at another work site where your company contracted.

A staffing company may employ thousands of people, but only a small percentage of people actually work for the employer at the staffing industry site because most are contracted out to other companies. Staffing companies recruit potential employees on a temporary/permanent, part-time/full-time basis. The downside may be an interim position that does not offer benefits, pays lower wages, and has an impersonal nature. The upside may be that you might be more secure in the sense that your job does not depend upon any particular "client" company having layoffs, going out of business, or so forth.

Second to networking, the staffing industry is a good segue into full-time employment. It is a good trial-basis opportunity to determine if a suitable match exists between you and any variety of industries or company types. Sometimes these positions turn into full-time jobs after about 90 days, but the company must pay the leasing firm a fee in exchange for your employment status.

Recruiters are job placement professionals paid by a company searching for suitable candidates. Their allegiance is to the hiring organization. They tend to specialize in a specific industrial niche and are paid a contingency fee when a placement is made. This fee may be split between the employer or employment agency and candidate. Some retained recruiters specialize with physicians and medical groups and are paid whether or not an actual match is made. They may or may not represent you, but since they mostly just want to fill a position, don't be surprised if they are not interested in discussing your ideal goal or aspirations. Recruiters scout for candidates with specific qualifications to fill a specific position. You must be clear about the job title and level you are seeking.

Your documentation should include a clear profile summary about your core competencies so the reader can quickly understand your qualifications. This encourages a recruiter to take a risk on you and refer you to a client. Your resume should place more emphasis on chronological work history as opposed to functional; however, a long list of duties and responsibilities are not effective. Similar to any good resume, you must also 1) capture special emotional competencies that reveal how you relate to others and what you stand for; 2) quantify how you effect change within an organization and provide examples how the company benefited from your performance; and 3) describe your professional accomplishments in terms of what makes you unique to a position.

Recruiters will likely contact you if interested, but don't hesitate to phone them to briefly discuss your background and your qualifications. If you decide to use a recruiter, find one who specializes in your work field. Although a recruiter's loyalty is to the company, good ones will want to work with you. To locate a recruiter using Google, enter "find a recruiter."

EMPLOYER LOCATOR/DATABASE

An easy way to access the database of employers for all states is to go to America's Labor Market Information System (ALMIS) at www.acinet.org. The "employer locator" is located under the "career resources" section on the home page. The direct link to this employer database is www.acinet.org/acinet/employerlocator. You can search by occupation, location, or keyword. Your local librarian can help you research hard copy business directories. Employer research can be found at www.wetfeet.com. Also, the Chamber of Commerce keeps a list of employer member information.

Job search and career exploration internet sites are abundant. Three good websites for general career exploration activities are www.acinet.org, www.qualityinfo.org, and www.online. onetcenter.org. These sites provide valuable information about job openings, wages, skills sets which match job titles, job descriptions, and employers in your locations. The sites will help identify and refresh vocabulary and transferable skills for your resume and interview. Insofar as the survey information—like most surveys—take it with a grain of salt. The salary information, for example, reflects a very small sampling of employers who posted jobs on the site, not the actual wage paid, and can-

not be used to extrapolate salary ranges. Use a variety of resources to acquire salary information, including www.salary.com (also see Chapter 21—"Negotiating Salary and Job Offers").

To use the www.acinet.org website, look for "Career Information" and click on "What It Takes." You will find important knowledge, skills, abilities, tasks, and more for your selected occupation. This website will provide vocabulary to help write your resume and easy access to America's job bank where you can find job openings and job search information in your desired area. This site also links to America's Career Info Net, which provides 450 career videos showing real people doing real work, including selected careers within specific industries.

As part of America's Labor Market Information System (ALMIS), a database of employers for all states is available. To access the "employer locator" database, the direct link is www.acinet.org/acinet/employerlocator. You can search by occupation, location, or keyword.

To use the www.qualityinfo.org website, go to the menu column under TOOLS titled, "Skill Explorer," and "Occupational Info Center." You will be prompted to receive a "One page summary report," or better yet, a "Full report" for job openings, wages, skill sets, and more. After researching these two menus, check out the menu "Careers." Transferable skills analysis is located in the section "IMatch."

To use http://online.onetcenter.org, go to the menus "Find Occupations" to find keywords or view a complete list, "Skills Search" to use a list of your skills to find matching occupations, and/or "Crosswalk" to use other systems to find matching occupations. Chapter 7 references this site for job description and resume writing information as well.

INTERNET JOB BOARDS

Two ways you can use the Internet in your job search include searching for job postings and posting your resume. At the time of this writing, about 7 to 10 percent of job openings are filled through the use of electronic resumes. Correspondingly, you shouldn't spend more than 10 percent of your job search activities looking at Internet job boards since this is not the best use of your time. Posting your resume on Internet job boards with the hope that recruiters and companies will review it is only one job search strategy out of many.

The exception to this statistic is technology-related job openings that are increasingly filled through Internet boards. For the latter, several boards, such as onlinejobs.com only work with technical professionals. Recruiters and employers pay for job board service, not the applicant who can post resumes and search for job openings for free. Not all companies use job boards to advertise job openings, so, as I have said, do not limit your job-hunting to an online search.

"Recent research revealed that niche sites that specialize by career field or industry, and those that specialize by geographic focus, are favored by 78 percent of corporate employment specialists. Only 17 percent of respondents preferred general job boards, like www.Indeed.com, www.monster.com, or www.careerbuilder.com, and only 3 percent selected their organization's own website. On the job-seeker side of the picture, more candidates get jobs through niche sites than through comprehensive job boards. Candidates prefer to use niche sites catering to their region or work discipline to avoid wasting time exploring opportunities that don't fit who they are or what they are looking for." ("The Herman Trend Alert" by Roger Herman and Joyce Gioia, www.hermangroup.com)

There are hundreds of Internet job boards that allow you to search for job openings and/or post your resume. The popular and well-advertised sites include www.monster.com, www.careerbuilders.com, www.headhunter.com, and www.alljobsearch.com. These sites also offer job description information that will aid you in acquiring vocabulary for your resume and interviews. See the sources. Niches sites include:

Federal/State: www.Federaljobseach.com and www.Statejobs.com

Non-Profit/Social Services: www.philanthropy.com/jobs and www.nonprofitcareercenter.org

Minorities: www.imdiversity.com

Women: www.ivillage.com/work and www.careerwomen.com

Executives: www.netshare.com, www.Careerjournal.com, www .Sixfigurejobs.com, and www.execunet.com

Military related: www.vetjobs.com

Building trades: www.constructionjobs.com

Sales/Marketing: www.accountmanager.com, www.salesjobs.com

Information Technology: www.computerjobs.com, www.dice.com, and www.computerwork.com

Spanish/Portuguese speaking: www.latpro.com

Some boards are simple and relatively fast to use to copy and paste your resume documents. Monster.com takes longer to complete more information to help employers target and match specific applicants. The site allows you to subscribe and receive an updated list of daily job openings for your preferred targeted locale.

ELECTRONIC RESUMES—HOW TO CREATE

The advantage to having an Internet-friendly resume is the ability to respond via Email to job openings posted all over the world. Some hiring managers won't even look at a resume unless they receive it electronically. If your resume is on a computer, disc, or thumb drive, you already have it in electronic format. However, what you see is not necessarily what the employer will see upon electronic receipt.

Most Email systems can accommodate document attachments in Word, Word-Perfect, Quark, or plain text, but the intended receiver may not be able to open all documents. While you can attach a nicely formatted Microsoft Word document to an Email as a separate document, all of the nice formatting of a Word document makes the documents nearly unreadable when you copy and paste from an HTML or XML document. You may inadvertently include tags or invisible characters that cause a reader difficulty reading your resume, or that may not allow your resume to be saved successfully.

Read the directions in a job announcement carefully. For example, are you required to copy and past a Word document to that website's format, embed the resume within the body of the Email, or send your resume as a Word document attachment? Call or visit the organization's website to learn which version is preferred, and consequently increase your odds of getting your resume and cover letter read.

> *"Become a possibilitarian. No matter how dark things seem to be or actually are, raise your sights and see possibilities."*
> **Norman Vincent Peale**

To paste from Microsoft Word:

1. Open your resume in Microsoft Word and click *File* in the menu bar.

2. Select *Save As*.

3. In the "Save as type" filed, select *Text only with Line Breaks (•.txt)*.

4. Save the text document to a location where you can easily find it.

5. Close *Word*.

6. Using *Notepad* or *WordPad*, open the new text document.

7. Correct the format of your resume by adding spaces to align fields or by adding asterisks to denoted bulleted items.

8. Select *Edit* and then *Select All* to select all of the text in your resume.

9. Select *Edit* and then *Copy* to copy the text to the clipboard.

10. *Paste* the text into the resume filed on the online application

You may need *three versions* of your resume to submit electronically: The regular Word one, a PDF (Portable Document File), and an ASCII (American Standard Character) format that can be scanned by a computer. The latter "text" method will not be as attractive as your regular Word document but it will be universally compatible between computer systems, allowing you to maintain its appearance. Many companies store and perform searches on PDF. If required, Kinko's has the software service to convert your document into PDF, or you can purchase Acrobat software that will do this for you, and safeguards against any change in content.

1) To prepare an electronic resume or cover letter, use a standard word processing application and compose a resume as you normally would. Plain text format is very basic and does not recognize formatting features such as bullets, boldfacing, underlines, tables, borders, or italicized text. For bullets or emphasis, consider using asterisks (•), symbols (+), hyphens (-), equal (=) signs, arrows (>), or CAPITALS to achieve similar effects or to separate sections of the document. In short, use any symbol that one can find on a standard keyboard.

2) A *two-page* resume should be formatted with a fixed-width typeface, and use 12-point Courier, or Serif for PDF. Fonts such as Helvetica or Arial have different widths for different characters and should be avoided. Set your margins at 0 and characters at 65. This allows the longest line length, including spaces, to reach 65 characters before

wrapping to a new line; your resume will be easier to read and print. Put a **hard return** at the end of each line.

To achieve the best result in a one page resume, use 12-point preferably, and 10-11 point only if you must. Use Courier and set the page width at 4¾". Achieve alignment vertically by using an equal number of spaces from the left-hand margin.

3) Never enter more than six lines without inserting a double space. Too much block/dense print is difficult to read.

4) Keep all lines **left justified** against the page. Do not use tabs because they are ignored by Web browsers and behave unpredictably. The space bar will handle indents more predictably and consistently than tabs.

5) Save your document as an ASCII or MS-DOS text document and append the .txt extension onto the file name. For example, "resume. txt."

Kim Issacs, Monster.com expert writes, "To convert your file from MS Word:

• Open your document, go to Edit > Select All and change the font to Courier 12 point; go to File > Page Setup and change the left and right margins to 1.5 inches.

• Go to File > Save As > Under "Save Type," select "Text Only with Line Breaks."

• Select "Yes" at the prompt that warns about features being compatible.

• Close and reopen the file, which now has a text (.txt) extension.

• Review and clean up your document."

Send the message to yourself and a friend first to test that the formatting works and use the spell check. If the document looks good, resend it to the employer. To view a sample Word and electronic version, see Steve Reynolds in the sample resumes at the end of this chapter.

When sending an electronic resume, remember to:

1) Include a cover letter. When applying for jobs via Email, you can write your cover letter in the body of an Email message, or condense it in a shorter version. Limit your cover letter to 250 words. Include a signature with your Email address and telephone/cell phone numbers. Include the title of the position you are applying for in the subject line of your message, or

> *"Treat people as if they were what they ought to be and you help them to become what they are capable of being."*
> **Johann Wolfgang Goethe**

> *"The within is ceaselessly becoming the without. From the state of a person's heart doth proceed the conditions of their life; their thoughts blossom into deeds, and the deeds bear the fruitage of character and destiny."*
> **James Allen**

Send the resume and cover letter in one file, or

Send your cover letter and resume as separate file attachments.

2) Use the job title and/or job reference numbers as the subject line of your Email.

3) Follow up with an Email or phone call within a few days after you submit your resume.

USING EMAIL IN YOUR JOB SEARCH

Hiring administrators, recruiters, and human resource professionals may receive hundreds of Emails and resumes daily. How do you increase your chances of getting your Emailed resume and cover letter opened and read? Emails should be brief and to the point. The purpose of the Email is to cause the reader to open and read your cover letter and resume.

Chapter 15, The Ten-Thousand-Pound Telephone, and Chapter 17, Cover Letters, provide tips about getting the name of the person in charge of hiring in order to personalize the letter. Out of respect and in order to increase your chances of getting an interview, insert the name of the individual in the introduction/greeting area. In other words, use the person's name ("Dear Ms. Smith:") when sending Email.

The *subject line* of your Email must compel the reader's attention. You are in error if you use your name, "Susan Cox—resume" or, "See attached resume." Rather, you should identify your work field that matches the company needs. For example,

"Mechanical and Structural Engineer with Project Management Expertise"

"Accounting and Chief Financial Operations"

"Sales and Marketing for Retirement Real Estate Services"

Use the job title and/or posting number in the subject, if applicable. Do not attempt to capture the reader's attention with humor, all capital letters (there is no need to rudely "shout"), exclamation points (!), or "emoticons." Spam filters may delete Emails with these items. Use a *conservative* Email name, such as your last name. Avoid cute, funny, gender, or other statement attempts.

The body and content of the Email should not be more than two short sentences within two or three paragraphs. Here is a sample Email:

Subject: Mechanical and Structural Engineer with vulnerable packaging expertise

"Dear Mr. Jones:

My background consists of more than 15 years in Mechanical and Structural engineering with an emphasis in:

• Packaging vulnerable technology in order to protect against shock and vibration damage.

• Producing creative and practical designs within specifications for timely project completion.

• Skillful application of various computer software programs, including MathCad.

I will contact you in the near future to discuss my qualifications. Please feel free to contact me anytime at (insert a reliable telephone number or other contact information).

Sincerely,

Your name

attached: Resume and Cover Letter

• *Your Email address*

An Email address serves the purpose of sending and receiving information, but also reflects that you are financially responsible enough to pay for the service. Consider changing your Email address if it reflects age, gender, or personal humor or appears unprofessional. Examples such as blondie24@aol.com, or fratman@hotmail.com may make a poor first impression. Other salutation information should include your name, address, and cell and residence telephone numbers in larger, bold typeset for easy reading.

It is usually best to send and receive Email from a computer other than from your work. Using your current employer's computer for job hunting may leave a prospective interviewer wondering if you would do the same in the new company. Also, companies frequently monitor personal Email at work sites. If the prospective employer hits the "reply" button, you may get caught in an uncomfortable situation with your current company. Yahoo and Hotmail provide free Email address services. It is best to use Email from a secure site, such as your home or library.

> *"Dreams come true when they are introduced to expectations."*
> *Anonymous*

> "Every day is future history. So don't step lightly. The trick is to leave tracks that can be followed."
> **Clive Cussler**

Discussion questions/exercises

1. Of the job search methods discussed in this chapter, which one(s) seem like they'll be most useful for you?

2. What has worked for you in the past and why? Depending on when you last used those job search methods, how useful do you suppose they would be today?

3. In light of your answers to the questions in the beginning of this chapter, what new insights have you gained that will alter your approach to your job search?

CHAPTER 14

Networking: The Most Effective Way of Finding Employment

Networking is about developing relationships. Personal contact is the most successful way to get a job, since over 80 percent of the good jobs are located by accessing the hidden job market. Four out of five employers do not advertise job openings, which means that only 20 percent are advertised. Looking for a job is similar to fishing. You take a fishing pole (your qualifications) and attach a hook (your resume) to the end of the line and drop it in a lake where about one-fifth of all fish (job openings) exist. Comparatively, you could drop your hook into the ocean where 80 percent or more fish exist. Fishing in the ocean, however, requires a different approach using "people skills."

Networking is a game. It means getting out there, rubbing elbows with people, and getting personal referrals. It requires using the telephone and introducing yourself to someone who could potentially get you an interview. Email and faxing are not as effective as a face-to-face conversation. In order to get a job introduction, consider who you know. If you don't know key people who can introduce you to a hiring manager, investigate how you can get acquainted with people in charge of hiring.

Networking isn't preparing a badly canned sales pitch; rather, it's discovering which methods work best for you when marketing and selling yourself. Networking involves telling people you are looking for a job, asking for references, and making connections that can serve you and others. Be sure and read the section about Information Interviews in Chapter 4 as part of your networking strategy.

Employment usually provides a job title and a sense of identity. When we attend a party and someone asks, "What do you do?" we often wonder whether we "measure up" in terms of responsibility, income, and competency. The job seeker

> *"Don't judge each day by the harvest you reap, but by the seeds you plant."*
> Robert Louis Stevenson

has a couple of options. One is to say something like, *"I just got laid off my job and don't know what I'm going to do. My boss is such a jerk."* A better example is to say something like, *"I have been in management and sales in the [insert industry] for [insert years]. I know a lot about growing corporate revenue through marketing strategies. I'm looking for a small to mid-size company that deals with manufacturing and distribution."* The first example is complaining; the second example is networking. You must use up-to-date business terminology and practice a response until you are comfortable with it. But you have to get started. Take baby steps if necessary and keep taking steps to accomplish results.

PERSONAL BUSINESS CARDS

Create personal business cards and distribute them during conversations and with correspondence. A personal business card establishes and reflects your career identity. Free business cards may be obtained through www.vistaprints.com. Since you are now in the business of marketing your skills and abilities, your personal business card should reveal personal contact and professional work industry information. First, work on the content and then decide on any graphics. The cards can also match or complement your resume, cover letter, and reference documentation paper and typeset style. Your professional title should identify your desired work area or field. College graduates with an English, Psychology, Philosophy, Biology, or other degree can use the title, "Research Analyst" or other applicable term that captures more of what they do rather than what their major was.

Networking requires an outward focus—talking with people at opportune times and going out where the jobs are. In order to network effectively, you must ask questions, as well as impart your qualifications and goals. What do you want to know or find out? What are your transferable skills and can you impart your skills set effectively? What does other people's work involve within the industry you are targeting?

NETWORKING REQUIRES GETTING INVOLVED

It's important that you research membership directories of professional organizations for names and employer contacts. Consider joining the local Chamber of Commerce, Rotary Club, or Toastmasters group, and talk with people about your career transition and interests. Speak with former connections with whom you had a working relationship (customers or vendors) and who are familiar with your service/product. Explore the Internet and view websites for business activities of people and affiliations in your field.

Statistically, most job openings are filled as a result of networking. Identifying specific job interests and networking, including going directly to organizations that employ people in those areas, get the best results! Your local Chamber of Commerce usually has a list of the largest employers in your area including addresses and telephone numbers. Call and request a copy. The library has reference books with extensive employer contact information (Business Directory) about companies including number of employees, type of service provided, locations, size of company, history since inception, etc.

Less than 20 percent of job openings are advertised and filled through newspaper want ads, state employment departments, employment agencies, or staffing companies. An even smaller percentage of job openings are filled through state, federal, or civil service (non-uniformed federal workers) listings or by mailing resumes at random. In spite of the recent hype, Internet job banks fill less than 10 percent of job openings. The problem with limiting your job search to these resources is that a large percentage of the job seekers are applying for less than 20 percent of the job openings. If you want a job, networking is the required footwork.

> "It's not what you are that hold you back; it's what you think you are not."
> **Dennis Waitley**

DISCUSSION QUESTIONS/EXERCISES

1. What is preventing you from networking? What can you do to overcome this?

2. List five people you can talk to about your job search, regardless of whether they know of a job opening.

3. What else can you do to begin networking? Consider baby steps to get started.

The Ten-Thousand-Pound Telephone

A VALUABLE RESOURCE

The telephone is the most basic tool used as part of your networking. It is a source of obtaining information, advice, and ideas as well as a method to speak with people who can support you in your job search. Although you might dread it at first, you can build connections and possibly land the perfect opportunity as a result of picking up what may at first feel like a "ten-thousand-pound telephone."

Fear is probably the number one reason people avoid making telephone calls: fear of rejection, feelings of insecurity when trying to find solid ground, fear of the unknown, fear about the person on the other end of the telephone line, fear of lack of control, and fear of intimidation. Pick up the telephone and give it your best shot. *Feel the fear and do it anyway. Show courage in the midst of feeling fear. Fake it until you make it fearless.*

At first, making telephone calls can be difficult and awkward. In order to become confident and effective with using the telephone for job search activities, you must learn some techniques to get the best results.

One of the best approaches to telephone calls is to introduce yourself and clarify your reason for calling. You might say you are not necessarily looking for a job with the company, but taking the opportunity to get information and ask a few questions. You might add, *"although it would be great if my skills and your company needs were a match in the event an opening came available."* Granted you may be looking for a job, but first you want information and connections that may lead to a job. This call is a networking strategy to learn more about how your skills are best transferred into an employer or industry that could use your qualifications.

Keep in mind that all kinds of callers frequently telephone employers for many different reasons, including people seeking information about jobs. Employers expect these kinds of calls as part of their job and are usually willing to talk to callers. Be brief and limit your call to a few minutes unless encouraged to speak at length. If necessary or appropriate, ask if there is another, better time to call and talk at greater length.

YOUR FIRST IMPRESSION

You want your first impression to be a good one.

Use a professional greeting on your answering machine and reduce background sounds that can be heard (e.g., television, music, traffic). Have a telephone available in a quiet area free of distractions to talk with prospective employers.

Treat every incoming call as though it is a prospective employer. Answer the telephone, *"Hello, this is [insert your name]."* If you are away from your telephone and unable to answer, record a voice-mail greeting that is professional, brief, grammatically correct, and appropriate for a prospective employer. This includes your name, possibly the date (if you can change it daily), and thanking the person for calling. For example, *"You have reached Sue Barnett at 555-261-3333. Today is [insert date]. Please leave a message at the tone and I will return your call as soon as possible. Thank you very much for calling."* Write the script and practice reading it until it sounds positive, audible, and natural. After recording, listen to the quality of your message. Ask a friend, family member, or colleague to listen to the message from another number and give you suggestions for improvement.

Do not delay returning calls! A prompt return call is a good impression and can deter the employer from pursuing another candidate.

PREPARE TO SOUND CONFIDENT

The suggestions below will help prepare you to sound confident while networking via telephone. When you get an idea to call someone, do it! Do it in spite of the fear. It is alright to feel nervous or insecure but make the telephone call anyway. Some fear can be a positive motivator. Acknowledge your fear and BREATHE before and during the call. Put a sign over your telephone that reads, ***BREATHE***.

Write a script for improved effectiveness. Write a script that is an outline of what you want to say on the telephone. This includes your name, who referred you if applicable, and the reason you are calling. Plan to ask the listener if they have a couple of minutes to talk and keep your call within a few minutes unless they are engaging the conversation longer. Keep in mind that most people want to be helpful and are willing to help you.

Practice before. The time to rehearse is not when you are actually making the phone call. Try taping yourself with a voice recorder beforehand to listen to your pitch, tone, volume, and content. Use a watch with a second hand and time yourself not to exceed 60 seconds. Read the section, "The One-Minute Interview Introduction" in Chapter 20 about job interviews. Practice a 10–20-second

> *"The bravest thing you can do when you are not brave is to profess courage and act accordingly."*
> **Cora May Harris**

> *"Go as far as you can see. When you get there—you will see how to go further."*
> **Thomas Carlyle**

version of your script. You want to sound upbeat and energetic, but not high pitched, nervous, or discouraged. Practice with a friend, career counselor, or family member. Nervous people tend to speak too quickly so speak slowly and naturally. Avoid nervous "bridges" such as "uhm" and "so" and "you know."

Be prepared. Know what you are about to say; have notepad, pen, script outline, and written questions to ask next to the telephone.

Pick up that 10,000-pound telephone. First, briefly tell people the reason you want to talk with them. Tell them you are looking to make a job change and are seeking information; tell them specifically how they can help you. Be organized and clear in presenting yourself and your goals. Be sure to use your one-minute introduction so that the person knows your reason for calling. You must condense your script or introductory pitch to 10 or 20 seconds, depending on your listener's receptivity. Ask them specific questions. Do not expect them to read your mind or be able to answer questions you have not formulated.

One of the reasons for your call includes asking the person if they know of anyone else you may contact. Make a request by asking, *"Do you know anyone I could talk to in order to further my research and job search efforts?"* Before you hang up, be sure to let the person you've been talking to know that you appreciate the time they took to help you. For example, say *"Thank you for your helpfulness"* or *"Thank you. You have been very helpful."* This is a powerful conclusion to any conversation. People want to be helpful. When you acknowledge a person for their helpfulness, it makes them feel good. *"Thanks for your help,"* isn't as effective as *"I appreciate your helpfulness."*

One of the reasons for your call includes asking the person if they know of anyone else you may contact. Make a request by asking, *"Do you know anyone whom I could talk to in order to further my research and job search efforts?"*

Finally, keep a list of the names of people and organizations to whom you are referred, and track who you call. The goal is to get as many people and organizations as possible on your networking list.

GETTING PAST THE GATEKEEPER

The first person to answer the telephone may be an assistant, secretary, receptionist, or other party. This person may be screening before connecting you with your contact person, or thwarting your entry to the decision makers (also known as a "gatekeeper"). In the latter case, you may be more successful if you call early, late, or during breaks when the receptionist is unavailable to answer the phone. Your goal is to speak with the person in charge of hiring, which may require you to take a few steps.

> **"Until we show up fully in the present we will not create the future we want."**
> **Stephen Covey**

When the greeter answers the telephone, use a respectful greeting such as, *"Hello, my name is Jane Doe. Would you please tell me the name of the manager or president involved in your company's hiring decisions?"* Keep in mind this greeter receives many telephone calls a day and does not know the reason for your call—whether you are the unemployment department calling about a claim, a job counselor seeking data, or a sales representative selling payroll software. It is your job to approach the gatekeeper in a friendly way and ask for direction and information, rather than announcing you are a job seeker who needs to speak to the hiring manager. This requires diplomacy and balance between being too blunt and being dishonest. Never speak impatiently or rudely to the gatekeeper. Better to err on the side of killing with kindness than to have the greeter speak unfavorably about you.

Ask for the extension number of the hiring manager and the best time to call. When provided the hiring manager's name, say *"thank you for your helpfulness"* and hang up. You are now in a position to call and ask to speak to the hiring manager and/or use the name on your cover letter of introduction. If the greeter asks you about the nature of your call before giving you the manager's name, you might say something like, *"I want to address a letter to the manager with information that may be of interest."*

Good companies and managers are always interested in talented applicants. It is usually best to write a letter in advance to introduce yourself and your intentions prior to the phone call. This is an excellent marketing strategy and the manager is more likely to accept your call if given a "heads-up" courtesy letter beforehand.

Be sure to make an effort to build a respectful, collaborative relationship with the greeter. Express gratitude. He or she is in a position to speak favorably about you and help you accomplish your goal by connecting you to the person to whom you want to speak. If possible, try to arrange an appointment directly through the receptionist. Use the person's name occasionally in the conversation.

> *"Courage is the human virtue that counts most—courage to act on limited knowledge and insufficient evidence. That's all any of us have."*
> **Robert Frost**

SAMPLE CONVERSATIONS

Example: *"Good morning. This is Susan Jones. May I speak with Mr. Dynamic, please?"*

Response: *"He is not available. Is there someone else you'd like to speak to?"*

Tell the greeter the nature of your call in an effort to cut to the chase. Be brief, concise, and respectful of her time and possible limitations in transferring you.

Example: *"Perhaps you can help me. I believe your company has a current opening for a sales realtor and I would like to schedule an appointment with him. I have a strong* *background in real estate. It is my understanding that Mr. Dynamic is the person in your organization most likely to be interested in speaking to people with my experience and qualifications. Are you able to schedule an appointment for us or refer me to someone who can assist in this matter?"*

Response: *"I'm afraid he does his own scheduling and is the only one who can help you."*

You can then say, *"Thank you. What is the best time for me to call back and reach him?"*

If after a few attempts you are still unable to speak with Mr. Dynamic, ask the receptionist if she can schedule a telephone call for you. If these attempts fail, keep in mind your goal is to talk and or/meet personally with Mr. Dynamic. Ask to leave a voice message with Mr. Dynamic apprising him you are sending a letter/resume for his consideration.

After mailing a letter of introduction and resume, call the prospective employer to learn if the correspondence was received and when you might speak further about your qualifications. Offer to answer any questions he might have about your possible candidacy for the position.

Example: *"Good afternoon, Ms. Executive. My name is Job Seeker. I would like to make an appointment with you."* In order to avoid the likely response, *"What do you want to see me about?"* tell her up front.

Example: *"I was hoping that you might have a few minutes to speak with me about my interest in working in the financial investment industry. I have a strong background in banking and am exploring career opportunities in consulting services. Do you have some time now or may I schedule to talk with you later this week?"* Be prepared and have your questions ready.

You may receive a response such as, *"I don't know if I am the best person to help you."* You want to avoid getting turned over to the human resources department. You can say, *"I don't know either, but I have heard that you have expertise in financial matters and I would very much like to speak with you now if it is convenient, or perhaps next week. It wouldn't take more than a half hour. Then if it appears my skills could be a good match, I could speak to the human resources department."*

You might say something such as, *"Sue Smith suggested you might have information that would be helpful for me. I would appreciate it if you would talk to or meet with me for about 20 minutes in order that I may get your input or any suggestions about my interest in pursuing financial management. I would be happy to meet you anytime at your convenience."*

> *"The reward of a thing well done is to have it done."*
> **Ralph Waldo Emerson**

VOICE MESSAGE

Leaving a voice message can cause your heart to race and your breathing to cease before you hang up unable to utter a word. Opinions vary about using voice mail. Obviously job search success increases with a live person, but if voice mail is the only option, use it.

If you must leave a message after a few unsuccessful attempts to talk directly to the person, leave a brief message. *It is acceptable to leave up to about three or four voice mails* for which your persistence may pay off, but 10 is going too far. The goal of leaving a voice mail message is to connect with the hiring manager. Use the name of the person who referred you, if possible. Spell your name slowly and provide the time and date of call.

Tailor your message and be specific. For example, say, *"I would like to talk with you about my qualifications for the director of advertising position and learn whether there might be a mutual interest in my candidacy."* Ask them to please return your call at their convenience and slowly leave your telephone number. It is frustrating when someone recites a name and telephone number too quickly to write it down and it may cost you a call back. Also state that you will keep trying to reach them. And do keep trying to reach them.

If you leave a second message, *briefly* state your skills sets and qualifications for the position, and suggest a date and time for an appointment to meet. Ask them to call again to confirm. Try to avoid phone tag by offering two proposed meeting times and express that you will keep attempting to reach them to confirm as well. This provides you with a reason to call again. Say something such as, *"I am available until four o'clock today and three o'clock the remaining of the week. If you haven't reached me, I'll keep trying to reach you until we can connect."* Follow-up messages should always provide the date and time of your call. A written script may give you the advantage of a polished message. Practice it until it sounds positive with good enunciation.

If "avoidance" is your strategy, you are too terrified, or not very interested in talking to a hiring manager, you can leave the ball in their court but you may lose a job opportunity waiting for an employer to return your call. Someone who did follow up gets the job instead. Often, you may be able to reach the executive before or after regular nine-to-five office hours, so don't hesitate to call before or after that time, especially if you have the extension number.

Personal meeting. This may seem redundant, but they are important job search strategies in order to get an employer's attention. Your professional goal is to acquire a face-to-face meeting but don't be discouraged if that doesn't happen right away. Use your one-minute introduction, as described in Chapter 20 about job interviews, and then ask if you can send a resume. Of course, follow up with another call to learn if they received your resume and ask to schedule

> **"Even the highest tower begins from the ground."**
> **Chinese proverb**

a personal meeting. Avoid being interviewed on the phone in lieu of a personal meeting, but be prepared for the interview over the phone if that is the person's preference.

Write a letter. If you do not receive a return call, leave a second message that you are sending the individual a letter about the nature of your call and interest, as well as a resume if applicable. Tell the person you will call again after they have had time to receive and review your letter and resume. Be sure to follow up with a call.

One of the best job placement activities you can do is call the employer and say you are interested in speaking about your qualifications in order to learn whether your skills can benefit the company. Tell the employer you are taking the liberty of sending a cover letter and resume. Be brief, say thank you, and end your call (unless prompted to speak more about your objective). Your cover letter will remind the employer about your call. Then, be sure and call the employer in a few days after sending your letter. Your cover letter and resume alone are not likely to yield much fruit, but a phone call in advance of the resume and then a follow-up call are more likely to put you on their radar.

Some sophisticated companies send generic letters to applicants acknowledging receipt of resumes. Many companies will send a generic letter once the position has been filled, thanking the applicant for submitting a resume. This courtesy is occurring less frequently because corporations want to save the cost of postage and staff time. If you do not receive a response to your resume, call and politely ask something like, *"Is it customary for your company not to respond to a resume? I was wondering about the status of the hiring process."* This approach may get you connected with a person in charge of the interview process.

DISCUSSION QUESTIONS/EXERCISES

1. Write a script of introduction (no longer than five sentences) about yourself that identifies key/core competencies, quantifiable/measurable results, and purely performance-based statements.

2. Practice your script in front of a mirror and in front of another trusted person.

3. Identify three companies and their respective hiring managers with whom you may want an interview.

4. After reading this chapter, what are your fears and obstacles?

5. What is the worst thing that could happen if you fail at your attempts during telephone contacts?

6. Write a letter of introduction. Include apprising the employer to expect your telephone call.

7. What actions can you take in order to gain the employer's attention?

8. What is your reliable method for receiving telephone calls from a potential employer?

9. Write a script for a professional telephone message greeting. Record it and have a friend/colleague provide feedback.

CHAPTER 16

Resumes: An Introduction to You

"The one who gains a victory over others is strong, but the one who gains a victory over themselves is all powerful."
Lao Tzu

How you "package" yourself is essential to your job placement. Your resume lays a solid foundation for the reader to select you for an interview. The main point about an effective resume is "What makes you unique?" An effective functional resume should incorporate both "people" and "technical" skills, or "soft" and "hard" skills, respectively. This includes interpersonal and communication abilities, knowledge, procedural, and systematic skills. *Your resume should help you "reach" toward a job title.* In other words, what do you know, what can you do, and how well do you get along with people? You must reveal your most applicable transferable skills and work industry knowledge in the first half. This informs the employer how your skills match the company needs.

For some, writing a resume is a complete mystery. A common question is, *"What do you put in and what do you leave out?"*

If you are sending out your resume but not getting interviews, consider a few possibilities. There is no labor market demand for your skills set, your chosen career has dried up and you need to renew your career choice, or your resume needs an overhaul. You might be perfect for a position, but not get the interview due to an ineffective resume. Even though networking is the most effective method for getting a job, a well-designed resume can itself open doors.

That said, a resume, no matter how good, will not get you a job by itself. However, an informative resume with references, attached to a unique cover letter, is more likely to achieve its purpose: to attract the attention of the hiring manager and to secure a personal interview. *An employer will glance over your resume for two to six seconds* before deciding whether to interview you or toss your resume in the trash.

Your resume is one of the most important documents you own. It should contain just the facts about core competencies and transferable skills. Use purely performance-based statements and quantifiable statements. The first 15–25 lines of your resume is very important. They should contain keywords germane to your job goal. ***Hiring managers and computer screening technologies scan for keywords related to the specific job description your resume is matched against.*** You can increase your chances by selectively *italicizing* or **bolding** keywords in order to help focus the reader's attention. Note that with the arrival of the

Internet, underlining is no longer a proper method for emphasizing regular text—as this is reserved primarily to denote website links.

AN ACCURATE REFLECTION OF YOU

Your resume should be an honest reflection of your qualifications and should present your skills in the best possible light. Resumes are brief snapshots of knowledge, skills, abilities, and professional achievements, not a personal biography. This chapter, including the sample resumes, will help you write a resume that is best for your circumstances. Then, consider if want to include a portfolio with additional information.

Think of your resume as a promotional brochure reflecting your experience, accomplishments, and qualifications. A resume is divided into a variety of sections, each of which should convey particular highlights of your background. The first half of your resume should consist of qualifying phrases, expertise, and/or selected career accomplishments designed to get an employer's attention. The latter half reflects employment experience and possibly other highlights to convey important aspects of your background.

Your resume is also an example of your communication and organizational skills. A well-written resume is a glimpse of you as a potential employee. Likewise, a sloppily produced resume will land in the trash without any consideration. This chapter will help you write an effective **"functional"** resume, not a boring chronology of your work history. Most employers are not willing to put any effort into reading a resume. Employers read resumes that are easy to understand at a glance and are well thought out by the job seekers who put hard work into a unique resume. A successful resume is an accurate portrayal of you.

There is not one resume template that works for everyone. Design and layout styles can change every few years. *You may use one style or mix and match designs and layout styles* for an attractive, effective resume. Ultimately, you must decide what will work for you.

OBJECTIVE/JOB GOAL/SUMMARY PROFILE

Write your resume with an eye and mindset toward the future position or industry you are targeting. Using an introductory statement such as "Objective," "Job Goal," "Summary Profile," "Professional Qualifiers," or "Career Summary" in your resume is optional, but considered most effective. Keep in mind that hiring managers, recruiters,

and human resource personnel are not interested in matching unspecified resumes to job openings. A career summary, goal, or objective statement provides key terms and power words for a *professional identity*, qualifies your core competencies, uses industry specific terms, and discloses what type of position you are seeking. If you choose to open your resume with an introductory focus, it can be as simple as a *specific* job title (objective), in just one or two words, that tells a potential employer you are seeking an exclusive position (e.g., *Sales/Marketing* or *Accounting/Finance*). See the Robert Houdin chronological sample resume toward the end of this chapter. Otherwise a well-designed sentence, or short paragraph as an introductory statement will apprise the reader about your objective and can be very effective. See the Robert Houdin functional sample resume as a contrast for comparison.

For more examples of how to use such an introductory summary statement, see the applicable sample resumes at the end of this chapter. The purpose is to identify your competencies, marketable skills, and professional identity with technical/functional aspects, as well as personal skills/strengths. Fragmented sentences are acceptable. Examples of well-written opening statements include:

CAREER SUMMARY: *Effective executive with* **proven leadership abilities***, management style, and keen analytic thinking skills in* **industrial engineering***. Exceptional accomplishments in strategic planning. Instrumental member of management teams for price/cost services.*

PROFILE: *Proven professional with demonstrated experience in* **project leadership***, customer* **relationship management***, and process improvements.*

PROFILE SUMMARY: Mechanical/Electrical Engineer. *Solid management experience in private corporations and Fortune 500 companies.*

PROFESSIONAL QUALIFIERS: *Highly effective Chief* **Financial Officer***. Proven history with national medical groups. Accounting and management, systems analysis/evaluation/implementation. Exceptional computer systems operation.*

PROFESSIONAL PROFILE: *Results oriented Executive with proven success history in Profit and Loss management,* **contract negotiations***, and procurement. Expertise in* **marketing** *and targeting needs assessment.*

BACKGROUND SUMMARY: *Demonstrated track record in successful* **operational improvements** *and problem solving. Adept communicator with leadership capacity and* **customer relationship building***.*

(Notice the bolding and italics of keywords or style in above examples.)

Avoid vague phrases such as:
"Seeking a position to utilize my skills" or "Seeking a rewarding position." These sentences are too generic and appear insincere. Also, do not write something like, *"Seeking a full time, secure position with a salary that will support my*

lifestyle." This objective is about meeting your needs and interests, rather than what you can do for the company.

Another option in lieu of an "Objective" or "Summary Profile" is to introduce your resume by apprising the reader about the number of years' experience and/or knowledge you have in your primary work industry. This method can simultaneously express your goal or objective. A second qualification sentence (optional) may reveal the number of years of experience you have in your secondary skills set, or, identifies your knowledge base. The first and second sentences can ensure that your objective closely matches the job title for which you are applying. Use terminology that highlights your primary and secondary job roles, as well as your core competencies. Terms such as "with an emphasis in" or "including" can give added definition to your particular achievements.

You may choose to use only one primary job role phrase, which may very well be appropriate. The main point about an effective resume is "What makes you unique?" Another candidate may have 20 years' experience as a teacher, but what makes you unique? Your resume should reveal, ***"What do you do, what do you know, and how do you get along with others?"***

Be specific about knowledge, skills, abilities, and qualifications. Don't list vague qualities such as "strong work ethic" unless you add more emphasis but do describe actual achievements.

Writing your "Selected Career Accomplishment" statements can be a significant boost to securing a position (see the Rand Smith resume sample). Employers want indicators about how you can perform. Identify your contributions in past jobs or how you made a difference in organizations. You must think about the results you obtained and actions you took in response to challenging situations. Consider how you contributed to or participated in change that brought value to your department or organization. Read your former job descriptions to remind yourself how much you did and to create accomplishment statements. Use your PAR stories to help develop this section of your resume.

Do not include the word "Resume" at the top of page, or "duties include" in your work history. The employer will know the document is a resume and work tasks describe your duties. Avoid special interest work (e.g., religious, environment, political) unless the organization supports such groups and it specifically relates to the job.

Also, be sure to harness the power of white space. Big blocks of text are not easy on the eyes. Readers may overlook important content if your writing is too dense.

> *"If yo
> a mira
> miracle."*
> **Bruce Almighty**

> *"Darkness cannot survive in the presence of the light."*
> **Anonymous**

LENGTH

The question, *"Do I use a one-page or two-page resume?"* is frequently asked. Executive search firms and employer websites may require a one-page resume. For a one-page resume example, see the Trish Jones sample at the end of this chapter. A one-page resume is also appropriate for college students or if you have limited experience (see the Thomas A. Stevens resume sample). Two-page resumes are often appropriate for most job seekers, including college graduates. Longer resumes referred to as curriculum vitae (CV) are typically reserved for professionals such as physicians, professors, information technology directors, and executive-level consultants. (See sample CV on p. 165.) It can be particularly difficult to reduce a lengthy resume into a one- or two-page version, but is well worth the effort if you want to get it read, in most organizations.

Your ability to capture essential highlights about your experience and training, which match the job requirements, will demonstrate your organizational skills to the employer. One page of well-organized information with pertinent details reveals more of your qualities than more pages of unnecessary details. Do not disadvantage yourself by limiting your resume to one page but a lengthy resume is not advantageous if it contains irrelevant information. Resumes should contain information applicable to the position for which you are applying.

Personal information/hobbies

Don't mention personal characteristics such as age, height, children, or marital status. This is the same information that employers may **not** legally solicit from you. List your personal hobbies and interests *only* if you can specifically relate them to the position you're applying for, or if you lack enough relevant employment experience.

FORMATS—TWO CLASSIC STYLES

These are two classic styles—chronological and combined functional—and each has advantages and disadvantages. Below is a general overview of each format and style.

Chronological

The chronological resume emphasizes job history. It is the **least effective** resume style for most interviews except for some recruiters, global, and state and college positions. It is easier to write than a functional resume and may be referred to as a "lazy" resume. It starts with your most recent job, and then describes the next job, and so on until all relevant jobs and responsibilities have been listed in reverse chronological order. A chronological resume lacks qualifying phrases about your pertinent strengths and skills.

The problem with a chronological resume is it requires an employer to analyze your employment history, assess your skills set, unearth your job goal, and identify a job title match. It tells an employer what job duties you did for another company, but not what you can and want to do.

The chronological resume format is best used when your entire job experience is almost exactly the same as the job for which you are applying and you want to stay on the same similar career path. For example, if you have held five accountant jobs and are applying for a similar accountant job but with a different company, you may want to use a chronological resume. See the sample resume of Robert J. Houdin, MBA. Potential employers can easily read what you have done, how you have progressed, and the experience you have garnered. The downside of a chronological format is that it can highlight limited or unrelated experience, an absence in the workforce, periods of inactivity, a history of short-term jobs, major gaps in employment, or numerous job changes.

Combined Functional

Were you surprised to read that an employer will only take two to six seconds to read a resume? Most people are. So with that in mind, how do you make the most impact in a short amount of reading time? *A combined functional resume is the most effective way.* As implied, a combined functional resume consists of qualifying phrases followed by chronological work history. It offers the familiarity of the chronological format, yet immediately describes education, unique skills, pertinent qualifications, achievements, skills set, job objective, and how your abilities match the company goals. A combined functional resume eliminates the employer having to "guess" or "unearth" how you fit into the company.

A combined functional resume defines you in the first half and lists employment history in the second half (presented in reverse chronological order). Arguably, some employers prefer to go straight to your work history. The combined functional resume may include "component headers" such as ***"Qualifications," "Professional Profile," "Distinctions," "Core Competencies," "Achievements," "Qualification Highlights," "Publications," "Military History," "Computer Skills," "Memberships/Affiliations," "Awards," "Selected Career Accomplishments," "Volunteer Service," "Education," "Certifications/Licensure," "Special Training,"*** and ***"Professional Profile."*** List corresponding statements about capabilities *and provide fewer succinct details on job history.*

Clear, qualifying statements in the beginning summarize relevant knowledge, achievements, and abilities, and are usually presented with bullets or arrow symbols. The reader doesn't have to guess why you are a match for a job opening, mind-read what your job goal is, or unearth pertinent information as to why you are a suitable candidate. An employer is not willing to put much effort into reading a resume unless it is well thought out and organized. You have to do the work for them. Information and statements of capability or achievement are

> *"Rule Number One: Take one more step. Rule Number Two: When you don't think you can take one more step, refer to Rule Number One."*
>
> *Jackson Brown, Jr.*

organized to present how your skills are directly related to the position applied for. *Do not conclude your resume with your last job.* Rather, include one or more "component headers" to divide sections to emphasize how you are unique or your accomplishments.

The functional format is the most challenging resume to develop. It takes careful planning and thought but is well worth the effort. It is always a good idea to ask a professional resume writer to provide fine-tuning or tips that could enhance your resume. For an example of an effective chronological resume, see the Robert J. Houdin resume at the end of this chapter.

RESUME WRITING TIPS

Make your words count

The careful selection of each word is important so you can quickly get the employer's attention. Avoid long paragraphs (over three or four lines). Hiring administrators often computer-scan resumes, so provide relevant experience and information in short, powerful statements. Avoid using "I" in declarative sentences like, "I developed the . . ." or "I assisted in . . ." Instead, leave out the "I," and use phrases, not complete sentences. For example, "Responsible for . . .," Provided all aspects of . . .," "Developed innovative programs . . .," or "Wrote the employee manual. . . ."

Avoid passive constructions, such as "was responsible for managing." It is more effective to say "Managed."

Do you need different resumes?

If you put the hard work into writing a combined functional resume, you shouldn't have to rewrite a complete new resume for each job prospect. You can edit or "tweak" the resume, capturing the essence of your best skills, to emphasize experience relevant to different positions. Emphasize your knowledge, skills, abilities, and qualifications for an employer. If you are going after more than one job opening, customize or tailor your resume accordingly.

Be specific and explicit—quantify

Specifically express what you have accomplished. Describe results that can be measured objectively. Quantify your contributions with succinct statements. Telling someone that you "improved inventory efficiency" is vague. Clearly stating "Cut requisition costs by 25 percent, generating savings in excess of $3,800 for fiscal year" is explicit and powerful.

Be meticulous about the appearance

First impressions are significant. The presentation of your resume can make an excellent or weak first impression to a prospective employer. It can make or

> *"Life's problems wouldn't be called 'hurdles' if there wasn't a way to get over them."*
> **Anonymous**

break your opportunity. Edit carefully for proper grammar and correct spelling. Pay attention to detail, format, and overall appearance.

Format and organization

For two page resumes, use normal margins (1" on the top and bottom, 1.25" on the sides). Use a 12-point font size and don't cram your text onto the page. Allow for some breathing room between the different sections. Avoid unusual or exotic font styles. Use simple fonts with a professional look. A few standard fonts you should consider are Sans Serif, Times New Roman, or Arial.

For one-page resumes, extend your margins and use 12-point font size, if possible. You may use 10-point font, but run the risk that the employer will find it too difficult to read and toss it in the trash. An 11-point font size is not uncommon. You may omit component headers such as Education or Professional Highlights to save precious space.

Printing and copying

Use original resumes printed from a computer printer. If you need to copy your resume, make sure your copies are clean and clear. Use only powerful copiers maintained for professional copying.

Use standard, non-textured, 25 percent cotton, fine-grained or linen paper that is white, light gray, or ivory/cream colored. Consider using two complimentary papers that will allow for contrast. For example, use the same color/texture papers for the cover letter and references documents, but a complimentary one for the resume.

Do not use brightly colored (sea foam green) resume paper or make a statement about topics such as endangered animals using a black striped zebra print background. Also, dark colored paper does not copy well and employers may have reason to make copies for other participants in the hiring process. For more information about paper selection, see Chapter 17 and the section, After the writing: Now what?

References upon request

The phrase "References available on request" should be omitted from resumes. Prepare a list of references as a separate document (see reference sample). Employers assume you have references they may contact and will request them if interested. You may provide your reference list to an employer at the end of an interview and say something like, "I have taken the liberty of preparing a list of references for you in the event you would like to contact them," if you have not already included references in your job search packet.

> *"To have what you've never had, you must do what you have never done."*
> **Anonymous**

Education

Prioritize your skill sets, qualifications, work history, and education in the order that best matches your job goal. If your education relates to the job goal, use "Education" as a heading at the top of the page; otherwise place it in the center or toward the end. For example, placing education on the top of the page may work well for a candidate with a new master's degree in Engineering. Conversely, a candidate with a bachelor's degree, but with more relevant skills and experience, may want to put education at the end.

What's in a name?

An unusual name given by your blessed parents in an attempt to distinguish you from the masses, a self-appointed unique new name, or a single name without a surname is likely to immediately land your resume in the trash. In an unscientific study conducted by television news magazine, "20/20," it was revealed that when two identical resumes were submitted with the only exception that one had an out of the mainstream name (e.g., "Treasure Star") and the other had a more common name, the latter got the interview. When it is a matter of getting the interview over the competition, it could come down to what's in a name as a knock out. I will leave it you to decide how to approach this potential problem, but my personal opinion is to give up your individuality in the name issue and select a mainstream name for your job search efforts. After getting the job, you can always change it.

> "The error of the past is the wisdom and success of the future."
> Dr. Dale Turner

STYLE/FORMAT /LEAD-IN TIPS

Employers are more interested in content than graphic design. For an article about writing and formatting a resume, including layout, design, and fonts, check out www.owl.english.purdue.edu/handouts/print/pw/pdfs/p_resdesing .pdf. You can apply borders and formatting to your liking, but do so conservatively. Include your name and telephone number on the second page in case the pages are inadvertently separated. For a professional appearance, use a "header" (find "Header and Footer" in the "View" menu on your computer).

Use opening lead ins to describe your job duties, with accomplishment statements such as: "**Director of** {insert}," "**Responsible for** {insert}," "**Oversaw all aspects of** {insert}," "**Provided** {insert}," "**Contributed to** {insert}," "**Responsibilities included** {insert}," "**Produced** {insert}," "**Managed** {insert}," "**Trained** {insert}," "**Performed** {insert}," "**Coordinated** {insert}," "**Supervise** {insert}," "**Acted as** {insert}," "**Created** {insert}," "**Developed** {insert}," "**Implemented** {insert}," "**Conducted** {insert}," "**Cut costs** {insert}," "**Grew** {insert}," "**Played key role in** {insert}," "**Introduced** {insert}," "**Spearheaded** {insert}," "**Revitalized** {insert},"

"**Improved** {insert}," "**Recognized for** {insert}," "**Designed** {insert}," "**Won** {insert}," "**Resolved** {insert}," "**Consolidated** {insert}."

Your employment history can be written in narrative format (see Sharon B. Sullivan—page two) or with the use of bullets (see the Professional Template—page two). Conclude your resume with a new Component Heading such as Professional Affiliation or Computer Skills. This adds a final "punch" instead of ending with job duties. For college graduates or others who lack extensive employment experience, the Thomas A. Stevens resume sample exemplifies a one-page functional combined resume.

Finally, avoid the tendency of writing a perfect resume and wasting time making changes at the expense of your job search. While your resume is an important document, it is only one part of all the job search techniques.

"The more the marble wastes, the more the statue grows."
Michelangelo

FREQUENTLY ASKED QUESTIONS

"What about the dates of my employment?" It is only necessary to include the years in the dates of your employment, not the months. This is usually to your advantage. For example if you were employed less than one year for a company, enter the dates as: 2007–2008. Or, enter the date for your months of employment as: 2008. The employer isn't interested in counting the number of months you worked in each year and you can answer a question if asked.

"How many years do I go back?" In general, it is only necessary to list jobs held for about 10 years, and possibly 15 or 20, if relevant to the job you are applying for. Too much work history may send a red flag—"overqualified"—regardless of whether the candidate wants a less demanding position. Too much history may also bring up an age bias.

"What about gaps in my employment dates?" is a common question. In today's world of work, it is not uncommon to have gaps or absences in employment dates, and this is acceptable. If asked, briefly explain your reason. You may have taken time out to care for children or elderly parents, taken a year off to travel, or took sufficient time to find the right job between dates of employment, a well-deserved break, or any number of possibilities. Employers are looking for your skill sets in your resume that answers the question, "How is this applicant a match for the job opening?"

"How do I list different job titles performed for the same employer?" (See the sample resumes for Sue Ann Montgomery and Steve Reynolds to address this format question.) It is to your advantage to list multiple job titles with the same employer because it demonstrates how you were promoted within the company.

"How do I list the same job title performed for different employers?" In order to shorten a lengthy chronology of work history that contains the same job title

and similar job duties with numerous employers, list all of the employer names, after identifying the specific job title. Next, list the job duties and write job responsibilities that correspond to each employer. For example:

Accountant, Meyers CPA Agency, Briggs and Associates, SORA Services, Inc., and Edward Smith, CPA   **2003–present**

Performed personal and corporate tax returns. Responsible for accounts payable and receivable audits resulting in **30 percent increase in customer revenues.** Oversaw all aspects of fiscal management and financial statements. Coordinated services between in-house accountants, vendors, and customer services.

> "I do not feel obliged to believe that the same God who has endowed us with sense, reason, and intellect has intended for us to forgo their use."
> *Galileo Galilei*

"Do I include the date I graduated?" You may include or omit the date of your academic graduation or certification completion depending on whether you think the information will be to your advantage (relatively current), or possible disadvantage (by revealing age and the length of time since the education was acquired).

"Do I include unpaid or volunteer experience?" Yes, you should include any unpaid work, volunteer opportunities, practica, or internships if relevant. The employer is interested in your skills, not whether you earned income from the experience.

"My resume has six different types of jobs and companies on it." Your resume would be more effective if it focused on the industry you have had the most success in. This narrows the parameter of your job search and makes you a stronger candidate. In this scenario, however, you may need to get training and start a new career focus.

"I only want full-time or part-time work." Avoid writing that you are "Seeking full-time (or part-time) position." This may tend to tell the employer that you are more interested in meeting your demands rather than the needs of the position. Depending on the circumstances, a part-time position may prove quite satisfactory or turn into a full-time position.

"Do I place my job title or the employer name first?" You want to *emphasize your* **job title first (in bold),** *and the name of the company/employer second.* In other words, advertise your job title and minimize the attention to the company. You may bring the reader's attention to the company name if the employer name is particularly prominent and would enhance your candidacy.

"How do I qualify previous employers?" You may want to bring attention to impressive organizations, such as Fortune 500 companies. See the Employment History section of the Sharon B. Sullivan resume sample. Notice that the company has an added qualifier sentence. This is a very effective method for enhancing your resume. If possible, qualify every employer or do so as often as

possible. For example, when I provided outplacement services for US Cellular, the qualifying sentence for the employer was "fifth largest wireless telecommunication company in the United States."

"How do I describe my job duties and responsibilities?" You want to prioritize your pertinent accountabilities in order of the most-to-least relevant. Or, you may opt to list only job titles and employers, for the purpose of saving space (i.e., one-page resume). You can use a component header "Other Career History" that captures job titles and employers omitting any detail about job duties. For an example, see the third page of the Rand Smith sample resume and the executive resume template at the end of this chapter.

"How do I indicate a geographic preference?" You may reference your desired relocation or placement locale in your resume by including something like, "Seeking {insert preferred location} placement." For an example, see the David M. Andrews resume. If you are concerned about being prematurely screened out as a "relocation expense risk," consider obtaining a viable mailing address at which you can receive correspondence, in your preferred location, for both your cover letter and resume.

SAMPLE RESUMES/TEMPLATES

The following pages contain sample resumes with fictitious names and histories, including professional and executive level resume templates. If you would like to receive the resume template(s) to help compose your resume, you may place an order through my website, www.lindarolie.com.

> *"You've got to get to the stage in life where going for it is more important than winning or losing."*
> *Arthur Ashe*

Sharon B. Sullivan
4381 Andrews Boulevard   Chicago, IL 60605 97520
Home (708) 631-7300   Cell: (708) 218-4329
Email: sbsullivan@cds.com

QUALIFICATIONS

- More than 7 years' experience in creative **advertising, marketing** strategies, and **public relations**
- Almost 9 years' experience developing **innovative** marketing plans
- Established history of **leading** others toward a vision; able to make a difference through insightful and **creative** ideas
- Proven **self starter**; autonomous and effective **program development** and project completion abilities
- Strong problem solving skills and coordinating communications between a variety of people to accomplish mutual goals
- Bring an **exuberant** approach to work, add enthusiasm, energy and positive spirit to the workplace

PROFILE

*Excellent skills in creative **design** and **copywriting** for print*
*Proficient at **writing, directing**, and **producing** radio and television*
*Experienced at targeted **media planning** and purchasing to achieve gain*
*Creative **promotional events** resulting in generating increased customer loyalty*
*Demonstrated ability to sustain **interpersonal relationships** with customers and vendors*

HIGHLIGHTS

CREATIVE MARKETING PLANS AND ADVERTISING

- Strong ability to grasp new marketing and operations concepts using "team" approach
- Ability to work within budgetary constraints, maximizing **profitability**
- Talent for **needs assessment** and propose viable solutions
- Strong company presence to **generate** community interest and involvement, including press releases, media, and news coverage
- Skillful at working independently with excellent **time management** skills

PROMOTIONAL SERVICES

- Strong problem solving and dispute resolution skills
- Demonstrated ability to **meet quotas** under adverse conditions
- Skilled in prioritizing tasks; able to meet deadlines

PUBLIC RELATIONS

- Develop flexible **operation plans** commensurate with market swings
- Excel at prioritizing and **implementing** procedures
- Strong sense of **loyalty** and commitment to people and organization
- Excellent steward of resources while serving others with **integrity**
- Provide clear focus, action, momentum, and pro-active approach to **meet goals**

EMPLOYMENT HISTORY

Vice President, Media Services, Eastern Retirement Services, IL   2001–Present
Largest retirement real estate company in the eastern United States
Responsible for overseeing all aspects of full service in-house advertising agency. Grew client base from three affiliate retirement communities to 41 senior industry clients in first six years. Responsible for planning and budgeting marketing operations for start-up retirement community projects totaling $126 million. Supervised largest lead tracking database conversion ever undertaken by proprietary software. Accountabilities included acting as art director, graphic designer, events coordinator, public relations representative, client liaison, production manager, market planner, and project bidder.

Manager, KTL, CA   **1996–2000**
Highly acclaimed award winning movie and commercial production company

Served as location manager and production assistant on multiple projects (client list available). Coordinated commercials for production companies and commercials.

Created and implemented database system for tracking purposes. Developed instructional curriculum for talent management.

AFFILIATIONS / PROFESSIONAL MEMBERSHIP
United Way
International Association of Marketing Professionals

COMPUTER SKILLS
Proficient in Word, Excel, and Photoshop.
Equally cross-trained in Mac and PC platforms

AWARDS
Best Practices recipient—Video Producer in New Zealand by Video World
Named No.1 of 29 Youth Media Awards

EDUCATION
Bachelor of Science Degree in Business, University of Arizona, 1990

David M. Andrews
637 Wagner Creek Road, Newark, NJ 97530   (201) 541-3286
Email: andrews@aol.com

QUALIFICATION HIGHLIGHTS

▸ More than 15 years' experience in Electrical/Electronic engineering with emphasis in scientific instrumentation

▸ Possess 10 years' experience in computer technologies (e.g., hardware and maintenance)

▸ Adept at working autonomously, including collaboration efforts with peers and groups

▸ Excel at multi-tasking, evaluating and prioritizing workloads

▸ Proven ability to quickly analyze situations, implement creative problem-solving skills and provide effective solutions

▸ Outstanding diplomacy in customer support and related services

Seeking Ohio, Kentucky or Indiana Placement

PROFESSIONAL EXPERIENCE

MANAGEMENT / TRAINING / QUALITY CONTROL

• Effectively trained field personnel in the technical installation and service in state-of-the-art High Resolution ICP-MS instrumentation.

• Supervisory abilities including engineering staff in both Test / Installation, and Field Service departments.

• Produced detailed test specification documents for the 2nd generation High Resolution ICP-MS instruments.

• Proposed quality control feedback/solutions to instrument design team and manufacturing department.

• Extensive experience in telecommuting and strong organizational skills.

COMMUNICATIONS / SALES / CUSTOMER SERVICE

• Ability to provide rapid high-quality technical support to customers and field-based engineers.

• Strong interpersonal communication skills: liaison with customers, sales personnel and upper management: site planning and instrument commissioning.

• Ability to apprise customers about current support services and instrument upgrades

SPECIAL TRAINING

Management: Proprietary methodology designed to implement team efforts and collaborative project completion.

Technical courses include third-party vendor products (maintenance, operations, customer training and usage).

Instrumentation including factory based training for ISO 9000 company certification.

EMPLOYMENT HISTORY

Senior Field Service Engineer/Technical Specialist, Intel Inc
2003–Present

Responsibilities include liaison with customers and engineering staff via Email and telephone. Assisting customers with instrument upgrades and providing onsite customer support when required. Additional duties include ordering parts on behalf of customers, repairing parts when applicable and document and report writing.

Technical Support Representative, FIGEL Elemental (UK)
1998–2002

Provided technical support for both customers and field based engineers. Acted as liaison with design team. Provide research data from customer instruments. Produced documentation for the next generation of high resolution instruments including test specs, training manuals and customer instrument manuals.

Test & Installation Engineer, ORION (UK)
1999–2001

Tested and installed high resolution mass spectrometry instruments. Organized training for new test and installation engineers and customers. Wrote documentation for the next generation of high resolution instruments.

Technician Engineer, EAR Farnborough (UK)
1988–1990

Supervisory position overseeing apprentices producing circuit boards.

EDUCATION
Bachelor of Science Degree in Electrical Engineering, University of Derby, UK

Sue Ann Montgomery
463 East Loop Drive
Portland, ME 04100
(207) 661-5688
Email: Montgomery@orion.com

QUALIFICATIONS

- More than 12 years' experience in human resources, management, and administration responsibilities
- Excellent interpersonal communication skills; Strong interviewing skills resulting in top employee candidate selection
- Strong team building including personnel training
- Able to establish and maintain professional relationships with peers and supervisors
- Skillful at overseeing financial, material, and personnel resources
- Proven organizational and coordination skills
- Enjoy managing multiple tasks simultaneously; Excel at evaluating and prioritizing work tasks
- Able to interpret a wide variety of subject matter and data

PROFESSIONAL HIGHLIGHTS

Administrative Responsibilities

- Organizational development: Excel in developing collaborative team environments, instilling team cooperation and employee commitment resulting in goal achievement.
- Develop reward and recognition incentives for improved employee performance.
- Ability to forecast and conform to budgets.
- Proficient at analyzing data and projecting needed changes.

Communication and Employee Relations

- Strong problem solving, dispute resolution, and mediation skills.
- Excellent at communicating company policies, procedures, and employee benefits.
- Strong negotiation and facilitation skills.

Marketing and Public Relations

- Able to establish community relations and partnership program between public and private sector.
- Skilled at managing high volume in/outbound call centers focusing on customer service.
- Interpretation of market trends and forecasting of new strategies.

EMPLOYMENT EXPERIENCE

Executive Director - Delta Computer Training Institute   2004–present

Area Marketing Director
Responsible for staffing and transition; expenses and budget forecasting; management and goal setting; data and information interpretation; sales; establishing and maintaining partnerships internally and within the public and private sectors. Overall leadership.

Call Center Coordinator
Provided staffing and payroll; statistical tracking; sales training; organizational development and team building; coordination with other marketing departments.

Sales Representative
Performed telephone contact with prospective customers to generate interest in products and services. Facilitated enrollment. Provided statistical tracking. Assisted with training new employees.

EDUCATION
Business-Computer and Office Automation
Business Computer Training Institute, Vancouver, WA — 2003

COMPUTER SKILLS / SELECTED ACCOMPLISHMENTS
Microsoft Word, Excel, Publisher, Outlook, Internet Explorer
QuickBooks
Internal Database Systems

- Designed company wide Excel spreadsheet tracking and employee production program for Business Computer Training Institutes' marketing program
- Utilized FoxPro tracking database for Business Computer Training Institutes' training center
- Proficient in electronic communication using Outlook and streaming website information

(Professional Template) **Your Name**

Address, City, State, Zip

Home (512) 326-4905   Cell: 321-9508

Objective, Goal, or Profile statement (optional)

QUALIFICATIONS

- ▸ More than X years' experience in
- ▸ Knowledgeable about
- ▸ Established history of
- ▸ Proven abilities in
- ▸ Strengths in
- ▸ Excellent skills in
- ▸ Proficient with

PROFESSIONAL PROFILE

YOUR WORK INDUSTRY HEADING

- Strong ability to
- Ability to
- Talent for
- Skillful at
- Adept in

EMPHASIS HEADING

- Strong problem solving and dispute resolution skills
- Demonstrated ability to
- Skilled at
- Excellent
- Proven history in

EMPHASIS HEADING

- Develop
- Excel at
- Strong sense of
- Excellent
- Provide

EMPLOYMENT HISTORY

Your Job Title, Company name   Year – Year

- Director of
- Responsible for
- Oversaw all aspects of
- Accountabilities included
- Provided
- Contributed to
- Produced
- Managed
- Trained

Your Job Title, Company name   Year – Year

- Performed
- Coordinated
- Supervised
- Acted as
- Developed
- Created and implemented
- Conducted
- Incorporated
- Prepared   (Repeat employment history, as applicable)

OTHER CAREER HISTORY (omit job duties information)

Your Job Title, Company name   Year – Year

Your Job Title, Company name   Year – Year

(Below are examples of section components to convey aspects of your background.)

ACHIEVEMENTS
TECHNICAL SKILLS
EXPERTISE
AFFILIATIONS/PROFESSIONAL MEMBERSHIPS
PRESENTATIONS
CERTIFICATIONS/LICENSURE
AWARDS/HONORS
DISTINCTIONS/PUBLICATIONS/PRESENTATIONS
SPECIAL TRAINING
COMPUTER SKILLS
EDUCATION

Bachelor of Science Degree [insert title of degree] School, City, and/or State, date, (or pending graduation date—optional)

Trish C. Jones   *Phone (775) 432-5767*
767 View Avenue   *Incline Village, NV 89450*

QUALIFICATIONS

Objective: FINANCIAL CONSULTANT

- Eleven years' experience in bank brokerage programs
- Produced over $350,000 gross commissions per year at both Wells Fargo and Bank of America
- Excellent motivational skills
- Collaborate well with bank employees toward generating investment referrals
- Pro-active regarding creative problem solving
- Effective at discovering clients' liquid assets
- Strengths in persuasive customer service interactions

PROFESSIONAL HIGHLIGHTS

- Licenses: Series 7 and Life Agent–Authorized for variable contract in Oregon, California, Nevada, and Utah
- Knowledge of securities and annuities. Adhere to compliance regulations
- Marketing: Small business retirement plans
- Strong interview skills: Profiling and qualifying investment suitability

EMPLOYMENT EXPERIENCE

Financial Consultant, Zion Investments, Reno, NV   2006 – present
Recommending mutual funds and annuities at six bank branches. Providing training for bank employees to identify candidates for investment referrals.

Financial Consultant, Bay Federal Bank, San Francisco, CA   2000 –2005
Recommending mutual funds and annuities at four branches. Providing sales and production services. Proposing portfolio diversification to meet individual client needs.

Financial Officer, Wells Fargo Securities, Grass Valley, CA   1998 – 2000
Recommending and monitoring mutual funds, variable annuities, (e.g., sub-account) performances at two bank branches.

Investment Specialist, Bank of America, Bakersfield, CA   1991 – 1997
Offering mutual funds and annuities at seven bank branches. Ranked number two producer out of sixteen brokers.

EDUCATION

Bachelor of Science Degree in Anthropology, University of Oregon, 1990

Thomas A. Stevens
103 Manzanita Avenue, San Diego, CA 92115
(619).512.1643
Email: t_stevens@hotmail.com

EDUCATION

Bachelor of Arts degree in Economics

San Diego State University, San Diego, CA 2008

QUALIFICATIONS

- Strong interpersonal communication and relationship building skills
- Excellent organizational and management skills
- Able to multitask and simultaneously perform two or more activities
- Creative problem solving and conflict resolution skills
- Presented and lectured clinics and workshops
- Created and developed clinics and projects
- Implemented strategies and techniques appropriate to various age groups
- Organized and conducted participants in daily activities
- Exposure to diverse multicultural groups and individuals
- Coached sport clinics (soccer camps); taught related skills and activities

COMPUTER SKILLS

Knowledge of computer operations

- Good computer skills
- Microsoft Word, Excel, Access and PowerPoint

WORK EXPERIENCE

Brothers Soccer Academy, Santa Rosa, CA   2004 – 2008
Provided soccer camp training and implementation.

Allen Property Management, Santa Rosa, CA   2005
Provided grounds maintenance services including watering, equipment operations, chemical solution application. Conducted Senior Thesis project in Business Management research.

ACHIEVEMENTS

- Jr. College All-American First Team In Soccer • Jr. College Team Captain
- Conference Player of The Year, 2005; Santa Rosa Jr. College, Santa Rosa, CA

ROBERT J. HOUDIN, MBA, CPA

48 Granite Street, Seattle, WA 97301 Phone: (206) 485-7516 houdin@mail.com

Objective: Accounting/Finance

Summary Profile

Twenty years' management experience in physician groups, hospitals, and healthcare systems. Extensive background in financial management, systems analysis, operational review, project planning, implementation, and evaluation. Demonstrated ability to capture gains through process improvement techniques. Exceptionally skilled with computer systems.

Experience

2003 – 2009	First Health System
Director of Finance – Physician Network	Modesto, CA

Responsible for accounting, financial reporting, budgeting, and billing office functions for physician clinics, a network of 39 FTE providers in 10 satellite clinics. Managed centralized billing office with 22 FTEs.

- Focused organization on budget accountability and industry benchmarks
- Participated in development and implementation of physician compensation plan
- Team leader for selection and installation of new practice management system
- Significantly reduced registration errors and increased collections
- Initiated coding reviews and chart audits to improve billing accuracy
- Primary management during dissolution of physician network, including valuation and liquidation of medical equipment and furnishings

1998 – 2002	Central Hospital
Vice President – Physician & HMO Services	Spokane, WA

Responsible for implementation of hospital's primary care initiative. Oversaw application process for obtaining state licensure of a community-based HMO insurance company. Strategic planning, construction, recruiting, setup, and opening of two primary care clinics.

- Recruited physician, clinical, and office staff.
- Selected and installed computerized billing system.
- Set up fee schedules, credit policies, and operating procedures.
- Oversaw architectural design and construction of two separate facilities.
- Managed growth of practices to a combined size of 3 OB/GYN, 4 Family Medicine, 3 Internal Medicine physicians and a support staff of 22.5 FTEs.

1998 – 2001   **Spokane Clinic**
Director of Finance   **Spokane, WA**

Chief financial officer of a 120-physician multi-specialty group practice with 515 employees, 84 departments, three satellites, and gross revenues of $73 million.

- Responsible for financial reporting, accounting procedures, physician compensation plans, profit sharing and 401K plans, working capital requirements, long-term financing, equipment leases, operating and capital budgets, and financial projections.

- Issued $24 million in variable rate bonds, negotiated $10.2 million refinancing, increased cash reserves from 4.1 to 23.0 days, initiated and implemented move from cash based to accrual accounting, converted G/L and A/P systems to MAS90, and installed Novell LAN.

1996 – 1998   **Harbor House Retirement Center**
Director of Finance   **Seattle, WA**

Chief financial officer of a non-profit life care retirement community with 450 residents, $4.5 million in revenues, $32 million in assets.

- Issued $15 million tax exempt variable rate bond. Implemented cost accounting systems for a $35 million, 510-unit construction project. Installed LAN and computerized accounting programs.

- Served as site review team leader for AHA national accreditation survey program.

1995 – 1997   **Jensen's Restaurant Enterprises**
Treasurer   **Seattle, WA**

Chief financial officer in turn-around attempt for restaurant group and affiliated partnerships with combined sales of $3.2 million.

Education and Professional Certification

Master of Business Administration Degree, University of Puget Sound,
Tacoma, Washington, and Bachelor of Arts in Business Administration

Certified Public Accountant, University of Washington, Seattle, Washington

Professional Affiliations

Medical Group Management Association
American Institute of Certified Public Accountants

Steve B. Reynolds, M.A.
1167 Ash Street, Durham, NC 54389 / Cell: (302) 912-9780
Email address: Steve_reynolds@yahoom.com

Organizational training, sports education, and project management.
Deliver strategies using innovative multimedia
for marketing and sales applications.

EDUCATION

Master of Science Degree in Applied Psychology, Organizational Training and Development

Southern Oregon University, Ashland, OR, 2008

Bachelor of Science Degree in Educational Studies, Family and Human Services,

University of Oregon, Eugene, OR, 2004

QUALIFICATIONS

- Knowledgeable about organizational curriculum development and training delivery
- Highly experienced as a competitive athlete, coach, and sports trainer; background in outdoors recreation and wilderness environments
- Demonstrated ability to coordinate people, information, and resources
- Proven self-starter; autonomous and innovative program development and project completion
- Well-developed ability to lead others with enthusiasm; operate from process to action
- Excellent verbal and written communication skills, including adaptive use of presentation styles to fit diverse audiences
- Able to implement creative, practical and concrete action; resourceful and adaptive during periods of change

PROFESSIONAL HIGHLIGHTS

ORGANIZATION TRAINING AND DEVELOPMENT

- Demonstrated ability to assess, design, develop, implement, and evaluate training programs.
- Expert organizational skills; enlist collaborative efforts to achieve plans. Pro-active problem solving and barrier removal.
- Advanced computer technology; ability to incorporate multimedia to deliver trainings.
- Strong project management skills; able to train staff to meet short- and long-term goals.

SPORTS MARKETING

- Perform as an exuberant presence to promote knowledge of products.
- Experienced in event planning, including road races, silent auctions/fundraisers.
- Highly effective in sports marketing with proven participant history.

GROUP DYNAMICS AND FACILITATION

- Able to communicate effectively with a variety of socio-economic and culturally diverse populations.
- Demonstrated ability in coaching, group facilitation, and conflict management.

EXPERIENCE

Program Developer, Spring Life Program, Ashland, OR   2005–2008

Content Developer for Online Learning Network, Grant Health Systems, Medford, OR

Program Manager Assistant, Youth Partners, Eugene, OR

Youth Advocate and Educator, Clear Horizons, Eugene, OR

- Responsible for developing, implementing, and evaluating a behavior tracking system integrating Microsoft ACCESS and Excel software programs. Established treatment options and goals.
- Assisted in the development of learning management system. Created newsletters, including online and paper distribution methods.
- Created activity manuals geared toward experiential techniques.
- Managed and maintained database.
- Tutored homeless youth for GED preparation.

EMPLOYMENT HISTORY

Licensed Lead Raft Guide, Destination Wilderness, Eugene, OR   2002–2004

- Responsibilities included overseeing all aspects of operations.
- Facilitated group dynamics and outdoor recreation activities.
- Coordinated and organized a variety of services, including safety procedures, scheduling guides, transportation services, food, and gear.
- Taught and fostered environmental ethics.

Track Coach, Park City Track Team, Eugene, OR   2003

- Served as track coach for long and high jump.
- Supervised youth in performance development and competitive training programs.

Climbing Instructor, Drew Rock Gym, Eugene, OR   2000–2002

Performed as skill developer and instructor for belay technique and climbing commands.

TEACHING ASSISTANT

General Psychology 201 and Psychology 228, Methods, Statistics and Laboratory I, Southern Oregon University

- Designed class format and taught psychological concepts and theories. Developed innovative techniques to work with project groups to research, develop, and implement lab projects. Mentored and tutored students. Graded and edited papers.

COMPUTER SKILLS

Software: Microsoft Word, Excel, PowerPoint, Publisher, Dreamweaver
Operating Systems: Windows 98 and XP, Macintosh OS 11

(Electronic Version of the previous Word formatted resume)

Steve B. Reynolds

1167 Ash Street, Durham, NC 54389   Cell: (302) 912-9780

Email: steve_reynolds@yahoom.com

Organizational training, sports education, and project management. Deliver strategies using innovative multimedia for marketing and sales applications.

EDUCATION

Master of Science in Applied Psychology; Organizational Training and Development,
Southern Oregon University, OR   2008
Bachelor of Science in Educational Studies; Family and Human Services,
University of Oregon, Eugene, OR   2004

QUALIFICATIONS

- Knowledgeable about organizational curriculum development and training delivery.
- Highly experienced as a competitive athlete, coach, and sports trainer; background in outdoor recreation and wilderness environments.
- Demonstrated ability to coordinate people, information, and resources.
- Proven self-starter; autonomous and innovative program development and project completion.
- Well-developed ability to lead others with enthusiasm; operate from process to action.
- Excellent verbal and written communication skills, including adaptive use of presentation styles to fit diverse audiences.
- Able to implement creative, practical and concrete action; resourceful and adaptive during periods of change.

PROFESSIONAL HIGHLIGHTS

ORGANIZATION TRAINING AND DEVELOPMENT

- Demonstrated ability to assess, design, develop, implement, and evaluate training programs.
- Expert organizational skills; enlist collaborative efforts to achieve plans. Pro-active problem solving and barrier removal.
- Refined knowledge of advanced computer technology; ability to incorporate multimedia to deliver trainings.
- Strong project management skills; able to train staff to meet short-term and long-term goals.

SPORTS MARKETING

- Perform as an exuberant presence to promote knowledge of products.
- Experienced in event planning, including road races, silent auctions, and fundraisers.

GROUP DYNAMICS AND FACILITATION

- Able to communicate effectively with a variety of socio-economic and culturally diverse populations.
- Demonstrated ability in coaching, group facilitation, and conflict management.

EXPERIENCE - Internships

Program Developer, Spring Life Program, Ashland, OR
Content Developer for Online Learning Network, Grant Health Systems, Medford, OR
Program Assistant, Youth Partners, Eugene, OR
Youth Advocate and Educator, Clear Horizons, Eugene, OR   2005 – 2008
- Responsible for developing, implementing, and evaluating a behavior tracking system integrating paper distribution methods.
- Created activity manuals geared toward experiential techniques.
- Managed and maintained database.
- Tutored homeless youth for GED preparation.

EMPLOYMENT HISTORY
Licensed Lead Raft Guide, Destination Wilderness, Eugene, OR   2000 – 2004
- Responsibilities included overseeing all aspects of operations.
- Facilitated group dynamics and outdoor recreation activities.
- Coordinated and organized a variety of services, including safety procedures, scheduling guides, transportation services, food, and gear.
- Taught and fostered environmental ethics.

Track Coach, Park City Track Team, Eugene, OR   2003
- Served as track coach for long and high jump.
- Supervised youth in performance development and competitive training programs.

Climbing Instructor, Drew Rock Gym, Eugene, OR   2000 – 2002
- Performed as skill developer and instructor for belay technique and climbing commands.

TEACHING ASSISTANT

General Psychology 202 and Psychology 228 Methods and Statistics, Southern Oregon University

- Designed class format and taught psychological concepts and theories. Developed innovative techniques to work with project groups; Perform research, develop and implement lab projects. Mentored and tutored students. Graded and edited papers.

COMPUTER SKILLS
Software: Microsoft Word, Excel, PowerPoint, Publisher, Dreamweaver
Operating Systems: Windows 98 and XP, Macintosh OS 11

YOUR NAME

3223 STREETCITY, STATE 97520

HOME: 124.123.3456   EMAIL@YAHOO.COM

OBJECTIVE: Organizational Effectiveness Consultant

Visionary Leader with over 10 years of combined Organizational Development (OD), Project Management, and Supplier/Vendor Management experience in Fortune 500 and mid-sized organizations. Demonstrated ability to assess, analyze, develop, and deploy OD initiatives. Effective project leadership skills promoting optimal team performance by planning, providing direction, assigning responsibilities, and delivering results. Resourceful and adaptive to lead others through cultural change. Proven ability to persuasively communicate to all levels of management.

AREAS OF EXPERTISE

- Organizational Development
- Supplier/Vendor Management
- Employee Engagement
- Project Management
- Culture Change
- Training and Development
- Leadership
- Process Redesign
- Coaching

SELECTED CAREER ACCOMPLISHMENTS

ORGANIZATIONAL DESIGN AND EFFECTIVENESS

- **Sustained turnover at 8 percent** by coordinating the development of concise job requirements for every role with core competency and technical knowledge requirements to identify career development and advancement opportunities within Coca-Cola Fountain.

- Key contributor in **strategically mapping 80 hours of training** for 200 managers and employees in the Supply Chain Management Office (SMO) resulting in building manager capability and employees exceeding performance goals by **increasing market share by 15 percent.**

- **Maintained 60 percent employee engagement** by implementing organizational effectiveness initiatives from the SMO Workplace Survey.

- Developed and supervised the New Associate Orientation Program to provide insight on the organizational goals, vision, values, and key learning activities for new employee adaptability within the first 90 days.

LEADERSHIP AND PROJECT MANAGEMENT

- **Modeled the role of servant leader** over 8 years by empowering, training, and coaching 14 facilitators promoting a shared vision, meeting team goals, and increasing members' knowledge by teaching transformational life skills in non-profit's 8-week New Member Orientation Program.

- **Built cultural change** and sparked a collaborative team environment by instilling team cooperation and employee commitment through the Who Moved My Cheese initiative with 100 Coca-Cola warehouse managers and employees.

- **Launched and delivered a 35 percent increase in supplier conformity** to reduce fraud by quality assurance initiatives including process redesign with an authorization method, a supplier training program, and laboratory annual conference (VALUE).

- **Conducted 20 percent of customer training classes** to promote user-friendly instruction and implement the Company's software. Provided accurate output, quick turnaround, and customer satisfaction as Design Forms Manger. Hired, trained, and managed a staff of three.

PROFESSIONAL WORK EXPERIENCE

Employer., City, State   2006 – Present
International medical technology group providing advanced clinical solutions for cancer care

Document Control Coordinator

- **Increased efficiencies** 60 percent by identifying time consuming barriers to streamline the Product Creation Process allowing software engineers to manage information faster and more intelligently.

Employer, City, State   2004 – 2005
One of the nation's largest and strongest financial holding Fortune 200 Company

Project Manager, Marketing Communications

- **Minimized consumer fraud and heighten awareness** by managing a multiple-distribution communication campaign with a cross-functional team informing over 1/2 million clients about online portal changes, branch consolidations, and the closing of 67 branches as result of the new SunTrust logo and the National Commerce Financial Bank acquisition.

Employer, City, State   1997 – 2003
World's most recognized brand and Fortune 100 Company

Project Manager, Quality Management Systems

- **Exclusively managed an $80M quality management program** for the development and commercialization of innovative Point-Of-Sale products, packaging, and vessel concepts.

- **Directed and maintained system-wide capability** of Company expectations, program consistency, and trademark compliance by aligning cross-businesses including 55 suppliers, 4 vendors, and 10 cross-functional departments. Suppliers: Georgia-Pacific, International Paper

Project Coordinator

- **Increased alignment capabilities** by launching organizational effectiveness initiatives to improve employee engagement and commitment, execute cultural change, enhance cross-function collaboration, and identify common departmental performance metrics in SMO.

The Atlanta Committee for the Olympic Games, Atlanta, Georgia   1992 – 1996
2006 Host Committee City for the Games of the XXVI Olympiad, the 100th year celebration

Project Coordinator

- Organized Special Events Team in numerous events and logistics including the **Torch Relay Press Conference** assuring sponsor brand visibility for BMW, Coca-Cola, and Champion Hanes, and managing the VIP hospitality suite.

- **Total responsibility for the $45M allocation** of global and national beverage sponsors' products (Coca-Cola and Crystal Springs) for over 200 pre-Games events including the Olympic Stadium Grand Opening of 70,000 attendees.

EDUCATION AND TRAINING

M.A. in Organizational Leadership, Name of University, City, State, Graduation 2008
B.S. in Computer Science, Name of University, City, State
Courses: Project Management, Performance Management, Diversity, Coaching, Servant Leadership

AFFILIATIONS

Member, Society of Human Resources Management
Charter Member in Gwinnett County, American Business Women of America

PROFILE ADDENDUM

PROFESSIONAL VALUES

- Forward-thinking Leadership
- Proven Integrity
- Excellent Performance
- Total Commitment
- Creative Collaboration
- Mature Attitude

ENDORSEMENTS: "She brings value through her excellent leadership and teamwork roles." Fountain Packaging Innovation Manager, Coca-Cola; "Willing to go the extra mile." Legal Counsel, Coca-Cola; "Successful in getting competitors to work together in non-threatening and productive manner." Consumer Product Manager, STR Laboratories; "Earned your OD stripes and have presumably done enough to convince your client as to the merits of your recommendation." Professor, Regent University

PRESENTATIONS

- Guest student speaker at the 17th Annual Southeast Human Resource Conference
  Topic: Women's Leadership and Service through Team Building

CASE STUDIES

- **Building a Women's Leadership Team**

  Challenge: A newly formed and diverse, non-profit women's leadership team of nine was challenged to bond as a team and to serve 7,500 women through numerous life skills programs and activities.

  Solution: With understandable urgency, conducted a needs analysis to identify immediate concerns. Designed a team-building intervention embracing core foundations of team vision, role allocation, blending personality types, leadership training and development, and principles of servant leadership. Identified barriers to effective team building and rules to sustain and grow. Developed simple measurement and feedback mechanisms to monitor and evaluate effectiveness of the team-building process.

  Results: Team-building success through responsiveness, collaboration, and performance after the implementation of team-building exercises and change strategies. Project concluded May, 2008.

- **The Value of Manager and Employee Communications**

  Challenge: Identify communication issues between Elekta Inc.'s managers and employees. Specifically, do Elekta's Inc. managers give effective communication that employees understand and are engaged to complete work assignments and meet company objectives?

  Solution: Conducted survey and qualitative interviews with a diverse population of managers and employees identifying their manager's communication effectiveness in style, motivation, active listening, and performance feedback. Performance feedback scored highest; however, analysis revealed performance gaps among managers' communication skills and low scores for active listening.

  Results: Proposed to Senior Management the design and implementation of an annual 360° Feedback Program to address communications skills, behavior changes, and developmental opportunities for managers promoting individual development and self-awareness. Project concluded October, 2008.

Gregg M. Jones
Address ~ City, State zip code

(area) 484-3409   **gjones@gmail.com**

Highly effective professional with expertise in **productive communication** skills resulting in successful **sales** and **increased revenues**. Skilled in creating **profitable alliances**. Orchestrate relationship building and developing collaborative **partnerships**. Act as Agent in creating and implementing innovative **strategic planning**. Exceptional skills in acquiring **new market shares** and retained customers.

SENIOR SALES MANAGER ~ NATIONAL MARKETING DIRECTOR

- More than 25 years' experience in progressively responsible sales positions; consistently rated as Top Sales Producer
- Accomplished in creating and implementing resourceful and innovative programs
- Outstanding customer relationship management and company representative
- Experienced in creating, negotiating, and finalizing contracts
- Established history of tracking and managing database of over 11,000 clients
- Excellent organizational, interpersonal, communication and presentation skills
- Excellent in Accounts Receivable (A/R) and retrieving payments

Areas of Effectiveness

• Customer Services	• Sales	• Marketing
• Management	• Budget	• Publications
• Promotions	• Contracts	• Ad Placement
• Pricing Strategies	• Business Operations	• Communication
• Territory Development	• Technical Presentation	• Leadership

Selected Career Accomplishments

- Proven history in penetrating new market shares resulting in greater sales profits and customer base
- Effectively redesigned existing program directly leading to the doubling of the number of clients while increasing the profit margin by 100 percent
- Established history of building revenues from $500,000 annually to $1M
- Effective in managing organizations talent of over 75 staff employees
- Introduced and implemented visionary strategies and techniques for merging productive partnerships and enterprises
- Launched a successful cooperative incentive with national manufacturers
- Developed key relationships resulting in over $15M in revenues for selling advertising space
- Created novel "concept packaging" presentation for greater impact and orders of new products
- Established a telemarketing program through direct mailings, special discounts, and catalog requests
- Motivated and enlisted 140 national/international independent sales reps; supported 53 national shows

PROFESSIONAL EXPERIENCE

REGIONAL SALES MANAGER, ComGroup 2007 – Present
Owner in national advertising company
Accounts include: Harry and David, Macy's Brighton, Collectibles, Marmi, Eddie Bauer, Maserati, Verizon, Mace Rich Corp., Carnival Cruises, Rockport Shoes, Relax The Back, Hearts on Fire Diamonds, Tagheuer, Lassen Galleries

- Consistently top sales producer for company
- Direct the planning, coordination, and management of advertising
- Sell business-to-business advertising, including services and retail industries
- Plan, direct, and evaluate the activities of sales department
- Establish sales goals and assigned territories
- Coach representatives to improve sales performance
- Always meet industry deadlines
- Deliver exceptional communication skills for increasing customer base and profit
- Work closely with advertising agencies to ensure the best complete customer satisfaction
- Assist in product development and marketing strategies to identify potential new markets

DIRECTOR OF MARKETING, Jeld Win, Inc 1999 – 2006
NATIONAL SALES MANAGER (promoted to above)

- Developed pricing strategies to maximize profit on each product or service sold
- Established distribution network for products and services
- Initiated market research
- Assisted in product development and marketing strategies to identify potential new market

OPERATIONS MANAGER, Adroit Synergies, Inc 1996 – 1998

- Improved organization of $500,000 company to achieve first profit in three years by lowering cost of goods from 125 percent to 54 percent
- Conducted all planning, financial management and staff development
- Coordinated budget development, contracts and administration of 24 contractors
- Supervised all inventory purchase and administration

OTHER CAREER HISTORY

SALES MANAGER, GROTON, LTD., VA 1993 – 1995
RETAIL MANAGER, ELITE BOARDS, VA 1990 – 1992

EDUCATION
Bachelor of Science Degree in Psychology, Chico State College

COMPUTER SKILLS
Microsoft Office Suite (Word, Excel)

Rand Smith, PMP
321 C Street ~ Tulsa, OK 95230
(612) 484-3456   **rand.smith@gmail.com**

Highly effective professional with expertise in **project management** and core competencies in **information technology** and **human resources**. Skilled in orchestrating projects and managing service delivery to meet company goals with **superior customer service**. Diverse experience in **business operations** and highly effective at building **excellent client relationships**.

Senior IT Manager ~ Project Manager

- More than 13 years' experience in progressively responsible IT management positions
- Consistent project management successes, complemented by PMP certification
- Experienced in retail, direct marketing, manufacturing, and international environments
- Exceptionally broad business operations and management experience
- Established history of superior customer service and problem solving abilities
- Excellent organizational, interpersonal, communication, and presentation skills
- Outstanding systems analyst, strategic planner, leader, and coach

Expertise includes:

• Project Management	• LAN/WAN/Infrastructure	• Documentation/Policies
• Process Development	• Website Development	• Business Systems Analysis
• Resource Management	• ERP/CRM/EDI Systems	• Relationship Management
• Problem Resolution	• Vendor Management	• Financial Management
• Team Development	• Negotiation	• Strategic Planning

Selected Career Accomplishments

• Project manager for: ERP/CRM system installations and upgrades, website development and rollouts, Email system installations/consolidations, Windows server/data conversions and consolidations, PBX replacement, new product development, corporate acquisition, corporate health insurance conversion.

• Established all Information Technology operations and procedures for a highly successful start-up business, supporting sales Installed a 1,000-user Email system, including vendor selection and contract negotiation as well as authoring the user manual and creating formal 90-minute classes introducing the system to corporate users.

• Launched a start-up retail computer business and grew sales 500 percent in seven years, including the establishment of independently profitable service and training divisions.

• Directed the highly successful product acquisition/rollout and warehousing operations for Australia's largest retail computer organization headquarters during a two-year overseas assignment as the number two executive in the organization and transaction growth of over 400 percent in four years while instilling an IT culture focused on delivering the highest levels of customer service.

PROFESSIONAL EXPERIENCE

PROFESSIONAL DESIGN MANUFACTURING, LLC, Anchorage, AK   *2002 – Present*

DIRECTOR OF PROJECT MANAGEMENT   (2005 – Present)

- Direct the planning, coordination and management of all key projects for the company, and oversee all project and resource assignments. Serve as project manager for selected projects and provide training, guidance and mentoring for other project managers.
- Establish standardized functional PM methodology, planning processes, reporting, PM tools, risk management and communications across all areas.

DIRECTOR OF IT / ADMINISTRATION   (2002 – 2004)

- Directed all Information Technology operations, resources and projects, made all key IT decisions and participated in the annual strategic planning process as a member of the senior management team.
- Implemented technology solutions to reduce business labor requirements, simplified operations, increased productivity 30 percent-50 percent and cut error rates by 75 percent.
- Led the development of the company's e-commerce website and all site refreshes and upgrades.
- Directed all corporate Human Resources functions, including operating budget, benefits, insurance, 401(k), payroll, recruiting, hiring, training, terminations and labor compliance.

SHIATSU HOLDINGS, Kyoto, Japan   *1994 – 2001*

PROJECT MANAGER   (1999 – 2001)

- Directed the activities of 15 team members and managed the implementation of a $1.1 million shipping system in collaboration with senior managers and a broad range of corporate resources, utilizing standardized project management methodologies.
- Identified key system requirements and coordinated analysis and selection of software vendor.

PROJECT MANAGER, NEW BUSINESS INITIATIVES   (1998 – 2000)

- Leveraged exceptional cross-organizational rapport as IS Division Representative on a hand-picked team that created the business plan for the company's first five-year Internet expansion plan.
- Led the development of the strategic e-commerce business plan and road map, organized the plan outline, gathered and verified all data and authored the majority of the final version of the plan.

MANAGER, NETWORK SYSTEMS   (1996 – 1997)

- Directed the activities of 6 IT Analysts tasked with resolving all LAN, WAN and server-related issues on a network comprised of 60 servers and 5 midrange systems connected to an IBM mainframe.
- Oversaw all network server operations and related projects, upgrades, installations and support.
- Developed and implemented technology solutions to meet corporate goals and objectives.

MANAGER, PERSONAL SYSTEMS   (1994 – 1995)

- Managed vendor selection, contract negotiation, implementation and rollout of the company's first Email system, serving 1,000 users via an IBM mainframe bridged to PC and Macintosh networks.

OTHER CAREER HISTORY

COMPUTERLAND INDIA, Bombay, India   *1991 – 1993*
CEO & GENERAL MANAGER

COMPUTERLAND AUSTRALIA, Sydney, Australia   *1988 – 1990*
DIRECTOR OF OPERATIONS

CERTIFICATIONS / PROFESSIONAL TRAINING

PMP Certification, Project Management Institute
Situational Leadership, Center for Leadership Studies
Project Management certification, Cadence Management Corporation
Advanced HR Leadership certification, Cascade Employers Association
Fourth Shift ERP System Administration certifications, SoftBrands, Inc.
Technology certifications from IBM, Hewlett-Packard, Microsoft, Apple and others

EDUCATION

Bachelor of Science in Electrical Engineering (BSEE)
Lehigh University, Bethlehem, PA
Master's in Business Administration Program
Golden Gate University, San Francisco, CA

AFFILIATIONS

Member, Project Management Institute
Board Member & Treasurer, Cascade Employers Association

John L. Scott
541 Realtor Blvd
San Francisco, CA 96094

(520) 895-0190   johnscott@bay.net

Enthusiastic and energetic professional with expertise in sales and negotiations. Top-producing real estate sales agent. Highly effective in building trust and motivating others to action with relationship building skills.

BRANCH MANAGER ~ REAL ESTATE
- More than 10 years' experience in progressively changing real estate industry
- Proven history as top producing sales agent utilizing exceptional negotiation skills
- Successfully closed over 400 real estate deals: land, house, commercial, and ranch properties
- Outstanding communication skills; highly effective with individuals and large groups
- Established reputation as a trusted real estate consultant
- Passionate about serving the needs of others with energy and enthusiasm
- Highly skilled at motivating, inspiring, and supporting others, by listening to their needs

EXPERTISE INCLUDES
• Proven Leadership	• Event Planning / Coordination	• Marketing
• Neural Linguistics	• Extensive Network	• Lead Generation
• Video Production	• Contracts / Negotiations	• Financing Process

SELECTED CAREER ACCOMPLISHMENTS
- Sold over 200 lots with N.R.P.I. in 3 resort communities with one of the highest closing ratios
- Top producing land sales agent in Lake Shastina since 2000 (126 sales and over $6 million in volume)
- Top residential sales agent in Lake Shastina since 2000 (80 house sales and over $18 million in volume)
- Top ranked sales agent in 2003, 2006, & leading for 2008, & second in 2001, 2002, 2004, 2005

PROFESSIONAL HIGHLIGHTS

Business Operations
- Proven history of managing two branch offices including hiring and training agents
- Offer clients after sales service program to work toward establishing referral business
- Implement client relationship systems utilized before, during, and after transactions

Sales / Marketing
- Build confidence in clients resulting in sales; overcome obstacles and objections
- Collaborate with agents and implement preferred marketing strategy
- Create video tours of properties and provide listing for superior Internet presence
- Build strong relationships with lenders, escrow officers and agents for seamless closures

PROFESSIONAL EXPERIENCE

Real Estate Consultant, Real Estate, *Employer Name, CA*   **1999 – Present**
- Develop after sales service program including creating phone directory to strengthen exposure in the marketplace
- Implement new marketing strategies including setting up virtual tour of houses resulting in increased prospects
- Facilitate clientele through home construction process as a Lindal Cedar Home representative
- Instrumental in establishing top-producing real estate office in our market and top ten in Siskiyou County

Property Consultant, Real Estate, *Employer Name, Inc., CA*   **1999 – 2007**
- Generated sales leads, acquired land, hosted seminars, led sales presentations, and closed deals as tour guide
- Successfully closed deals and quickly accommodated up to 4 clients per day
- Outperformed in sales measured against the nation in highest volume and best closing ratio
- Top agent for 3 consecutive record-breaking years in land sales for nation's largest land acquisition company

Loan Analyst, Real Estate Loans, *Employer Name, CA*   **1998 – 1999**
- Collaborated with processors, loan officers, underwriters, and loan production to compile complete loan packages
- Contributed to the success of two record breaking quarters

PROFESSIONAL TRAINING
Professional Standards Real Estate Contracts, Association of Realtors
Professional Coaching and Training, By Referral Only
Buyer Representation, Ethics, Agency, Fair Housing, Trust Fund Handling
Professional coaching and prospect management, House Values
New Dealer Training, Lindal Cedar Homes

LICENSE / CERTIFICATION
Salesperson License, California Department of Real Estate

EDUCATION
Bachelor of Arts degree, Economics & Business
Westmont College, Santa Barbara, CA

AFFILIATIONS
MLS Committee - Consultant
Association of Realtors – Realtor

COMPUTER SKILLS
Microsoft Office Suite; Word, Excel, PowerPoint, Publisher
Act (Contact management), Pinnacle Studio (Video editing), Paragon (Online MLS)

NATALIE M. BREWER
1500 Alana Mountains Dr.
Santa Rosa, CA 94954

(707) 450-7513   natalie.brewer@yahoo.com

OBJECTIVE: ACCOUNTING, FINANCE OPERATIONS AND INVESTMENT MANGEMENT IN A FAST-PACED DYNAMIC ENVIRONMENT

PROFILE: Highly effective motivated professional with experience in financial management and operations. Highly enthusiastic in negotiations and contracts. Skillful in diplomatic and persuasive negotiations. Diverse experience in business operations and highly effective at creative problem solving. Skillful in advisor capacity and as exchange specialist.

PROFESSIONAL HIGHLIGHTS

- Experienced with banks, brokers, and associates in financially related institutions
- Proficient in transaction, process improvement, impact analysis, and solution-focused results
- Experienced in a wide range of financially related services, including real estate
- Proven history in coordinating information between individuals and resources
- Knowledgeable about principles and practices of finance and accounting
- Exceptionally skilled in analytical processes, including applying complex calculations, evaluations, and assessing value
- Excellent in translating technical and complex information, including applying rules, statutes, policies and regulations
- Adept at managing expectations and accompanying emotions; ability to build and sustain long-term business relationships
- Thorough investigative and research skills; attention to pertinent fact gathering

AREAS OF EFFECTIVENESS

Comparative Analysis	Generate New Business	Decision-Making
Account Reconciliation	Assess Value	Project Management
Exceed Sales Quotas	Meet Timely Deadlines	Detail Oriented
Needs Assessments	Act as Resource Broker	Financial Reporting

SELECTED CAREER ACCOMPLISHMENTS

- Successfully achieved 90% and above on all four sections of Series 7 license
- Achieved over $13 Million in sales within one year
- Initiated time-saving operational procedures that increased the accuracy and productivity of processing physical securities
- Modernized business operations accomplishing over 30% revenue increase by an innovative marketing strategy within a two-year period.
- Awarded membership of President's Circle for sales at Coldwell Banker Real Estate with over $120,000 in commission within one year

INVESTMENT MANAGEMENT
- Knowledgeable about day- to-day operations including assessing market trends and impact
- Skillful in determining individual portfolio needs; adept in managing investments and expectations

SALES / CONTRACTS
- Responsible for customized investment acquisitions
- Highly effective collaboration skills with a wide range of professionals and personality types

BUSINESS OPERATIONS / COMMUNICATIONS
- Develop process improvement programs resulting in increased productivity and morale
- Strong problem solving skills; ability to bring understanding to principles and act with decisiveness

PROFESSIONAL EXPERIENCE

Agent, Real Estate, *John L. Scott, CA*   2001 – 2009
- Oversaw the planning, coordination and management of real estate escrows
- Developed strategic marketing and promotional activities
- Advised clients on courses of action based on needs
- Cultivated and maintained long-term relationships that produced repeat transactions

Manager, Morgan Stein, Inc., *Oakland, CA*   1998 – 2001
- Recognized for highest sales margin, generating $1.4 million in Bay Area market
- Assisted in new Bay Area market launch of 22 new stores
- Received Top Gun Award for top sales producer company wide
- Trained 18 employees in product knowledge and sales techniques

Agent, Nationsbanc Securities LLC, *San Francisco, CA*   1997 – 1998
- Managed safekeeping of physical securities; reconciled daily securities transactions
- Coordinated the daily deposits and withdrawals with DTC
- Implemented new procedures to increase efficiency amid expansion of operations
- Facilitated and tracked ACATs for new client accounts

OTHER CAREER HISTORY
- Registered Representative, Baraban Securities
- Broker Assistant, Bear Sterns

PROFESSIONAL TRAINING
Series 7 licensed, NASD
Real Estate licensed, California Dept. of Real Estate

EDUCATION
Bachelor of Science, Business Finance
California State University, Sacramento

AFFILIATIONS
California Association of Realtors
Sonoma County Board of Realtors
Petaluma Council of Realtors

MATHEW OGDEN
450 Madrone Lane, Jackson, MI 97340
(603) 989 – 6838   mogden@charter.net

PROFILE: Highly effective **manufacturing manager** and **safety compliance officer**. Expertise in **process improvement**, **safety administration**, coaching and mentoring **improved employee performance**. Core competencies in building **efficient work teams** and **continuous improvement processes**. Adept in creative problem solving and solution-focused results. Proficient in **bi-lingual** Spanish skills.

SENIOR MANAGER / SAFE WORK PRACTICES ~ MANUFACTURING

- More than 20 years in progressively responsible positions primarily focusing on promoting and improving workplace safety and productivity
- Adept at straightforward, direct, and logical problem solving
- Experienced in evaluating manufacturing and processing systems
- Exceptionally skilled in maintaining quality assurance and statistical process control (SPC), including measuring and adjusting parameters
- Established history of organizing and prioritizing workload to accomplish company goals
- Excellent skills in the use of delegation techniques as a management tool
- Strong understanding of manufacturing methods and techniques

AREAS OF EFFECTIVENESS

Supervision	Trouble-Shooting	Needs Assessments
Industrial Hygiene	Ergonomics	Problem-Solving
Conflict Resolution	Diplomacy / Tact	Logical Analysis
Communication	Collaboration	Listening
Organization	Auditing	Safety/Risk Management
Succession Planning	Occupational Health	Enforcement Action

SELECTED CAREER ACCOMPLISHMENTS

- Administered a thorough safety and health program in an industrial environment of 160 employees that met and exceeded OSHA standards and guidelines
- Provided succession planning for talent management resulting in exceptional employee retention and greater company sustainability
- Significantly improved safety performance; eliminated accidents in the workplace resulting in a reduction of the accident incident rate from 7 percent to zero over five-year period
- History of evaluating hazardous work/ industrial health environments including chemical exposure, noise factors, air quality sampling, airborne contaminants, personal protective equipment, hazard abatement, etc.
- Created and implemented Standard Operating Procedures (SOP), including Job Hazard Analysis (JHA) documents
- Implemented the Safety Benchmark initiative from Best Practices principles and deliverables
- Developed work team initiative resulting in increased work productivity by 25 percent within six-month period, including exceptional employee support and increased morale

PROFESSIONAL HIGHLIGHTS

Management / Safety

- Proven history in creating and implementing safe work environments within OSHA guidelines and company policies
- Perform well as a presenter in staff meetings
- Excellent in process improvement methods
- Motivated self-starter; pro-active and results oriented
- Proven history implementing practical and concrete action; resourceful and adaptive during periods of change

Employee Performance / Coaching / Mentoring

- Ability in assessing employee skills level, including succession planning
- Highly effective managing personnel and human resources
- Adept in planning and assigning duties to employees
- Skillful in interviewing and mentoring employees for skill competencies
- Strong capacities for delegation, accountabilities, and follow up
- Established history of leading others toward a vision

Project Management

- Well-developed communication and listening skills; ability to promote effective results
- Adept coach and mentor for employee professional growth creating win-win scenarios
- Strengths in training, supervising, and managing personnel while instilling positive attitude for goal achievement
- Well-developed communication and listening skills; ability to promote effective results
- Demonstrated ability to coordinate people, information, and resources
- Enjoy managing multiple tasks simultaneously
- Capacity for understanding how individuals, processes, and systems interrelate

PROFESSIONAL EXPERIENCE

PLANT SUPERINTENDENT, *Boise Cascade/White City Veneer, White City, OR* **2004 – 2008**
Leading manufacturer of building materials

- Direct the planning, supervision, and coordination in all phases of plant operations
- Responsible for performance of 75 employees, two production shifts, and three lathe lines
- Accountable for profit and loss against established budget
- Prepare operation schedules
- Coordinate manufacturing activities and ensure production
- Oversee all aspects of meeting quality specifications
- Review and analyze reports and records related to production and process improvement
- Managed interdepartmental activities and schedules
- Implement systems and procedures while instilling accountability in a rapidly changing environment

KEY ACCOMPLISHMENT: Succeeded in a process efficiency project that identified bottlenecks and contributing factors in the production process resulting in an increase in productivity by 25 percent within a 6-month period.

PROFESSIONAL EXPERIENCE, CONTINUED...

PLANT SUPERINTENDENT, *Boise Cascade/Rogue Valley Plywood, OR*   **1999–2004**
- Accountable for 3 production shifts, 160 employees, PLV & plywood panels, 3 hot press and 3 dryers and 2 automatic lay up lines

KEY ACCOMPLISHMENT: Significantly improved employee safety performance by realigning work crews. Achieve vision of zero accidents

PROJECT MANAGER, *International / Corporate Boise Cascade, Boise, ID*   **1998–1999**
- Identify in-country sources of Eucalyptus Wood in South America, Chile, Brazil and New Zealand
- Evaluate in-country facilities to peel, dry, grade, and ship samples to United States/West Coast plant for processing and assessing highest degree of strength
- Provide comparative analysis of equipment strengths and weaknesses between in-county and United States for quality, profitability, productivity and sustainability
- Analyze in-country sites for locating a manufacturing facility controlled by Boise Cascade

KEY ACCOMPLISHMENT: *Requested by regional management to accept this project as keenly important to Boise Cascade and growth in the LVL business*

PLANT SUPERINTENDENT, *Boise Cascade/White City Veneer, White City, OR*   **1992–1998**
Accountabilities include employment as Plant Superintendent above including:
- Direct the planning, supervision, and coordination in all phases of plant operations
- Responsible for performance of 75 employees, two production shifts, and 3 lathe lines
- Accountable for profit and loss against established budget
- Prepare operation schedules
- Coordinate manufacturing activities and ensure production
- Oversee all aspects of meeting quality specifications
- Review and analyze reports and records related to production and process improvement
- Managed interdepartmental activities and schedules
- Implement systems and procedures while instilling accountability in a rapidly changing environment

KEY ACCOMPLISHMENT: *Oversaw $5 Million plant remodel including modernized lathe lines*

DEPARTMENT SUPERINTENDENT, *Green End, Medford Plywood, ,OR*   **1989–1992**
Establish leadership and set the strategic direction for the Manufacturing team
- Oversee 3 lathes lines, two production shifts, and 80 employees

KEY ACCOMPLISHMENT: Learned all phases of plywood production from green end through finished panels

SUPERINTENDENT, *St. Helens Veneer Plant, St. Helens, OR*   **1985–1986**
Responsible for performance of 50 employees, two production shifts, and one lathe line

SHIFT SUPERVISOR, *St. Helens Veneer Plant, St. Helens, OR*   **1976–1985**
EQUIPMENT OPERATOR / LEAD *St. Helens Veneer Plant, St. Helens, OR*   **1972–1976**

PROFESSIONAL TRAINING

Total Quality

Statistical Process Control Training (SPC)

Total Process Efficiency

Managing Workplace Conflict and Violence

Sexual Harassment

Cultural Diversity

Coaching and Mentoring Employees

Supervisory Trainings

Leadership and Talent Management

Communications and Active Listening

Subject , Occupational Safety and Health Administration (OSHA) various conferences and training programs

COMPUTER SKILLS

Microsoft Office Suite (Word, Excel, Outlook, Internet Research)

Oracle

People Soft – Requisitions and Report Management

ROSALYN ALLISON

40 Brahm Street, Grand Rapids, Michigan 98650

(320) 481 – 8690   rallison@connect.net

Highly effective professional with expertise in sales. Skilled in creative problem solving. Diverse experience in communicating with a wide range of personality types. Known for excellent customer experience satisfaction. Keenly skillful with gentle persuasion and diplomacy.

SALES ~ MANAGEMENT REPRESENTAIVE

- More than 20 years in progressively responsible sales and customer relationship building positions
- Outstanding communication skills producing win-win results for all parties
- Experienced in sales techniques and methods
- Exceptionally skilled in developing trust and rapport with clientele
- Established history of learning quickly; consistently develop increased sales revenues
- Able to work independently as well as with co-workers and supervisors
- Strong sense of commitment and loyalty to people and organizations

Areas of Effectiveness

Service	Real Estate	Marketing
Product Sales	Mortgages	Needs Assessments
Resource Broker	Problem-solving	Analysis
Questioning Techniques	Interviewing	Follow-through
Time Management	Solution-focused	Evaluations
Multi-tasking	Detail-oriented	Sales Techniques

Selected Career Accomplishments

- Consistently achieved revenues of $300,000 yearly over a ten-year period through generating sales
- Launched a successful business operation resulting in over $45M in sales in one year period, and $500M over a ten-year period
- Performed competitive analysis through informational interviewing; acquired knowledge about market need and bridged gap resulting in impressive accounts generation
- Developed a highly functional networking base of internal/external customers, vendors, clients, accounts, resulting in repeat and referral business opportunities

Customer Satisfaction / Business Operations / Organization

- Adept at meeting people's personal needs and instilling a feeling of importance
- Highly effective listening skills; proven history in leadership and supervisory capacities
- Enjoy managing multiple tasks simultaneously
- Provide appropriate client needs assessment; earn respect by prioritizing client business needs

Sales / Marketing /Communication

- Motivated self-starter; proactive and results-oriented
- Able to quickly establish and maintain long-term relationships
- Skillful in sales techniques, including acquiring appointments, commitments, and closing sales
- Enjoy managing multiple tasks simultaneously

Professional Experience

PRINCIPAL BROKER, *Company Name., City, State*   **1995 – Present**

Longest existing mortgage brokerage business
- Direct the planning, coordination and management of all aspects of business operations
- Instrumental in day-to-day operations
- Perform marketing responsibilities
- Coordinate communications with agents, buyers, and lenders

KEY ACHIEVEMENT: *Created and implemented successful start-up business resulting in growing sales revenues to over $45Million within a 10-year period.*

BRANCH MANAGER, *Company Name, City, State*   **1992 – 1995**
- Oversaw the day-to-day mortgage business operations
- Coordinated communications with lenders, title companies, realtors, and clients
- Supervised administration functions for information acquisition, obtained approvals, secured and closed loans

KEY ACHIEVEMENT: *Innovative identifying a lucrative business niche and serving to fulfill a market need resulting in increasing revenues from $15K to $15Million within a 3-year period.*

LOAN OFFICER, *Company Name, City, State*   **1991**
- Responsible for all aspects of marketing and generating loans
- Engaged in extensive networking with a broad range of potential and actual clientele

OTHER CAREER HISTORY

Realtor, Century 21 and Sun Harbor, CA
Sales Representative, North County Lincoln Mercury, CA

PROFESSIONAL TRAINING

Floyd Whitman Sweathogs Effective Sales Strategies, Techniques, and Methods
Joe Stumpf's Marketing Gorillas and Referral Methods Program

EDUCATION

Bachelor of Arts degree, English Literature
Montana State University, Bozeman, MT

AFFILIATIONS

Chamber of Commerce
Board Member, Community Works

Your Name
Address ~ City, State zip code

(Area) 543–1356   Email @gmail.com

Highly effective professional with expertise in {insert} and core competencies in {insert}. Skilled in {insert} and {insert}. Diverse experience in {insert} and highly adept at {insert}.

TITLE or WORK INDUSTRY ~ JOB TITLE

- More than 13 years' experience in progressively responsible
- Proven history in
- Experienced in
- Exceptionally skilled
- Established history of
- Excellent
- Outstanding

Expertise includes

• Insert	• Insert	• Insert
• Insert	• Insert	• Insert
• Insert	• Insert	• Insert
• Insert	• Insert	• Insert
• Insert	• Insert	• Insert

Selected Career Accomplishments

- Insert Accomplishment
- Insert Accomplishment
- Insert Achievement
- Insert Achievement
- Insert Achievement
- Insert Accomplishment

PROFESSIONAL EXPERIENCE

JOB TITLE, Company Name   Year – Year
Qualify company (optional)
Accounts include: Optional

- Direct
- Oversee
- Sell
- Plan, direct, and evaluate
- Serve as
- Establish
- Manage
- Deliver
- Direct
- Led

Key Achievement:

JOB TITLE, Company Name   Year – Year

- Developed
- Established
- Initiate
- Assist in product

Key Achievement:

JOB TITLE, Company Name   Year – Year

- Improve
- Conducted
- Coordinated
- Supervised

Key Achievement:

OTHER CAREER HISTORY

JOB TITLE, COMPANY NAME, STATE   Year – Year

JOB TITLE, COMPANY NAME, STATE   Year – Year

EDUCATION
Bachelor of Science Degree in {Insert}, Name of College

COMPUTER SKILLS
Microsoft Office Suite (Insert)

(Executive Template 2) **Your Name**

Address ~ City ,State zip code

(Area) 543-1356   Email @gmail.com

Highly effective professional with expertise in {insert} and core competencies in {insert}. Skilled in {insert} and {insert}. Diverse experience in {insert} and highly adept at {insert}.

TITLE or WORK INDUSTRY ~ JOB TITLE

- More than 13 years' experience in progressively responsible
- Proven history in
- Experienced in
- Exceptionally skilled
- Established history of
- Excellent
- Outstanding

AREAS OF EXPERTISE

Selected Career Accomplishments

- Insert Accomplishment
- Insert Accomplishment
- Insert Accomplishment

Profile Highlights

HEADER (i.e., BUSINESS OPERATIONS)

- Developed
- Aligned
- Mapped

HEADER (i.e., CUSTOMER RELATIONSHIP MANAGEMENT)

- Collaborated
- Facilitated
- Teamed with

PROFESSIONAL EXPERIENCE

JOB TITLE, Company Name   Year – Year
Qualify company (optional)
Accounts include: Optional

- Direct
- Oversee
- Sell business-to-business advertising, including services and retail industries
- Plan, direct, and evaluate
- Serve as
- Establish
- Manage
- Deliver
- Direct
- Led

Key Achievement:

JOB TITLE, Company Name   Year – Year

JOB TITLE, (promoted to above, if applicable)

- Developed
- Established
- Initiate
- Assist in product

Key Achievement:

JOB TITLE, Company Name   Year – Year

- Improve
- Conducted
- Coordinated
- Supervised

Key Achievement:

OTHER CAREER HISTORY

JOB TITLE, COMPANY NAME, STATE   Year – Year

JOB TITLE, COMPANY NAME, STATE   Year – Year

EDUCATION
Bachelor of Science Degree in {Insert}, Name of College

COMPUTER SKILLS
Microsoft Office Suite (Insert)

Portfolio/Biography/Accomplishment Profile

Your job search documents should consist of a cover letter, resume, references—and depending on your qualifications and intention—a portfolio, career biography, addendum profile, accomplishment summary, or brag book. Your marketing documents may include a collection of work samples or addendum materials presented separately and in addition to your resume, cover letter, and reference list. A portfolio serves the purpose of limiting your resume to one or two pages, but allows for a comprehensive and professional packaging of your qualifications.

Historically used by such professionals as architects, artists, and photographers, portfolio attachments are becoming more frequent in job search packets and can enhance your candidacy over an equally qualified candidate who does not bring additional support documents to the interview process. For example, one engineer worked through the PAR assignment (problem-action-result—see Chapter 6) and identified three engineering design projects he developed and was most proud of. His "Accomplishment Profile" consisted of a narrative about each engineering project using the PAR method that also corresponded to a marketing brochure illustrating the products. Consider whether you want to include a one-page focused addendum that highlights your expertise in a specific field. An "Executive Profile" is similar, that is a one-page narrative that summarizes an executive career and unique or distinguishing highlights. The intention is to add credibility and quickly convey to the reader who you are in the world of work.

Decide which models, writing, illustrations, project scenarios, photographs, marketing brochures, or other work samples to include with your application packet that demonstrate or reflect your capabilities or achievements. For example, if your resume states that you earned a specific award, include a copy of the award in your portfolio. A brag book is ideal for college graduates who may want to include a copy of college transcripts. Depending on the job, you may include a driving record, background check (www.hotjobs.choicetrust.com), credit history, personal goals and history, values, skills and aptitudes, education/training, evaluations, recommendations, and references.

To assemble your materials, purchase a professional report holder or binder with clear sleeves that will allow for duplicating without holes punched. Place your cover letter and resume on the first pages and keep working in reverse chronological order using your resume as a guide. For ideas and Web-based portfolios, explore the samples on the website www.brandego.com

PowerPoint resumes can provide a platform for an effective presentation, especially in a conference room during a group interview. Slides should be fairly brief and cover key elements. Distribute hard copies of your resume in addition to a PowerPoint resume for reviewers to reference simultaneously or at a later time. When I was part of a selection committee for an accountant, the person who got the job presented qualification details and key elements in PowerPoint slides. The technology skills, in conjunction with highlighting other work talents and qualifications, established a uniquely qualified candidate. If you are not a wizard at creating a PowerPoint slide show, hire a company to do so but only you can create the content that reflects the value you want to showcase.

An Accomplishment Profile Summary is a usually one page in length and reveals your strengths and expertise in a specific area such as Information Technology, Engineering, Leadership, Sales, Marketing, etc.

Additional documentation is not required or necessarily appropriate for all interviews or job search packets. Is a portfolio right for you as a vehicle for job search? If you answer yes, what materials will you include?

Sample Professional Profile and Biography

The following pages contain a *Professional Profile* and *Career Biography (Bio)* sample.

PROFESSIONAL PROFILE   **Sample**

[Your name] brings more than 25 years combined Organizational Change, Strategic Planning, and coaching experience within high tech, health care, financial services, and energy companies.

[Your name] is known for strong communication, facilitation, and negotiation skills that have helped many organizations refine strategic plans, implement programs, and streamline procedures to deliver bottom line results. [Your name] has guided over 1,500 leaders and hundreds of teams to maximize productivity and effectiveness in their workforce during times of change.

His global clients have included [insert company/organization names]. America-based clients in Arizona, New Mexico, Florida, New York, and Missouri include [insert company/organization names].

He has been a senior consultant with [name of firm] since 2003, providing organizational development, training, facilitation, and coaching solutions designed to meet the unique requirements of each workplace. He has been a senior consultant with [insert company/organization names] since 1999. The group provides innovative solutions for organizations facing changes in leadership, strategy, structure, or process.

During the merger of [insert company names], [Your name] worked with [organization name] and key members of the two legacy companies to create a customized learning process. It became widely accepted as the primary tool for preparing the two companies' global workforces for the merger. This enabled employees throughout the organizations to lead rather than react to the inevitable pressures and complexities of combining two national companies.

He was a member of the consulting team at [insert company] as the company embarked on the largest operational initiative in history when it made the strategic decision to design and implement a platform and business intelligence process. A customized stakeholder toolkit was created to build the necessary leadership capabilities during migration to the platform.

Recently, he led [insert company name] transformational project during a restructuring. This included building the capability to manage performance and sustain leadership through organizational change across departmental boundaries. The facilitation led to the creation of a strategic map, which resulted in re-branding the HR department and identifying new strategic objectives.

[Your name] was on the ground floor of [company name] as an executive manager. He was responsible for the initial product sales, growing the client base from start up to the leading provider of portfolio accounting software. He created and staffed the sales organization and set strategic direction with the president as the organization went through rapid growth.

[Your name] did his undergraduate work at [insert college or university] and earned his [insert degree title] at [insert college or university]. Certifications include [insert].

CAREER BIOGRAPHY   Sample

Insert Your Name, (credentials)

[Your name] is a Professional Coach and Organizational Consultant with [insert company name]. He has more than 25 years' combined Organizational Change, Strategic Planning, and Coaching experience within high tech, health care, financial services, and energy companies.

[Your name] is known for strong communication, facilitation, and negotiation skills that have helped many organizations refine strategic plans, implement programs, and streamline procedures to deliver bottom line results. [Your name] has guided over 1,500 leaders and hundreds of teams to maximize productivity and effectiveness in their workforce during times of change.

His global clients have included [insert company/organization names]. America-based clients in Arizona, New Mexico, Florida, New York, and Missouri include [insert company/ organization names].

[Your name] did his undergraduate work at [insert college or university] and earned his [insert degree title] at [insert college or university]. Certifications include [insert].

Marian Rone, RN, BSN, MM, EMT-P

492 Madonna Lane
Ashland, OR 97520
541-482-2483(h)
541-901-6733(c)
mrone@jeffnet.org

Professional Profile: Highly accomplished, **motivated, and energetic** professional with proven ability to manage the complexities of a large nursing department. **Strengths in organizing, directing** and **implementing medical services**. Effective at fostering a culture **leading to high patient, employee,** and **physician satisfaction.**

Qualifications

- More than 8 years' experience in progressive management positions with a background in Emergency Nursing and Pre-hospital care

- Expert knowledge of Emergency Nursing principals, regulations, standards, and practices

- Established history of leading others toward a vision through clarifying processes, communicating information, building consensus, and instilling cooperation

- Proven self–starter; effective program development and project completion abilities

- Strength for synthesizing and organizing information; bring clarity to complex issues

- Knowledgeable about National Patient Safety Goals with an emphasis in assimilating regulatory requirements, including instilling staff buy-in.

- Visionary capacity for creative ideas, planning, and development

- Skillful in training, coaching, and managing personnel for goal achievement

- Resourceful and adaptive in change management

- Equally effective performing independently, collaborating with co-workers, and interacting with multi-disciplinary teams

Expertise Includes

ED Rules/Regulations	Staff /Patient Safety	Patient Satisfaction
Trauma	Performance Improvement	Solution Focused
Creative Problem Solving	Talent Management	Time Management
Staff Satisfaction	Patient Flow	Coding / Billing
Departmental Integration	Writing Policies	Pre-hospital Interfacing

Employment Experience

MANAGER EMERGENCY SERVICES, *Rogue Valley Medical Center, OR*   **2001-2009**

- Managed all aspects of a 38,500 yearly visits Emergency Department and Level 3 Trauma Center

- Led 67.51 FTEs (110 employees); performed hiring, mentoring, disciplining and termination, including 60 Unionized RN's

- Responsible for all supervision, direction and coordination of patient care, including cardiac, trauma, psychiatric, pediatric and neurological

- Oversaw the design and development of a $5Million and 30,000 square foot new Emergency department, as well as coordinated the move

- Managed an expense budget of $6.6Million and revenues of $25.3Million

- Monitored compliance with regulatory and accrediting organizations and hospital policies for the delivery of safe quality patient care

- Consistently maintained 90% or greater overall patient satisfaction

- Successfully piloted and/or implemented new computerized systems and programs

SUPERVISORY RN, *Department of Health and Human Services, D.C.*   **2007-2009**

- Responsible for full filling triage and or patient care for red, yellow, or green victims in ausutre disaster environments

- Function under the Incident Command Structure

- Responsible for working with 35 other Oregon team members and interfacing with other National disaster teams

- Member of National Disaster Medical Team sent to provide emergency care during disaster situations

TRAUMA COORDINATOR, *Rogue Valley Medical Center, OR*   **1999-2001**

- Coordinated and oversaw the trauma program at a level 3 regional trauma center

- Interfaced with HIS department regarding trauma data registry

- Lead multidisciplinary teams involved in the care of trauma patients

- Coordinated regional trauma conference along with local EMS education

- Active member of the county Emergency Preparedness committee

HOUSE SUPERVISOR, *Ashland Community Hospital, OR*   **1996-2000**

- Acted as the in-house administrative representative and resource person for all patients, staff physicians, and visitors

- Responsible for directing and coordinating patient placement and nurse staffing throughout the facility

- Directed and when necessary triaged admissions and transfers

- Responded on the behalf of executive nursing and/or executive management in their absence

Other Career History

Adjunct Faculty, *School of Nursing at Oregon Health Sciences University, OR* 1995-2000

Interim EMS Training Officer, *City of Ashland Fire Department, OR* 1995-1996

RN, Emergency Department, *Rogue Valley Medical Center, Ashland Community, OR* 1994-2000

RN, ICU/CCU, *Rogue Valley Medical Center, Ashland Community, Pioneer Memorial, OR* 1992-1995

Flight Medic, *Airlife of Oregon, OR* 1992-1993

Paramedic and Operations Manager, *Ashland Life Support, OR* 1989-1995

Accomplishments

- Instrumental in growing department from a 44.21 FTE, 33,900 yearly visits department to a 67.51 FTE 38,500 visits/year department

- Consistently maintained full complement of staff positions: nursing, technicians and other support staff

- Implemented a successful four month New Graduate program with a continued buddy program after completion

- Actively involved in the development and implementation of a cardiac STEMI program

- Developed, implemented and managed Facility coding guidelines

- Fulfilled a variety of Incident Command positions in drills and actual events

- Established a Shared Governance model resulting in greater staff satisfaction

Education

- Masters in Management degree, Southern Oregon University, 2008

- Bachelors of Science degree in Nursing, Southern Oregon State College, 1992

Licensure

- RN, Oregon

Certifications

- Advanced Cardiac Life Support Instructor
- Pediatric Advanced Life Support Instructor
- Pre-hospital Trauma Life Support Instructor
- Trauma Nurse Core Curriculum Provider
- Advanced Burn Life Support
- Level C Basic Life Support Provider
- Hazardous Materials Awareness Level
- Management of Assaultive Behavior
- Oregon State Paramedic

Special Training

- FEMA Emergency Management Institute Incident Command Modules:100, 200, 201, 700, and 800
- OR-OSHA Safety Modules:100, 101, 102, 201, 204
- Disaster Preparedness

Honors and Awards

- *Red Cross Heroes Award*
- *Who's Who in America*
- *Excellence in Teaching, OHSU*

Professional / Community Service

- *Regional Coordinator Oregon Disaster Medical State Team*
- *Review Jackson County EMS Standing Orders*
- *Volunteer Walker Elementary School*

Project Committees

- *Cardiac Arrest Committee*
- *Safety Committee*
- *Patient Safety Initiative Committee*
- *Disaster Preparedness Committee*
- *Joint Commission Stroke Accreditation Team*
- *Patient Flow*
- *Area Trauma Advisory Board*
- *Re-build committee*
- *Psychiatric Crisis Unit Committee*
- *Performance Improvement Committee*
- *Nurse Stiffing Committee*

Professional Activities

- *Oregon State board of Nursing Policies*

Published Materials

- Rone, M. Evaluation. In *Nursing Fundamentals: Caring & Clinical Decision Making, 2nd ed;* Daniels, R.; Grendell, R.; Wilkins, F., Eds.; Cengage Delmar Learning: New York, 2010; Chapter 15.

- Rone, M. Mass Causality Care. In *Medical Surgical Nursing: Contemporary Practices;* Daniels, R., Eds.; Delmar Thompson Learning: Albany, NY, 2007; Chapter 67.

- Rone, M. Evaluation. In *Nursing Fundamentals: Caring & Clinical Decision Makin,;* Daniels, R.; Eds.; Delmar Learning: New York, 2004; Chapter 15.

- Freiheit, M. Contributing author. In *Delmar's Guide to Laboratory and Diagnostic Tests;* Daniels, R.; Thompson Delmar Learning: Albany, NY, 2002.

- Freiheit, M. Contributing author. Some Heart Attacks are not Getting Treated in ED. In process.

"Great dancers are not great because of their technique; they are great because of their passion."
Martha Graham

DISCUSSION QUESTIONS/EXERCISES

1. What are the advantages and disadvantages of a functional vs. a chronological resume?

2. Which style would you use and why?

3. What are the advantages and disadvantages of one-page and two-page resumes?

4. Which format would you use and why?

5. What are your two strongest work qualifications? Write your primary and secondary skills.

6. What makes you unique?

7. Select 8-10 qualification phrases for your resume. Edit to reflect your abilities, as needed.

8. Write your employment history in chronological function.

9. Select your "Component Headings" and identify your "Work Industry Headers."

10. Write your resume content that relates your background and experience to the job you want.

11. Explain gaps between jobs.

12. Qualify your employers/company names with a statement sentence.

13. Go to www.monster.com, www.hotjobs.com, and/or employer websites. Become familiar with the process of posting your resume online. Post your resume.

14. Write your professional profile and/or career biography.

Cover Letters

PURPOSE OF YOUR COVER LETTER

A cover letter serves as an introduction and is a summary of your resume. How well you write a cover letter may play a large part in whether your resume will get reviewed. It is an important document in how you "package" "yourself. A cover letter should answer the most important question on the reader's mind: "Why, specifically, is this applicant the best-qualified candidate for the job?" Your cover letter must immediately convey your value to a company. It should highlight keywords and skills that describe your most distinguishing qualifications and characteristics related to your job goal.

Submitting a resume without a cover letter is a potentially disastrous oversight. A resume without a cover letter receives less attention than the candidate who submits both documents together. A cover letter requires good, solid writing and attention to detail. Your letter is an example of your organizational skills and how well you communicate. Employers want to read a cover letter that tells them that your qualifications match a job opening. A cover letter may reveal that you are a strong candidate for a variety of positions.

> *"Lack of directed goals is like trying to cut down a tree with a sledgehammer."*
> **Anonymous**

WRITING TIPS

Below are some tips on writing a succinct, informative cover letter. See cover letter samples at the end of this chapter.

Use third-person writing style. Employers' eyes glaze over when reading a letter that begins with "I" and uses "I" throughout. Avoid use of the first person and the passive voice as much as possible. This includes "I" statements ("I have experience as") or "My" statements ("My employment background is"). Instead write "Previous experience includes . . . " or "Relevant employment experience includes. . . . " Of course, you may use first-person and passive voice conservatively, as necessary (see sample cover letters). The reason for this suggestion is that the reader already knows you are referring to yourself. The cover letter is more powerful and professional using the "third-person" writing style.

Personalize the letter. Whenever possible, address the cover letter to the person in charge of hiring. Generic salutations, such as "To whom it may concern," or "Dear Hiring Manager" indicate that you are not familiar with or enthusiastic about the job or the company. Employers may assume the sender is only attempting to fill an insincere unemployment claim benefit quota. Use a personalized salutation. The greeting should address a specific person in a formal manner such as, "Dear Ms. Harper:" not "Dear Jennifer." If you are unable to identify a specific name, address the letter to "Hiring Manager," "Human Resources Manager," "Employment Manager," or "Administrator."

Use whatever reasonable means possible to find out the name and title of the person who does the hiring to personalize the letter. See Chapter 15 and the section about getting past the telephone gatekeeper for suggestions about learning the name of the hiring manager. Take the time to call the company or the Chamber of Commerce, perform research at the library, or use the Internet. Make sure to spell the hiring manager's name correctly! Your attention to detail in the beginning is what will set you apart from the competition.

Employ your best letter writing skills. Use excellent sentence structure and grammar. A cover letter should be more formal than the way you would naturally speak, but still sound natural. While the goal is to get the reader's attention, that doesn't mean you should try to be creative; cover letters must be straightforward. As with your resume, use action words to create dynamic but succinct sentences.

Be specific. Your cover letter serves as an informative introduction to the resume but not as a reformatted repeat of it.

Avoid writing about your work philosophies and save them for an interview, and then only if asked. Do not use clichés, like "I've taken the liberty of enclosing my resume" or "I'm a people person." If a sentence sounds very familiar to you, you're probably better off not using it. Don't write, "I understand your company has a good reputation and is excellent to work for." This is wasted space filler and they already know about their company's reputation. Write only about your knowledge, skills, interpersonal abilities, and qualifications for the job.

Avoid humor. Be respectful and professional. Avoid humor in a cover letter with a potential employer because it can easily be misunderstood.

Be efficient. Don't waste space and the reader's time on unnecessary details. Every sentence should be an explicit use of words about your skills, illustrating how your qualifications match the job duties.

Be available. Tell the employer how and when to reach you. Create a letterhead that includes your name, address, and telephone number, which should be reli-

> "A grateful mind is a great mind which eventually attracts to itself great things."
> Plato

> "And the day came when the risk it took to remain tight in side the bud was more painful than the risk it took to blossom."
> Anais Nin

ably answered by either a person or an answering machine. Include an Email address and cell phone number if possible.

Proofread. Check carefully for grammar and spelling mistakes. Proofreading your letter backward is an especially effective technique for catching spelling or punctuation errors that your eye might not "see" when reading forward. Have a friend or colleague proofread the letter again. Typos and grammatical errors are the first reason a hiring manager discards a cover letter and resume in the trash.

Don't depend entirely on the spell-check function of your word processor. For example, if you use "there" for "their," spell-check won't notice. Use the dictionary and thesaurus for proper word usage and consult a style manual for grammar questions. You may want to keep an Internet shortcut on your desktop to four important websites: www.dictionary.com, www.thesaurus.com, www.thesaurus.com, and www.ccc.commnet.edu/gramma.

Add your signature. Sign your name prior to mailing. Your signature follows the closing, "Sincerely." Allow two to four lines between the closing and your full name in print, with your signature in between.

If you forget this, the employer may think you've sent a form letter. Your handwritten signature should be legible, regardless of your personal flair. A typewritten name is not the "signature."

FORMATTING

A good cover letter should begin with a professional, attractive letterhead. For a consistent appearance, copy and paste the same format used at the top of your resume or create a complimentary personal letterhead at the top of the page. If your letter is shorter in length, letterhead data can be centered in three- to five-line blocks to fill up the page more. If your letter is longer in length, letterhead data can extend across the top of the page. Be sure to include your name, address, telephone/cell numbers, and Email address.

Keep paragraphs to no more than three to five short sentences long. A paragraph should consist of at least two sentences to be effective.

ORGANIZATION

In the letterhead, include your name, mailing address, city, state, zip code, and Email address (if you have one). **Bold** your name, telephone, and cell numbers for easy visibility; place your telephone number at the end of your signature as well as in the letterhead for easy access.

> *"Life may not be the party we hoped for, but while we are here we might as well dance."*
> *Anonymous*

Include the date within one day of when you mail the letter. Allow a minimum of two and not more than four spaces between the letterhead border and the date. Allow a minimum of two and not more than four spaces between the date and employer name.

Do not indent paragraphs. Two lines of space should separate paragraphs.

Use bullets conservatively for organizing and highlighting information in the body of your cover letter. Too many bullets can make a document look busy.

Regarding: Use a job title referencing your interest. For example, **"RE: Project Manager"** should be placed two lines above the employer name. Or, if you want to keep your job options more open but still relevant to an advertised position, use something like **"RE: General Manager or related."**

First paragraph: Get the reader's attention. Use the name of the person who referred you whenever possible. Reveal how you learned about the job opening or became familiar with the potential position. Express the purpose of your letter by stating your interest in a specific job possibility. If you don't want to limit yourself to one specific job title, write a job tile and include *"or related position."* For example, if you are seeking a job as a human resources representative but would make an interesting candidate for similar positions, write *"Seeking a challenging position in human resources or related position."*

Second paragraph: Highlight your most pertinent transferable qualifications for the job. Write about your relevant skills, abilities, attitude (motivation, patience, etc.), and knowledge.

Third paragraph: Expand upon pertinent work experience, applicable knowledge, accomplishments, and qualifications. This is where you can briefly emphasize any particularly important or relevant details that might set you apart from the crowd.

Last paragraph: Express your sincere desire to speak with the hiring manager in order to discuss your qualifications. Do not expect the employer to call you! Tell the employer what actions you will take to follow-up on the letter and then do so within a week.

Do not leave the ball in the employer's court. Conclude that you will contact the person in the near future and then follow up. For example, don't end with "I look forward to hearing from you soon." Rather, "I will call you in the near future and look forward to speaking with you."

SALARY HISTORY

If an employer requires a salary history, the best placement is at the end of your cover letter, after you have impressed them about your qualifications. Include a paragraph such as, *"I earned $26,000 per year with ABC organization before promoting to XYZ position based on my achievements. My most recent position had an annual salary of $47,000, exclusive of benefits. The job responsibilities outlined in the job announcement is an opportunity I desire and salary is not my primary motivator. I am flexible concerning a combination of salary and benefits commensurate with my qualifications."*

ENCLOSURES

Decide what enclosures to include with your cover letter. Enclosures may include your reference list, job application form, letters of reference, addendum, and/or portfolio. There may be advantages to enclosing these materials with a cover letter. If you have been referred by someone and/or think you have a reasonable chance that the reader will review additional material, send it. Be sure to include "enc:" at the end of your letter to apprise the reader of what is "enclosed" (e.g., resume, references document, letters of reference, profile or addendum, work product samples, portfolio, etc.).

It is not necessary to send substantial enclosure materials other than your resume with every cover letter. Rather, follow up with a phone call and ask the employer if they would like to receive additional information to support your candidacy. Whether or not you go to the time and expense of sending enclosures is a decision you will have to make. One rule to follow is the employer's guidelines in a job announcement. For example, if they request three references, send three and no more.

SUMMARY: A CHECKLIST OF COVER LETTER WRITING STRATEGIES

✓ Address the letter to the name of the person in a hiring capacity

✓ Inform the employer of the person who referred you

✓ Clearly write your specific interest for the position

✓ Identify your skills, qualifications, relevant personality characteristics, and abilities for the job

✓ Summarize relevant work experience and knowledge

✓ Use "enc:" for "Enclosures" and list attachments

✓ Apprise the prospective employer of the call he or she can expect from you in the near future

> *"Life is like a piano. What you get out of it depends on how you play it."*
> **Anita Robertson**

AFTER THE WRITING: NOW WHAT?

Paper and printing: If you aren't sending the cover letter and resume via Email, print them on the same high-quality paper stock. The only exception is to consider complementary colors, such as an off-white for your letter, and cream color for your resume, or cream color for your letter and a marble background for your resume (or some other subtle combination). Uniformity looks professional. Use high-quality, preferably linen, paper, and use only printers that produce neat, readable text with no stray marks or smudges.

Mailing: Don't even think about folding your documents into a small envelope. Purchase large size manila or white envelopes that will adequately hold and protect the material. You don't want to degrade your documents with wrinkles and poor packaging. A printed address on the envelope is more professional than one that is handwritten, and is also a reflection of your computer skills. I am not fond of resume packets that have extra plastic coverings and binders as it appears "overdone" and is an unnecessary cost (except for portfolio documents). There are circumstances when it may be appropriate, but it is not for the majority of job seekers. Be sure to use adequate postage. You can purchase small postage weigh scales at stationary stores and add your own postage.

Keep one for yourself, and track your applications or mailings. Keep a copy of each cover letter and resume you send, for future reference. Personal computers make this a particularly easy task without having to collect a pile of hard copies. Don't forget to back up your computer files on a frequent basis!

Make a master list of each employer contacted. If you can, create a computer file that tracks the names of the companies/organizations and representatives you have contacted, including phone numbers, Email addresses, postal addresses, and so forth. Also create a column or space that makes it easy to track dates of mailings, follow-ups, and notes or comments about your efforts with each particular contact.

SAMPLE COVER LETTERS

Sample cover letters are included in the pages that follow. ***Important introductory phrases have been bolded for emphasis but you would not bold such items in an actual cover letter.***

John L. Scott
541 Realtor Blvd
San Francisco, CA 96094

(520) 895 – 0190   johnscott@bay.net

October 28, 2008

Name
Title
Company
Address
City, State Zip Code

RE: Management Trainee

Dear Ms. Name:

It is with great enthusiasm and anticipation that I seek the position of management trainee. I was excited to learn about this opportunity on your website because I have been very interested in the senior care industry for some time. In particular I have an interest in sales and marketing because I believe that my work experience and education has prepared me well for this aspect of the senior care industry. As you will find on my resume, I have been in real estate 10 years with numerous roles including: top producing consultant, branch manager, training transaction coordinator and new agents.

In witnessing my grandmother's relocation to a retirement community, I understand the challenges this transition can have on seniors. However, now knowing the positive impact it has made on my grandmother's life it would bring me great pride to have the opportunity to make a difference in the lives of so many others. The combination of my extensive sales and management experience, as well as my relationship-building skills would be a tremendous asset to your organization in helping seniors with an excellent experience.

I am very optimistic that the senior care industry is one that will remain very stable because of the strong demand for housing and lifestyle change from this ever-increasing population. This opportunity would help give my family the opportunity to grow with a reputable organization for many years to come.

Thank you for considering how my qualifications can contribute to your organization's continued success. I will contact you in the near future.

Sincerely,

John L. Scott
enc: Resume

Natalie M. Brewer

1500 Alana Mountains Drive, Santa Rosa, CA 94954
(707) 450-7513
Email: Natalie.Brewer@yahoo.com

Date

Name
Company
Job title
Address
City, State Zip

RE: Job Title

Dear Name:

It is with great excitement and interest that I discovered the management trainee opportunity on Eastern Retirement Services/Hidden Valley Manor's website. I am interested in providing financial operations and/or related services specifically within the retirement industry. I think that I make an interesting candidate for a variety of management trainee positions and am especially enthusiastic about a relocation opportunity.

My primary focus is in financial services and operations. With an extensive background in business finance both in real estate and equities, I have a proven track record in assessing and delivering customer goals.

Relevant qualifications and professional highlights include:

➢ Excellent in translating technical and complex information, including applying rules, statutes, policies, and regulations

➢ In-depth knowledge of the financial industry from both the operational and client service side

➢ Skillful in advisory capacity; able to take complex information and make recommendations while conveying ideas in simple terms

➢ Bring a detailed approach to day-to-day operations; focus on goals and objectives

Please accept my sincere interest to speak with you about how my qualifications can continue to improve Eastern Retirement Service's financial operations. I will contact you in the near future and feel free to contact me at anytime.

Sincerely,

Natalie Brewer
enc: Resume

JOHN D. SAVIERS   440 Lincoln Avenue, Eugene, OR 97232
(503) 232-4432   johndsaviers@qwest.net

Date

Ms. Mary Jones
Department of Human Services
800 Superior Avenue
Eugene, OR 97232

RE: Human Services Specialist

Confidential, please. Thank you in advance for privacy.

Dear Ms. Jones:

This letter is to express interest in the Human Services Specialist position as announced in the county listings. Dennis Franklin referred me as a candidate for your organization. *A professional profile is enclosed* for your review. *I am seeking* a position in a challenging, team environment that will allow me to utilize my communication skills. I am satisfactorily employed but am looking for a professional growth opportunity.

With more than five years of employment experience in analysis and research, including project development, please consider my qualifications including

- ◆ creative problem solving skills.

- ◆ conversant and literate in Spanish.

- ◆ experienced with multicultural and diverse socio-economic populations.

Interpersonal communication experience includes diffusing confused or upset customers on the telephone and in person. Other strengths include developing plans, writing contracts, and implementing policies.

Please accept my sincere desire to speak with you about the position and how my qualifications may contribute to your organization. *I will contact you in the near future.* Thank you in advance for your confidentiality in this matter.

Sincerely,

John D. Saviers

enc: Application Form
Resume (confidential)

Matthew Ogden

450Madrone Lane, Jackson, MI 97340

(603) 989-6838

mogden@charter.net

November 12, 2008

Gayle Myers, Senior Recruiter
Human Resources Services Department of Consumer and Business Services
PO Box 14480
Salem, OR 97309-0405

RE: Health Compliance Officer—Announcement # EBCD2629 / Industrial
Hygienist 2

Dear Ms. Myers:

It is with great enthusiasm and anticipation that I seek the position of Health
Compliance Officer. I was ecstatic to learn about this opportunity after listening
to your presentation on National Public Radio. I am interested in providing
public service specifically within the industrial safety field and the opportunity
for relocation to the Eugene/Portland area.

My primary focus is in maintaining and improving workplace safety. With
an extensive background in managing the complexity of one of Oregon's
largest industrial work environments, including multiple facilities providing
manufacturing and construction safety compliance, I have a proven track
record in providing excellent customer satisfaction.

Relevant qualifications and professional highlights include:

- Extensive industrial health program experience, including
  administering, meeting and exceeding OSHA standards and
  guidelines
- In-depth training in occupational health and technology principles
  and practices
- Skillful in technical report writing; able to take complex
  information and convey in simple language
- Thorough understanding of health and safety regulations as
  defined through OSHA

Please accept my sincere interest to speak with you about how my
qualifications can continue to improve Oregon's public service commitment to
high quality safety and health compliance. I will contact you in the near future
and feel free to contact me.

Sincerely,

Mathew Ogden
enc: Resume

Susan B. Smith (820) 841-1692
860 Driving Lane   Email: susansmith@charter.net
Reedsville, TN 86420

Date (of cover letter)

Name of Employer
Title
Company
Address
City, State Zip Code

RE: Administrative Assistant Position

Dear ___:

With fifteen years' experience in administrative assistant responsibilities relevant to the position advertised in _____ on date _____, a *professional profile is enclosed* for your review. *I am seeking* a progressive position in a fast-paced environment that will utilize my strong administrative skills and abilities.

With a background in administrative office management, project assistance, coordination and organizational skills, please consider my qualifications for the position. Other abilities consist of detailed library research and utilization of resources.

Relevant strengths include managing tasks simultaneously, maintaining complex office systems, keeping records, and entering computer data. *Applicable experience* includes bookkeeping, office equipment, proofreading forms, correspondence, maintaining supplies, and developing and maintaining complex file systems. *In addition*, I possess excellent interpersonal communication, customer service, and writing skills.

Thank you in advance for reviewing my documents. *I look forward to discussing* how my proven track record could contribute to the profitability and strength of your organization. Please feel free to call me anytime. *I will also contact you* in the near future.

Sincerely,

Susan B. Smith

enc: Professional profile
    References

Don E. Mayfield, M.S.
252 Orion Street
Upper Saddle River, New Jersey 07458
Telephone (201) 785-9702

Date

Personnel Committee
Signa Counseling Center
P.O. Box 4592
Portland, OR 97500

RE: Executive Director Position

Dear Human Resources Director:

This letter is to express interest in the Executive Director position *advertised* in *The Oregonian* on (date). *A professional profile is enclosed* for your review. *I am seeking a progressive opportunity* that will utilize my extensive professional background in management functions and human resources.

With more than 20 years' experience in program development, administration, and implementation of goals, please consider my qualifications for the position. Professional highlights include:

- Management positions that required overseeing business development and implementation.

- Fiscal services, administration, project coordination, extensive interpersonal skills.

- Facilitating boards and regulatory divisions.

Previous experience was acquired through employment with national insurance companies, medical groups, and a school district. *My background* includes strong human resources, administering health and other benefits, including risk management with a proven history developing procedures and policies.

Please consider my interest to speak with you about how my qualifications could contribute to the strength and profitability of your organization. I will contact you in the near future and please feel free to contact me at anytime.

Sincerely,

Don E. Mayfield, M.S.

enc: Resume
Three letters of reference

Date

Mary Ann Worley
HR Administrator
Gahanna Corporation
213 Centre Drive
Cincinnati, OH 45224

Dear Ms. Worley:

Please consider my interest in a position with accountabilities for which I have a demonstrated track record of success:

- Organizational and Leadership Development
- Talent management / Executive coaching
- Training, including E-learning
- Performance Management and Improvement
- Instructional Design

- Team Building
- Project Management
- Public Relations / Event Planning
- Writing and Editing
- Research and Statistical Analysis
- Relationship Management

Prior accomplishments include:

- Conducted training and coaching sessions for thousands of employees, managers, and executives.
- Saved $250,000 in personnel costs by building strategic business alliances.
- Reduced employee turnover 20 percent through innovative training and motivation initiatives.
- Increased customer base 200 percent through program development and marketing efforts.
- Facilitated a change initiative that resulted in a profitable $1.2 million company sale.
- Managed a statewide organization that served 100,000 people on a shoestring budget by fostering partnerships.

Delivering profitable improvements to human and organizational performance is a responsibility in which I excel. As you consider your needs, please contact me to discuss how my qualifications can contribute to your organization's continued success. Thank you for your consideration.

Sincerely,

Joan M. Lovett

enc: Resume

Nathon J. Werner
1492 E. Hampton St.
Cincinnati, OH 34762
Email: Werner@yahoo.com   Telephone: (716) 348–0498   Cell: (716) 401–9842

January 30, 2009

Ms. Kathleen Revel
General Manager
First Title
1234 Oxford St.
Cincinnati, OH 03472

RE: Escrow Officer

Dear Ms. Revel,

This letter is in response to the January 2009 posting in the *Cincinnati Tribune* for the career opportunity as an Escrow Officer. I possess extensive experience with Title companies, including strong insights in the real estate market. It appears that my background could add significant value to First Title.

YOUR REQUIREMENTS	**MY BACKGROUND**
Experience in escrow or related field	Real Estate Broker since 1992
Relationship building	Recognized by organizations for diplomacy. Ability to develop and retain customer loyalty and market share
Organization skills	Adept at prioritizing and managing contact and database solutions for optimal results

In addition to title and escrow, my background includes banking, lending, and financial process. Please accept my interest to meet and discuss how we could merge this opportunity with my experience and dependability to our mutual benefit. I look forward to contacting you in the near future and do not hesitate to contact me at anytime.

Sincerely,

Nathon J. Werner

enc: Resume

Marian Rone
492 Madonna Lane, Ashland, OR 97520
Ronem@jeffnet.org
541-482-2483 (h)
541-901-6733 (c)

April 11, 2009

Byron Hearn
Chief Operating Officer
Hospital Alliance Group
180 West Randy Street
Medford, OR 93420

RE: ED Manager Position

Dear Mr. Hearn:

It is with enthusiasm that I am expressing my interest in your recently vacated ED Nurse Manager position. Brad McLaren referred me as a candidate for this position. I am seeking a position where I can utilize my leadership skills in order to help develop a strong cohesive department, with excellent patient, employee and physician satisfaction.

With proven skills and a demonstrated ability to provide leadership producing positive results even in the most challenging of circumstance, please consider my value.

Professional Highlights:

- **Policy and procedure development, strategic planning and performance metrics**
- **Sharing vision and bridging functions of business and nursing philosophy to improve business capability**
- **Program development and management, technology leadership and organizational management**
- **Excellent staff recruitment and retention**

Previous healthcare experience expands management, education, trauma coordination, pre-hospital care, disaster preparedness and direct patient care. In addition, my background includes participation in quality and performance improvement initiatives such as: **Patient Safety, Stroke Center Certification, Progressive Cardiac Programs, Patient Satisfaction and Staff Shared Governance,** leading to improved patient outcomes.

The attached Curriculum Vitae will illustrate my capabilities in delivering unrivaled value to your organization. I look forward to speaking with you in the future. Please feel free to contact me any time. Thank you for your consideration.

Sincerely,
Marian Rone, RN, BSN, MM, EMT-P
enc: Curriculum vitae
References

> "Life teaches us some painful lessons, but it is from adversity that strength is born. You may have lost the inning, but you will win the game."
>
> **Anonymous**

DISCUSSION QUESTIONS/EXERCISES

1. Write a sample cover letter for a job you desire, following the writing tips provided in this chapter.

2. Have a professional review your cover letter and provide feedback.

3. Consider whether some form of enclosure would be appropriate. Does it support your skills, knowledge, or abilities?

4. Practice preparing enclosures/support documents.

References and Recommendations

WHAT REFERENCES ARE AND WHY YOU NEED THEM

References support your application for a job. A prospective employer will want references. References are people and/or letters that serve as a recommendation for your candidacy for a job opening. They should provide some positive verification of your skills, abilities, character, and other pertinent employment-related data. A prospective employer may or may not read your letters of recommendation and will most likely want to speak with your references. Ask for letters of reference (a letter of recommendation) from past or present employers, co-workers, supervisors, managers, clients, customers, other professionals, or community leaders. Letters of reference should be available to prospective employers as part of your job search materials, but usually serve as "backup" only. Letters may bring additional support to your interview selection and candidacy, but employers will usually want to speak to references.

What to do to maintain a confidential job search

Frequently, job seekers do not want current employers or former supervisors contacted. You may not want your current employer to know you are looking for other employment. You may have differences with a current or former supervisor. An interviewer should understand this dilemma if you communicate effectively. Say something like, "Thank you in advance for your confidentiality in this interview process. I am satisfactorily employed and although I am seeking a new professional growth opportunity with your company, I do not wish to jeopardize my current position. Therefore, I respectfully request that you not contact my current employer."

As an alternative, offer up co-workers, friends, or other colleagues who are familiar with your work experience or character whom the interviewer can call on for a reference.

Some details about letters of recommendation and references

A reference describes your skills, abilities, and strengths. A reference defines what you do well and provides examples that describe your accomplishments.

> *"Every day may not be good, but there's good in every day."*
> **Anonymous**

> *"There is no such thing in anyone's life as an unimportant day."*
> **Alexander Woollcott**

What were some key things you did for the company? Contributions include saving money, developing programs, organizing projects, developing materials, and using interpersonal skills. Many of the suggestions about action verbs and qualifying or qualification phrases, covered in previous chapters, are applicable here as well.

A reference describes your interpersonal skills

A reference depicts your ability to get along with co-workers or provide communication skills to the public. A reference should be able to comment about your willingness to follow a manager's lead and your ability to provide leadership or motivate others. Use a reference to support your timeliness, reliability, dependability, calm temperament, or ability to solve problems with co-workers or the public. In many work environments, over 80 percent of job success may be about the ability to develop and sustain relationships, and the other 20 percent is skill.

Contact your references for permission

It is best to contact the people in advance and ask their permission to use them as a reference. You will need to tell them what kind of information will be helpful in the event that a prospective employer contacts them.

Inform references about the job for which you are applying and why you think it is a good match. Prepare them as best you can and help them to present you in the best light. Consider sending them a draft of some areas you would like addressed. Use the references most relevant to each job search.

Give them some information about the company(s) you are interested in working for. Tell them what questions they might face. Thank your references for their help and support. Also, be careful not to overuse or wear out your references.

Get a letter of recommendation upon leaving a job

A letter of recommendation or letter of reference contains relevant work-related information about you. It tells a prospective employer the nature and dates of your working/personal relationship. When asking for a letter of recommendation, it is best to do so upon leaving a company while the relationship and skills are fresh in the employer's mind. Down the road, your employer will have difficulty resurrecting pertinent information. See the sample recommendation letter at the end of this chapter.

Write your own letter of recommendation

In some circumstances, your reference-provider may be receptive and even appreciative if you write a letter on your own behalf that they can simply edit

> *"Though no one can go back and make a brand new start, anyone can start from now and make a brand-new ending."*
> **Carl Bard**

and sign. This saves them time and effort as well as allowing you to customize a supportive letter. If they elect to write the letter themselves, ask them to include useful information about you as follows: This letter is for the purpose of recommending Sue Smith for position of Vice President of Acquisitions with your company. Sue was employed at ABC Company as an Administrator for three years from May 2005 through May 2008 and excelled in her duties. Specifically, Sue's competencies include [insert qualifications] . . . " See the sample recommendation letter at the end of this chapter. A Google search for "letter of recommendation" has additional help, if necessary. In most cases, your references will want you to "coach" them about what you want them say about your competencies. Be prepared to succinctly impart this information.

REFERENCES DOCUMENT VERSUS RECOMMENDATION LETTERS

A references document is a separate list of references that includes the names, titles, addresses, and telephone numbers of people whom prospective employers may contact in order to ask about your qualifications and experience. You will usually be asked for the names of three to five references, professional and possibly personal, who can give you a favorable recommendation and speak about the accuracy of your resume. (See the sample References document in this chapter).

Letters of recommendation will not take the place of a reference document for providing telephone and postal mailing information of your references, but are particularly useful if a former employer is no longer accessible. Letters of recommendation are not considered as valid to an employer who generally wants to talk with a reference about your qualifications. Letters of reference are useful when personal contact is not possible, or in combination with a reference list.

A creative "Reference Dossier" summarizes the comments your references will say and may encourage employers to consider your references statements. Of course, you will want to contact your references for their approval and forward a copy to ensure that their verbal comments will correspond with written document.

Performance evaluations as references

A performance evaluation completed by a former supervisor can serve as a type of reference about your work capabilities. In the absence of a reference (or in addition to), attempt to secure a performance evaluation from your former personnel file as documentation about your work performance. The document may contain information that is useful in your resume as well as interview conversation.

> *"I can feel guilty about the past, apprehensive about the future, but only in the present can I act."*
>
> **Abraham Maslow**

REFERENCE CHECKS

Employment laws vary from state to state. Some companies require that you sign a consent form before employers can discuss your employment background or candidacy for a position. Without your signed consent, information shared between a former employer and prospective employer should be limited. A former employer is allowed to verify the dates of your employment, job title, and answer whether or not they would rehire you. A typical question by a prospective employer is whether the candidate is "eligible for re-hire?" with a former employer. A "No" answer may or may not thwart the prospective employer since some companies have a "no re-hire" policy once any employee leaves the job, regardless of exemplary performance. The goal is to have at least five references. Depending on the interviewer, one "ding" in a long work history won't hurt you.

One trend is job application forms is including the applicant's signature authorizing the release of information about past employment history (see sample in Chapter 19). Many employers are unfamiliar with laws about sharing employment performance information. Former employers are not likely to get sued sharing favorable feedback about your work performance, but run the risk if speaking poorly about your work traits. A growing number of employers fear legal consequences if asked to provide a telephone reference check. A former employer may refuse to speak about a former employee, regardless of favorable performance. Signing your signature authorizing the release of information does not necessarily mean the prospective employer will ask a former employer for any and all work-related contacts. It can be used to hold an employee accountable in case a discrepancy appears during employment.

Sometimes, unfortunately, the same supervisor who wrote a favorable performance evaluation speaks poorly about the job candidate when asked by a prospective new employer. If you are not getting job offers after a given amount of time, one red flag might be your selection of references. For example, you might have a supportive letter of recommendation from a former supervisor but the same individual is not speaking favorably about you when asked over the telephone. Or, the former employer may speak favorably as well as negatively about your work performance that could sabotage your selection for the new job. You may want to consider having a career counselor or other professional colleague contact the former supervisor in a mock-reference check to learn more about what is being said about your qualifications or people-skills. You can then decide if you want to contact the individual in an attempt to resolve any misunderstanding, which could be tricky, and whether to continue using that reference.

You might need to negotiate with a former employer for a reference. If there were issues or differences, try to remain positive about your accomplishments, strengths, and personal traits. If an area needed improvement, explain to the former employer that it is not necessary to share that information unless specifically asked. Then try to agree on the efforts you made toward improvement or the lesson you learned from the experience. Or, you might want to tell the interviewer in advance what may be said by the former employer and briefly explain your side of the story.

One part of your homework on the topic of references includes learning what employers may know about you from your online identity. To find your electronic footprints, enter your entire name in "quotes" in Google. Is there anything getting in the way of your success? Is there personal or professional information that can be used for establishing rapport during an interview? If unfavorable information exists, it is usually best to apprise an employer early in the application process about what they will soon discover. This allows you to demonstrate good communication skills and gain trust as well as discuss any discrepancies. For more information and resources about improving your on-line identity, see Chapter 19 and the section "Google Your Identity."

> *"Success is getting what you want. Happiness is wanting what you get."*
> *Dale Carnegie*

REFERENCES FORMAT

A reference list must include easily accessible and complete data, on a piece of paper separate from your resume. Do not expect the prospective employer to look up missing information in an attempt to contact your references. Follow the application directions. The references should include the following information.

Your name
Address
Telephone and Cell numbers
Email address

Reference Name #1
Title and company name
Address
City, State Zip
Telephone Number

Relationship: (optional) e.g., Former supervisor, co-worker, former manager, former colleague, team member, or personal friend.

Years known: (optional).

Background: (optional and is used to provide additional information about working/personal relationship).

Repeat the process by adding three to five references. It is best to use professional references familiar with your work performance whenever possible, but community members, such as your clergy, professor, comptroller, etc., are acceptable. Notice that the names and telephone numbers are easy to see by using a bold or larger font. This helps the reader and demonstrates your foresight. See the following sample "References" document samples and styles for Travis A. Miller and Hunter L. Roland.

(Sample References document)

References   **Hunter L. Roland**

Name/Role	Mailing Address	Phone / Email
John Levitt, Ph.D. Professor, Master's in Business Administration	Boston University 1250 Siskiyou Blvd. Boston, MA 02127	552–694–4103 Cell: 552–952–3732 levitt@bu.edu
Ann Barker Branch Manager	Premier East Bank 300 E. Main Street Boston, MA 02127	552–282–5265 Cell: 552–890–3505 abarker@premiereastbank.com
Bob Ekker, M.B.A. Economist	Workforce Development Employment Department State of Oregon	552–776–6060 bobekker@state.ma..us

---

SAMPLE REFERENCES DOCUMENT

References
Travis A. Miller
Address
Telephone and Cell numbers Email address

Mr. Gary Strong, Telephone (817) 391–8890
General Manager
Orion Group
8431 Kinsey Street
Fort Worth, TX 76100
Relationship: Former Supervisor
Years Known: Two
Collaborated in successful manufacturing of patented product

Ms. Sharon Reed, Telephone (319) 890–1660
Supervisor
Davis Corporation
7893 Dumont Street
Dallas, TX 75080
Years Known: Five
Relationship: Former Supervisor
Received supervision in team approach to forward company goals

Mr. Jeffrey Oxford, Telephone (280) 670–9843
Attorney
452 Arnold Street
Houston, TX 76537
Years Known: 14
Relationship: Business services
Oversaw patent rights for product development

Mr. Gerald Rolf, Telephone (415) 908–6713
Owner
Gills Manufacturing
345 Hill Drive
San Antonio, TX 76903
Years Known: 4
Employed for two years in manufacturing capacity

Ms. Betty Sutherlin, Telephone (541) 861–4567
Director of Nursing
Rogue Memorial Hospital
Austin, TX 78700
Relationship: Fund Raising
Years Known: 12
Coordinated fund raising event for disabilities

SAMPLE RECOMMENDATION LETTER

John R. Stevens, Operations Manager
Qwest Wireless
422 La Fiesta Drive
Los Angeles, CA 04188
Telephone (415) 261-1866

Date

To Whom It May Concern:

Erica Alder was employed by Wireless Telecommunications from 2003–2009 and was initially hired as a Retail Sales Associate before her promotion to Technical Support Specialist. Erica was able to accomplish a variety of projects simultaneously and interacted skillfully with diverse management styles and personality types.

Erica created and implemented a user manual for end users and was noted for her exemplary work, including installation, pricing, and in-house training programs. Her ability to maintain flexibility and work independently as well as in team projects always impressed me.

Erica possesses excellent communication skills, and I was always pleased with her work results. I believe she would make an interesting candidate for a variety of positions and will be an asset to any organization.

Sincerely,

John R. Stevens
Operations Manager

DISCUSSION QUESTIONS/EXERCISES

1. Enter your name in Google. Review the results. Is this the online identity you want to be known for?

2. List three to five names, addresses, and telephone numbers you would use as references in your job search. Limit personal contacts to no more than one, if possible.

3. Contact these people and ask permission to use their names as references.

4. Prepare a script to "coach" and prepare your reference for a prospective employer's telephone call.

5. Write your own letter of recommendation as though written by a current or former employer. Detail your abilities, strengths, and assets.

6. If you have any unfavorable references, what can you do to turn that situation around?

7. If you know a former employer is likely to give an unfavorable reference, how can you prepare the prospective employer for such? Prepare and rehearse a brief script to explain and practice with a trusted person.

8. Call former employers and ask for a copy of past performance reviews. Decide whether to include your performance reviews as a part of your job search packet.

9. Prepare your References document.

> *"Failure is success if we learn from it."*
> *Malcolm Forbes*

CHAPTER

Job Application Form

A "SACRED" COMPANY FORM: LEAVE NO BLANK SPACE

When applying for a job, you will often have to fill out a job application form. If possible, avoid handwriting by downloading the form and complete the job application from a computer at home. This form is "sacred" to a company and will become part of your personnel file if you are hired. Your resume and cover letter will not take the place of a job application form. It's a key factor for making a good first impression. A completed job application form is part of your job search "package."

Do not leave any blanks on the form; fill it out completely. When there is a space for an answer that does not apply to you, write "N/A" (for "not applicable"). This shows the interviewer that you read the question and did not overlook it. For security and privacy purposes, you may not want to reveal your date of birth and Social Security number. If possible, tell the employer that you are happy to provide this information at such a time when you mutually determine your viable candidacy for the position.

Prepare a master form for easy access to repetitive information

Prepare a "master job application form" in advance and keep it with you when completing new application forms. This master serves as a template from which to copy information. It saves you from remembering places and dates of employment, important information, names of supervisors, telephone numbers or having to reinvent terminology about job duties. You will be required to complete a job application form, often while waiting for an interview, if you cannot obtain one in advance. A sample master job application form is located at the end of the chapter.

State, county, federal, and many private job application forms are available on Internet websites such, as www.federaljobsearch.com and www.statejobs.com, as well as company websites for job opening postings. Read the job description thoroughly. The goal is to transpose key job description requirements onto the job application form. Candidates are often selected from job application forms that contain the same or similar vocabulary, skills, and abilities ("buzz words") that match those of the job description (see Chapter 6 for more tips about job descriptions). Some employers use computer technology to screen for the same skills set descriptors. The more similar your work vocabulary is to that on the job description, the greater your chances for an interview.

Google your identity

Employers are likely to enter applicants' names into an online search engine to learn about your personal and professional identity prior to inviting candidates to an interview. This provides an employer to make a decision on you based on what they find. If you have not yet done so, this may be a good time to learn what information is available about your name that an employer will find out soon enough. Do these results communicate what you want to be known for? It is challenging to remove or change electronic footprints. Organizations that provide online identity and reputation management include www.zoominfo. com and www.naymz.com. If you discover mistaken or undesirable information about your online name search, you may want to apprise the employer in advance and salvage the job interview.

Salary

It is not unusual for job application forms to contain questions about your salary. Before completing salary questions on a job application, read Chapter 21 "Negotiating Salary and Job Offers." The two common questions on a job application form refer to your "desired salary" and "salary history." One rule is "whoever mentions or reveals a number first loses," or at least is at a disadvantage. For the "desired salary" question, the employer may have a higher number in mind than the applicant. You may have a higher number in mind than the employer.

Avoid revealing this information. When prompted to complete questions about "desired salary," consider writing, "prefer to discuss" or "negotiable" or "open."

Your salary history is not relevant to the job you are applying for, and employers may use the information as a gauge for current salary negotiations. When the job application form asks for salary history information, keep in mind benefits can add about 40 percent additional compensation to salary when calculating retirement plans, profit sharing, medical insurance, worker's compensation coverage, Social Security, payroll taxes, vacation, personal and bereavement leave, travel, and other expenses. For example, if you earn an average annual salary of $40,000, the total compensation package including benefits may cost the employer closer to $55,000. If you must fill in a number, consider writing a salary "range" on the application that incorporates your total compensation. Calculating the salary you anticipate at your next performance evaluation is a fair tactic for negotiations.

> *"It's not what we get, but who we become, that gives meaning to our lives."*
> **Anthony Robbins**

> "The common idea that success spoils people by making them vain, egotistic, and self-complacent is erroneous; on the contrary it makes them, for the most part, humble, tolerant, and kind."
> W. Someset Maugham

REASON FOR LEAVING

If questioned as to why you left a job, some options include: "resigned," "prefer to discuss," "research career change," "pursue professional growth," or "sought better opportunity." These responses are valid and respectable to prospective employers, but you should only use this last response if you can provide a date or record of the better professional opportunity. Otherwise, your honesty will be put into question. If you were laid off in a time of economic turmoil, it is generally not considered a reflection of your work performance. If you can get a former employer or co-worker to vouch for you, then there is no reason to skirt the issue of having been laid off.

DATES

Applicants are often concerned about giving dates that may reveal age, whether it's for fear of seeming either too mature or too inexperienced. If you are wondering how much to disclose about your work history, generally the information should go back about 10 to 20 years, but not more. Regarding graduation dates, you can simply write "yes" if you choose to omit dates. An employer cannot ask, "When did you graduate from high school or college?" It is acceptable to ask, "Do you have a degree?"

The main factor when deciding what details to share about dates is the relevance of prior employment to the current job goal. If relevant, include the work history. If not relevant, omit the data. If the total time with the same company was long term, say 10 to 25 years, break the job duties into promotions doing different jobs for the same company. For an example, see the sample resume for Sue Ann Montgomery in Chapter 16.

COLLEGE: DEGREE OR NOT

Deceit on resumes and application forms has been rising and consequently employers seek verification of degrees. You may be asked to sign a release for the employer to acquire a grade point average and official transcripts. It should go without saying that if you did not graduate from college, never claim on a job application that you did. It is often best to enroll in a course from an accredited program and write, "presently enrolled in a course of study in [insert course name] at [insert program name]."

DRUG AND PHYSICAL TOLERANCE SCREENING/ BACKGROUND CHECKS

Pre-employment drug and physical tolerance screening and background checks for criminal activity or validating resume content are legal and required by some employers. These are performed in order to determine physical and work tolerances relevant to the job demands. Routine urine tests check for diabetes, vision, hearing, and blood pressure but are not used for the purpose of group health insurance enrollment. Drug screening is increasingly common since a drug-free workplace is especially important in occupations that involve driving or working around machinery. For example, the Department of Transportation requires a wide range of drug screening. Random drug screening is often included in company policy and procedure manuals.

Background checks are usually required for mental health jobs and those that involve handling cash. States require background checks for people working with children. For more information on this subject, read the section below about arrests and criminal records. Employers may hire private companies to perform background checks on job candidates regarding the truthfulness of a resume. Many people stretch the truth about salaries, job titles, educational credentials, references, and dates of employment. A resume should present you in the best light without falsifying your background. In cases of embellishment, a background check often causes the applicant to lose the position. If overstated capabilities didn't get noticed during the hiring process, but the performance level isn't met, questions will likely arise with negative consequences.

ARREST AND CONVICTION RECORDS

Some states prohibit employers from inquiring on a job application form about arrests or criminal history, or to use such information as a basis for denying employment. In other states, the job application form may ask about prior felony convictions. Many varied opinions exist about how to respond. An employer may not want to rely on an applicant's written version and may require the full criminal record. Because of abuse, feds are apt to applaud full-scope background checks including criminal, credit, and employer references. The burden is on the applicant to file a charge against an employer if revelations are improperly used against him or her in the hiring process.

Although questions relating to an applicant's arrest record are improper, it is permissible to ask about an applicant's conviction record, if job-related. To have a better chance for an interview, consider writing "prefer to discuss" rather than disclosing a conviction on the application. Regulations in many states prohibit the use of arrest records for employment decisions because they are inherently biased against applicants in protected classes.

Industry-specific employers and job-specific requirements may mandate checking an applicant's criminal record under federal or state law. The employer must establish a business necessity for use of an applicant's conviction record in its employment decision, which is based on the nature of the offense, amount of

> "Sayings remain meaningless until they are embodied in habits."
>
> **Khalil Gibran**

> **"Most people give up just when they're about to achieve success. They quit on the one-yard line. They give up at the last minute of the game one foot from winning a touchdown."**
>
> **Ross Perot**

time elapsed since, and how the offense related to the job in question. But, there are also employee privacy protections. Most states' laws protect an applicant's right not to disclose any information about 1) arrests or other information that has been expunged, sealed, or impounded, 2) criminal charges that did not result in a conviction, or 3) charges that have been pardoned by a governor or otherwise protected. A background check cannot be made until an applicant furnishes fingerprints, signs a release statement, and/or provides identifying information about criminal convictions.

Access to jobs involving children and elderly, or bank, savings and loan institutions, prison staff, law enforcement, security, public schools, and health care workers generally require criminal record inquiries. Employment may be denied until the check is completed. The applicant has a right to get a copy of a background check and to challenge its accuracy. A check can determine whether the person's conviction is such that it directly or indirectly breaches the responsibility, safety, and well-being of others in a caregiving capacity—or is prohibited from depository institutions due to prior dishonesty and breach of trust. Consumer-reporting agencies can provide this information, which may be incomplete. Ex-offenders can contact the state criminal justice department's record review unit and the Federal Bureau of Investigation rap sheet to determine accuracy and clean up any errors.

Federal and state civil rights laws may vary. The federal civil rights laws protect areas where minority persons may be more adversely impacted. State laws vary. Some state laws require employers to conduct criminal record inquires.

If you can get your criminal record history expunged, by all means do so. You can recover the expense with the new career. Take advantage of clearing your record and attaining your ideal job. That's an example of redemption. Second chances happen.

SUGGESTIONS FOR THE INTERVIEW

If you have written "prefer to discuss" about a criminal history on the application and the employer questions the offense, briefly describe the situation and end on a positive note about what you learned from the experience. Regulations may prevent a job offer, but better that than accepting a job only to have to leave and go through another job search when the truth comes out. If you write "prefer to discuss" on the job application form and are offered the job, you will eventually have to complete this section during the investigative part of the hiring process. This is done in case a discrepancy appears down the road after a background and reference check.

If you were convicted of theft but are applying for a job that does not involve handling money, the employer may be willing to overlook the offense. If you are applying for a position involving securities and investments, which requires fingerprinting and a criminal background check, briefly apprise the employer about what the company will soon learn. If you are a strong candidate, circumstances may enable the employer to get around the regulations or suggest an alternative position suitable for your skill set.

Be prudent and limit your responses about the scope of your record. Do not list any arrests that are not followed by a conviction—only misdemeanors and felonies need to be included. Drug use and treatment should be discussed in terms of both disclosure and rehabilitation; you will want to present how you are on the right track. Rehearse and be straightforward without unnecessary details. Get back to the subject of discussing the job. Tell the employer

- your criminal history,

- what you learned from the experience, and

- your background will not adversely affect your job performance.

Ask in a forthright manner whether the company is able to overlook your previous error in judgment. Express specifically how your knowledge and abilities are a good match for the job responsibilities.

SOCIAL SECURITY NUMBERS AND I-9 FORMS

It is permissible to require Social Security numbers on job applications, but some states are enacting measures to limit or prohibit the use of the number, due to a rising concern about identity theft. You can leave this incomplete or write N/A (not applicable) until such time as a hire is imminent or the employer requires the information for a reference or credit check.

All employees hired after 1986 must complete an I-9 form and provide documentation that verifies their identity and eligibility to work in the United States.

Skills checklists or lists

The job application form may have a proficiency inventory section about clerical/office skills, accounting/financial skills, computer/software knowledge, and so on. Check as many categories as you can. If you are familiar but not proficient with the skill, check the category. You can discuss the matter during an interview and convince the employer you are a fast learner.

Fair credit reporting

A credit reference check form may be included in the job application. Generally, this form is only required in instances where a credit check is a job-related

> "Things which matter most should never be at the mercy of things that matter least."
> Goethe

> "Sometimes a change in perspective is better than a change in environment."
> Bill O'Hearn

necessity. You can wait to complete this form until you know whether you want the job. Interviewers should not ask if the applicant own or rents a home or car or has ever declared bankruptcy, or if wages have been previously garnished, unless financial considerations for the job in question exist. (cite: Society for Human Resource Management)

Other job application form considerations

In general, employers cannot legally ask about the following:

- **race**
- **religion**
- **marital status**
- **number of children**
- **child care arrangements**
- **sexual orientation**
- **height and weight**
- **national origin and native language**
- **parents' surname**
- **club memberships**
- **previous addresses**
- **age**

None of these are appropriate.

It is unlawful to deny a female applicant employment because she is pregnant or planning to have a child. It may be best not to inform an employer about a pregnancy during an interview to avoid the possibility of selecting another candidate who is not pregnant. The Pregnancy Discrimination Act (Family Medical Leave Act) requires that employers hold the same or comparable job for a delivering mother for 12 weeks of unpaid leave of absence, as long as the applicant first meets minimum work time criteria with the organization. For information about Fair Labor Standards, go to www.eeoc.gov.

Finally, you may not want an employer to contact your current supervisor or boss. In the application form, if asked for the name of your supervisor or manager, you may want to consider writing "Prefer no contact" or "Confidential job search." You can provide an alternative name of a person that can speak about your work performance. Be sure and give a heads-up to the trusted individual when asking his or her permission to act as a reference.

Sample application for employment

PERSONAL INFORMATION

Position applied for _____

Name: _____ (•Last) _____(•First) _____(•M.I.) _____

Mailing Address _____

Street Address_____

City_____ State___ Zip_____Email Address_____

Telephone:
Residence_____Business_____Cell/Message_____

Social Security #_____Driver's license #_____State of Issue_____

Your Social Security number (SSN) is required to uniquely identify your record from other applicants' records who may have the same name. As allowed by law, this number may also be used to seek information about you from employers, schools, banks, and others who may know you. Providing your SSN is voluntary, but we cannot complete the application process without it.

EDUCATION AND FORMAL TRAINING

Do you have a high school diploma or GED? ___Yes   ___No

Colleges, Nursing, Military, Trade, Business, or Other Schools Attended

Name & Location of School	Major Course of Study	# of Years Completed	Diploma or Degree

Please describe any special courses, seminars, and/or training that would enable you to perform the position for which you are applying:

❐ Professional Licenses or Certifications

Type of license held   No.   Current? ___Yes ___No

Supplemental Employment Information

Are you a U.S. citizen or otherwise authorized to work in the U.S. without restrictions?___Yes ___No (Proof of citizenship or immigration status will be required upon employment.)

Have you previously been employed by XYZ Company?   ___Yes ___No

Have you previously submitted an application with XYZ Company? ___Yes ___No

If yes, give approximate date(s) and for which position(s)_____

Since the age of 18, have you been convicted of a misdemeanor or felony? (Note: A conviction will not necessarily bar you from employment. Each conviction will be reviewed on its own merits with respect to time, circumstances, and seriousness, along with all other information relevant to the work for which you have applied.)   ___Yes ___No   If yes, describe:

Are you able to perform the essential functions of the positions for which you are applying? (If you have any questions as to what functions are essential to the position for which you are applying with or without a reasonable accommodation, please review the posted job announcement.) ___Yes ___No If no, please explain:

PLEASE READ THE FOLLOWING STATEMENTS CAREFULLY BEFORE SIGNING THIS APPLICATION. IF YOU HAVE ANY QUESTIONS REGARDING THIS STATEMENT, PLEASE ASK THEM BEFORE SIGNING.

I certify that all answers or statements I have made on this application or on my resume or other supplementary materials are true and correct without omissions. I acknowledge that any omission, false statement, or misrepresentation on this application or supplementary materials will be cause for refusal to hire or for immediate dismissal from employment at any time during the period of my employment, regardless of when or how discovered. I understand that nothing contained in this employment application or in the granting of an interview is intended to create a contract between XYZ Company and myself for either initial or continued employment, or the providing of any benefit. I understand and agree that, if I am offered and accept a position, my employment may be terminated, with or without notice, during the established trial service period or at any time thereafter, at the discretion of either XYZ Company or myself. I also agree to conform to all existing and future rules, regulations, and policies of XYZ Company, and I understand that XYZ Company reserves the right to change wages, hours, and working conditions as deemed necessary.

I understand that, should employment be extended to me, I may be subject to the satisfactory results of any job-related pre-employment examination required by XYZ Company, including a blood and/or urine test to detect drug usage, and by my signature indicate my consent to such testing. I further acknowledge and understand that no representative of XYZ Company has any authority to enter into any employment agreement for any specified period of time, or to assure me of any future position, benefits, or terms and conditions of employment except as may be specifically set out in a current written agreement. I acknowledge that I have read and understand the above statements and hereby grant permission to confirm the information supplied on this application and authorize any of the persons or organizations referenced in this application, or any to provide XYZ Company complete information and records concerning any of the subjects covered by this application. I hereby authorize my past employers to release information to XYZ Company regarding my employment. I give my permission for representatives of XYZ Company to check references with any and all work-related contacts, including those listed on my employment application, those provided specifically by me, and any other contacts that may surface during the course of the hiring process. I understand that these references will be confidential and I will not have access to them. I indemnify and release XYZ Company and all providers of information from any liability as a result of furnishing and receiving this information.

This release of information covers any employment record in general, including information on the following: dates of employment; position(s) held; the quality and quantity of my work; my attendance habits (excluding eligibility for worker's compensation, pregnancy, disability, and protected absences); my relationship with co-workers and supervisors; my attitude toward work; reason for leaving and eligibility for rehire; strong and weak points; whether I have had outbursts of temper, threatened, provoked fights with, or assaulted others, engaged in hostile or violent behavior, have a criminal record or any traits that would present security or safety issues for others; and other relevant information regarding my performance, skills, ability, and suitability for employment sought.

_____

Signature of Applicant   Date

WORK HISTORY

List names of employers in consecutive order, with present or last employer listed first. Account for all periods of time, including military service and any periods of unemployment or self-employment. Explain any gaps in work history DO NOT REFERENCE YOUR RESUME. Submission of a resume will not substitute for completion of this section of the application.

Total Time:_____   Current or Last Employer

        Address, City, State, Zip

From_____

        Month   Year

To:_____

        Month   Year

  Supervisor's Name and Telephone:

Salary:_____

Average hours worked per week:_____

Your Title

Reason for leaving or seeking employment:

May we contact this Employer? ___Yes ___No

Duties (be specific):

Total Time:_____   Current or Last Employer

        Address, City, State, Zip

From_____

        Month   Year

To:_____

        Month   Year

  Supervisor's Name and Telephone:

Salary:_____

Average hours worked per week:_____

Your Title

Reason for leaving or seeking employment:

May we contact this Employer? ___Yes ___No

Duties (be specific):

Total Time:_____ Current or Last Employer

       Address, City, State, Zip

From_____
      Month   Year

To:_____
      Month   Year

  Supervisor's Name and Telephone:

Salary:_____

Average hours worked per week:_____

Your Title

Reason for leaving or seeking employment:

May we contact this Employer? ___Yes ___No

Duties (be specific):

_____

Total Time:_____ Current or Last Employer

       Address, City, State, Zip

From_____
      Month   Year

To:_____
      Month   Year

  Supervisor's Name and Telephone:

Salary:_____

Average hours worked per week:_____

Your Title

Reason for leaving or seeking employment:

May we contact this Employer? ___Yes ___No

Duties (be specific):

_____

REFERRAL SOURCE: Employee referral: _____

(Name of Employee)

(Name of College)

Newspaper ad: (Name of Newspaper)

Employment Dept.:_____

Internet ad: (Name of Website)

___Walk-in ___Job line   ___Other:

SKILLS ASSESSMENT INVENTORY

If you have acquired skills in any of the following areas through your work or volunteer experience in the last ten years, indicate the total years of experience in each area. Indicate speed or proficiency where applicable. This section is required.

LANGUAGES   Speak Read Write
_____   _____ _____ _____
_____   _____ _____ _____

MANAGEMENT/SUPERVISION

___Manager   _____yrs. exp.   No. of Employees_____
___Supervisor   _____yrs. exp.   No. of Employees_____

Other/Professional:

_____

CLERICAL/OFFICE SKILLS

Data entry   ___ yrs. exp. Typing/keyboarding   ___ yrs. exp. ___ wpm

10-key ___ yrs. exp. ___ kpm Multi-line phones___ yrs. exp. ___ # lines

Filing—alpha/numeric___ yrs. exp.

SOFTWARE. Identify the types of software you have used and your skill level.

Training Working Knowledge Proficient Expert: Mark
"T"   "WK"   "P" or   "E"   next to types.

Word Processing: Desktop Publishing:

Spreadsheets: Report writing:

Graphics: Other:

INFORMATION SYSTEMS. Identify the types of software you have used and your skill level:

Training "T"	Working Knowledge "WK"	Proficient "P" or	Expert: "E"	Mark next to types.

Operating systems: Databases:

Programming Lang: Hardware:

Other:

DISCUSSION QUESTIONS/EXERCISES

1. If you have not yet completed the task, perform a Google name search for yourself. Do you need to improve your online identity?

2. Obtain a job application form (download or go to an employer).

3. Complete the sample job application form and leave no space blank—make a copy to take with you for easy reference.

4. Based on your application, what questions do you most fear an employer will ask? Prepare brief and succinct answers that end on a positive note.

CHAPTER 20

Job Interviews

The job interview will be the most important factor in an employer's decision to hire. How you handle ("package") yourself in the first 60–90 seconds can determine the outcome. This chapter offers specific guidelines for every aspect of the interview process. Before we get started, be sure and find out what an employer may know about you by entering your name in Google. As discussed in previous chapters, employers are making decisions based on what they find. This may be to your benefit or it may require the challenge of removing or changing the electronic fingerprint. Follow these strategies for a dynamic, successful interview that will put you ahead of the competition.

> *"People think I'm disciplined. It's not discipline. It's devotion There is a great difference."*
> **Luciano Pavarotti**

HOW TO PREPARE

Make a good impression at your interview by doing a little homework beforehand. Always keep at least two copies of your master job application form, resume, cover letter, references, and other portfolio or addendum documents with you. You may be asked for the materials or encounter an unexpected interview opportunity. In the case of a telephone interview, keep well-rehearsed cue cards that highlight your qualifications next to your telephone.

Employers are most interested in job candidates who communicate well, have a professional attitude, and who have researched their organizations. If possible, find out in advance the names and titles of the people who will conduct a scheduled interview. Write the names down so you are less likely to forget them when introduced. Since several people may interview you, be prepared to distribute extra copies of your resume, cover letter, references, and other professional portfolio materials.

Prepare extra copies of your interview material

Prepare interview packets. You want your interview "package" material (resume, cover letter, references, and portfolio) reviewed by all the interviewers involved in the hiring decision. If you know beforehand to whom you will be talking, address cover letters to each individual. Note a cc: for each person at the end of the cover letter so that all parties are aware of whom else has received your data. This shows foresight and organizational skills on your part. It saves the interviewer from having to copy the paperwork for another's review, and shows your sincere interest in the position. Your material will likely be forwarded to the person in charge of the hiring process if you didn't happen to get it to exactly the right person.

TYPES OF INTERVIEWS

Different types of job interviews have different styles and settings. Following are descriptions of typical interviews and tips on how to handle them.

One-on-One Interview. Your well-prepared cover letter and resume landed you a one-on-one interview. Congratulations! It was established that you likely have the skills and abilities necessary for the position. The interviewer wants to know more about you in order to decide whether you will fit in with the company and if your personality and skills will complement the rest of the department. Your goal in a one-on-one interview is to establish rapport with the interviewer and elaborate how your qualifications will benefit the company.

Screening Interview. Screening interviews are sometimes conducted over the telephone, in person, or with other candidates. A screening interview is meant to weed out unqualified candidates. Providing specific information and facts about your skills is more important than establishing rapport. Screening interviewers typically work from an outline of points they want to cover, looking for inconsistencies in your resume, and challenging your qualifications. Provide direct answers to their questions. Do not volunteer additional information that is not relevant to the question asked.

Stress Interview. Stress interviews are intended to get a glimpse to see how you handle yourself in a potentially intense situation. It would be nice if they were omitted as an interview method, but be prepared anyway. The interviewer may seem arrogant and argumentative and be late for your appointment. Don't take it personally—answer all the questions appropriately. Ask for clarification for questions you don't understand and avoid rushing into answering out of nervousness. Accept some silence until the interviewer resumes questions but feel free to ask if any clarification of your answers would be helpful.

Lunch Interview. The same rules apply in lunch interviews as those held in more formal settings, such as the place of business. The business lunch setting appears more casual, but the same formal interview rules apply. Use the interview to develop common ground with your interviewer and build the foundation on both personality and skills. Follow his or her lead in both etiquette, selection of food, and price range. It should go without saying, of course, that under no circumstances should you ever order alcohol during lunch interviews.

Committee, "Panel," or Group Interview. Committee interviews are a common practice, especially when there are several partners, management teams, or com-

> *"It doesn't matter where you are in the race —it only matters where you finish."*
> *Carl Lewis*

munity board members deciding on whether you are hired. When answering questions from several people, speak directly to the person asking the question but make brief, solid eye contact with the other people so they feel you are connecting with them as well.

A committee interview is often conducted by mid-management teams to select the top three candidates for a second interview, or when seeking candidates for leadership roles to oversee employees or work with the public. The interviewers usually gather with the candidate in a conference room for a discussion.

Behavior-Based Interview. In Chapter 6, we discussed components of various competencies other than job skills. Examples include problem solving, decision-making, interpersonal communication, leadership, teamwork, and customer service. In some interviews, you may be asked to verbally demonstrate "how specifically" you bring into play your personable work behavior. Behavior- or competency-based interviews (also referred to as performance-based interviews) are largely about your personal skills and traits, with less focus on your job skills and knowledge. For example, you may be asked to demonstrate your problem-solving skills. You will likely be asked to describe how you responded during a difficult situation in a former job. Or, think about an example when you had a difficult team effort problem.

Often, behavior-based questions are phrased in one of the following ways: *"Tell me about a time when . . . "* or, *"Describe a situation when . . . "* or, *"Give an example of a situation when . . . "* The questions focus on the **past** and the purpose is to obtain information and examples of specific competencies and capabilities you possess. The interviewer is usually interested in learning about your analytical skills or ability to collaborate with a team. You may be asked to share an example about how you dealt with a problem in the past and the method you used to solve the matter. This may be an opportunity for to use your PAR examples (see behavior-based interviews in Chapter 6).

Much of this type of interview is about likeability. How do you impact people around you? The goal is to reveal your personal capabilities and competencies during these types of interviews, not just your knowledge and job skills.

Behavior-based interviews conducted by 5 to 6 people are common. Again, the goal of the group and behavior-based interview is to see how you interact with others and how you use your knowledge and reasoning powers to win over others or resolve problems.

If you do well in the group and behavior-based interview, you can expect to be asked back for a more extensive interview. The interviewer(s) will outline a theoretical situation and ask you to formulate a plan dealing with the problem. They may ask you, "How would you handle a situation in which your subordinate doesn't agree on a decision?" or "How would you handle a situation in which none of the board members agree on a decision?" Notice that these questions are *future* oriented instead of focused on the past. You don't have to come up with the ultimate or perfect solution. The interviewers want to see how your mind works and are looking for how you apply your knowledge and skills to a real-life situation. You might respond saying, "I would give each person the opportunity to express his or her opinion, and make sure he or she felt heard."

Sample Performance-Based Interview

MOTIVATIONAL FIT

1. Some organizations ask that you support and embrace their Mission and Core Values. How comfortable will you be working in this type of environment? What additional thoughts do you have about joining their organization?

2. You will want to know the negative and positive aspects of the job as a prospective candidate. You may be asked if you have experience in these types of working conditions and specifically how felt about them. You may receive examples (e.g., negative: answering calls all day long, potentially long work hours, including nights and weekends, etc.; positive: nice work environment, opportunity to contribute to improvement/changes, a growing part of the business, etc.).

MISSION & VALUES INTEGRATION

- An example is of a facility that provides compassionate service and honors the dignity and worth of each person by listening to them and supporting them, particularly those whose social conditions make their lives difficult/challenging.

- This organization promotes a work environment that respects and values the minds and bodies of others through work behavior and interactions with others.

- This organization asks that the job applicant will act as a role model to co-workers by demonstrating respect for others.

1. A typical performance-based interview question is: **Tell me about a time when "compassion" influenced your interactions** with your co-workers or those you serve.

2. This organization is inspired by their mission and heritage that includes a personal call to "excellence" in service to others. **Tell me about a time when you have demonstrated excellence**. (The key is that this organization is looking for excellence in performing tasks, customer service, documentation/report writing, etc.)

BUILDING EFFECTIVE TEAMS

- Forms and develops high performance teams when needed.
- Creates strong morale and spirit in his/her team.
- Shares wins and successes.

> *"When difficulties are overcome, they become blessings."*
> *Proverbs*

- Defines success in terms of the whole team; creates a feeling of belonging in the team.

- Fosters open and direct communication; encourages dialogue; and supports oppositional thinking when dealing with complex or challenging issues.

- Gives team members appropriate responsibility, authority, freedom, and support.

1. **Tell me about the most highly effective team you have lead or participated in. What was the team's purpose? What made it so effective? What was your role? How did you contribute to the team's effectiveness?**

2. Sometimes teams stall-out or function poorly. **Can you share a time when that happened? What did you do? Was it corrected and if so how?**

BUSINESS ACUMEN

- Knows how our industry works.

- Knowledgeable about current and possible future policies, practices, trends, and information affecting his or her profession and the industry.

- Knows the competition.

- Is aware of how strategies and tactics work in the marketplace.

1. **Tell me about a business move you executed that worked. How did those changes relate to the global financial challenges facing the industry?**

2. **What role does a "corporate culture" play in the success of a company? Describe how you have used that knowledge in decisions relating to your areas of responsibility.**

CONFRONTING DIRECT REPORTS

- Deals with problem direct reports firmly and in a timely manner.

- Does not allow problems to fester; regularly reviews performance and holds timely discussions.

- Can make negative decisions when all other efforts fail.

- Deals effectively with troublemakers.

1. **Tell me about a time when an employee or group of employees did not agree with a new rule, policy, or procedure that you were responsible for implementing. Walk me through how you handled that situation. Why did you take that approach? How did things turn out?**

2. Some employees just do as they are told while others want to understand why they are being asked to do things in certain ways. **Give an example of a time when an employee challenged one of your directives. What was the extent of their disagreement? How did you react? Why did you take that approach?**

CUSTOMER FOCUS

- Is dedicated to meeting the expectations and requirements of internal and external customers.

- Develops a deep understanding of customers' perspectives and needs.

- Acquires firsthand customer information and uses it for improvements in products and services.

- Acts with customers in mind.

- Establishes and maintains effective relationships with customers and gains their trust and respect.

1. **Tell me about a time when you went the extra mile to satisfy a customer. What specifically did you do? How did you know you exceeded the customer's expectations? What prompted you to go that extra mile**?

2. Many times it is hard to really know what someone wants. **Tell me about a time you thought you met someone's needs only to find out later that you hadn't. What was the situation? What did you do? What did you learn from the situation?**

MANAGING DIVERSITY

- Manages all employees equitably and inclusively.

- Demonstrates cultural competence in employee and customer settings involving individuals or groups with differing racial, ethnic, national, age, gender, and physical or mental abilities.

- Creates a work environment that optimizes the ability of diverse groups of people to work together.

Past Behavior Questions

1. Sometimes cultural or individual differences can lead to misunderstandings or misinterpretation of thoughts and ideas. **Tell me about a time when either you or a subordinate had a difficult time working with someone from another race, gender, or culture. Discuss how you handled the situation. What was the outcome?**

2. **Have you ever worked for a company that had "Diversity" as a core value? If so, how did this core value impact your work? Provide specific examples.**

PERFORMANCE IMPROVEMENT/REENGINEERING

- Effective at providing the highest quality products and services that meet and exceed the needs and requirements of internal and external customers.

- Reduces variation and errors; continuously improves outcomes through empowerment and management of data.

- Is willing to re-engineer processes from scratch.

- Is open to suggestions and experimentation; creates a learning environment leading to the most efficient and effective work processes.

- Can separate and combine tasks into efficient workflow; can simplify complex processes so that fewer resources can do more.

1. Tell me about ideas you have come up with to make your job easier or improve a process. Where did the idea come from? What did you do?

   (CHECKPOINT: How does he/she demonstrate expertise in re-designing (simplifying) complex work processes?)

2. Tell me about one of the most creative solutions you developed to address a work-related problem. What was the problem? What were some of the "more traditional" courses of action being considered?

   (CHECKPOINT: Does he/she create a learning environment leading to the most efficient and effective work processes or is he/she stuck on using "cookie cutter" approaches that may not offer the most effective solution?)

RESULTS DRIVEN

- Can be counted on to exceed goals successfully.
- Is action oriented and full of energy for the challenges facing the organization.
- Spends his/her time and the time of others on what's important; quickly zeros in on the critical few and puts the trivial many aside.
- Eliminates roadblocks; can quickly sense what will help or hinder accomplishing a goal.
- Is not afraid to try a new approach without being totally sure of the outcome of experiments and will try anything reasonable to find solutions.

1. **Sometimes it is difficult to determine what our priorities should be, especially when we're inundated with work and tight timelines. Describe a time when you were faced with this situation. How did you determine what you should accomplish first? What was the outcome?**

   (CHECKPOINT: Does he/she quickly zero in on the critical "few" and put the "trivial many" aside?

2. **Tell me about a time when you took the time to finish a task or project that had been put off or "pushed to the back burner." Describe the situation and your actions in detail. What roadblocks or obstacles did you need to overcome in order to finish the project? What was most challenging about the project? How did it turn out?**

   (CHECKPOINT: Did he/she identify and eliminate roadblocks? How well did he/she articulate and achieve specific outcomes?)

Telephone Interview. You might be called out of the blue for a telephone interview, which is often meant to eliminate poorly qualified candidates up front. A call that began as a check on your resume might turn into an interview. Your mission is to be invited for a face-to-face interview. If you are ever called for a telephone interview:

- Anticipate the dialogue. Write a general script with answers to questions you might be asked. See the section entitled "The one-minute interview introduction" in this chapter. Focus on skills, experiences, and accomplishments. Practice until you are comfortable. Then replace the script with cue cards and keep it by the telephone.

- Keep your notes handy. Have any key information, including your resume, notes about the company, and any cue cards you have prepared, next to the phone. You will sound prepared if you don't have to search for information. Make sure you also have a notepad and pen so you can jot down notes and any questions you would like to ask at the end of the interview.

- Be prepared to think quickly. If you are asked to participate in a role-playing situation, give short but concise answers. Accept any criticism without becoming defensive.

- If at all possible, do not discuss salary matters on the telephone. If you are asked to discuss salary, a good response is, "I would be happy to discuss the subject of salary, but before we do, perhaps we can talk more about the job responsibilities and my qualifications to determine whether we are mutually interested." (Refer to Chapter 21, "Negotiating Salary and Job Offers" for a complete treatment of salary consideration).

- Push for a face-to-face meeting. Sell yourself by closing with something like, "I am very interested in exploring the possibility of working in your company. I would appreciate an opportunity to meet with you in person so we can both better evaluate the matter. I am free either Tuesday afternoon or Wednesday morning. Are you available either of those times?"

- Telephone script. You may decide to read your interview script on the telephone. You can pull this off if you practice it enough so it sounds natural while talking to the employer. Be aware and sensitive while you are reading your interview script and be prepared if the employer interrupts to ask for clarification or wants to change the subject.

- Be prepared for role playing. Suave employers know job candidates can bluff their way through familiar interview questions. On-the-job simulations are an opportunity for the employer to throw three to four things at you simultaneously in order to see how you act in any given situation. You may be asked to spend a day in a "trial" job setting performing various tasks. In addition, a new generation of electronic assessment instruments is on the horizon for replacing tra-

> "An ounce of action is worth a ton of theory."
> Freidrich Engels

> "I simply imagine it so, then go about to prove it."
> Albert Einstein

ditional job interviews. Lastly, you may be asked to complete some aptitude pen/pencil tests that measure ethics, attitudes, job skills, or potential for performance.

THE ONE-MINUTE INTERVIEW INTRODUCTION

The purpose of this introduction is to inform the listener, in an organized, articulate, and succinct fashion, of your specific knowledge, skills, qualifications, and career achievements within about 60-90 seconds. This has been referred to as an "elevator pitch." An interviewer cannot retain more than about 60-90 seconds of information at one time. You will want to prepare a "script" and practice versions that are condensed down to 10, 20, and 30 seconds each.

You want to project competence, self-confidence, and enthusiasm in a short amount of time. This is your "introduction" from a well-practiced script—the opportunity to talk about your interest in the position, your goals, your current circumstances, and the purpose of the interview.

Your one-minute interview introduction is your "ticket to ride" for a successful interview. It establishes your credibility and candidacy for the job. Do not make the employer work harder at the interview than you! In fact, the purpose of the one-minute pitch is to put the employer at ease and make his/her job easier. Many employers don't even know how to conduct an interview very well. They may not be willing or know how to unearth information from you about your background experience and abilities.

Your one-minute script lays the foundation for a great interview. You are confident, and the interviewer is relieved of a difficult job and impressed by your ability to share valuable information.

Often, an interviewer may begin by making a request: *"Tell me about yourself."* The interviewer is asking you to verify your competencies. How intimidating is this question unless you are well prepared? It is a mistake to respond without having a solid, well-rehearsed introduction. This is your opportunity to provide an overview about your suitability for the job, to impress the interviewer with your accomplishments and skills that match the job responsibilities. The interview introduction is the means by which you tell the interviewer why, specifically, you are the candidate the employer is looking for.

Once you have your interview introduction prepared, rehearse it with a friend or colleague until you are confident. Be prepared to customize and adapt it for different listeners and opportunities. This is why you will have to condense your one-minute introduction into a 10-second delivery (e.g., leaving a voice mail) and a 20- or 30-second delivery (e.g., first telephone contact). Write your words out on paper and practice in front of a mirror. This pre-planning activity is well worth your effort.

Regardless of how the employer begins, try to interject your one-minute introduction early in the interview process. Even if you submitted extensive paper work (resume, cover letter, references, and so forth), assume they have not read it and that they may not know about your background and qualifications.

Toward the end of the interview, paraphrase your introduction to reinforce your skills for the job. This is a second opportunity to clearly apprise the employer about your skills and career goals.

Plan to spend equal time talking about your past employment history, qualifications, skills, and accomplishments, as well as express interest in the specific position for which you are applying, why you are looking for work, and how your skills apply. Most importantly, you must convince the potential employer that you can get along with other people in the work environment. It isn't just your ability to establish relationships on the job, but ability to sustain relationships that is a key element to success.

A good interview should last 45 minutes to an hour. Rehearse what you intend to convey during your interview introduction with a friend or co-worker. Videotape yourself if possible to check your diction, speed, and body language. Use the most pertinent information about yourself to grab the interviewer with your polished one-minute introduction when you speak about your qualifications.

EXAMPLE OF AN INTERVIEW INTRODUCTION

Thank you for seeing me today. I appreciate the opportunity to speak with you about my qualifications for and interest in the benefits administrator position. To tell you a little about my employment experience, I worked as an accounts representative for nine years and have been a budget manager for the past five years. Prior to that, I worked in the private and public sectors in benefits and administration functions.

I am interested in the benefits administration position because, from what I know about the job, it would allow me to utilize my skills in budget and payroll administration. My capabilities include strong analytic thinking, meeting payroll deadlines, and screening for errors. I really enjoy performing work that requires in-depth analysis and attention to detail and working in an environment that offers new and varied tasks and challenges.

My strengths include organizing, developing, and integrating efficient systems, including financial analysis. It is my understanding that the position would require payroll accountability and software implementation, which I can do well.

"The greatest weapon against stress is our ability to choose one thought over another."
William James

"The difficulty we meet within reaching our goal is the shortest path to it."
Freidrich Engels

I am interested in this position because it appears that it would allow me to work with a variety of people. One of my abilities is to be able to diffuse angry and upset people. I am skilled at conflict resolution and helping to clear up misunderstandings. While I work very well independently and am motivated as a self-starter, I really enjoy working in a team environment that I can help make cohesive and collaborative.

I am probably the most organized person I know, especially when overseeing aspects of day-to-day operations. In addition, I thrive on the challenge of performing multiple tasks simultaneously but am flexible when pressing activities come up that require immediate attention.

With that information in mind, I wonder if you could tell me a little more about the position and the expectations required to meet the job responsibilities. Perhaps you could tell me about the day-to-day routine for the position?

Who wouldn't want to hire this individual? In all likelihood, you will not repeat every word of your well-rehearsed interview introduction. The average listener can absorb about one or two minutes of information at one time. It is also enough time for you to get across the pertinent information about how your qualifications match the job duties. For more information and help on this topic, check out www.veronicanoize.com and read "Elevator Speech Tools."

WHAT TO WEAR

You will be judged by what you wear, so dress professionally and conservatively. For any interview, dress a step above what you would wear to the job on a daily basis. In the first interview, consider wearing a blue and white color combination. Blue and white represent being a "team player" and can put other people at ease. Black and white is a "power" color combination and is more appropriate during the second interview. This combination also serves as a subtle, but powerful leverage for salary negotiations. Notice that attorneys in trial settings wear black and white power suits. Avoid wearing prints, plaids, or floral patterns, which can have a "busy" appearance and are riskier in terms of taste.

For women

✓ Dress conservatively and professionally. You are an individual, and a female, so don't try to look like a man. Some flattering, but subtle and tasteful color is good!

✓ A straightforward business suit (skirt or pant suit) is best.

✓ Wear shoes that do not show wear! Buy a new pair if needed. Do not wear open-toed shoes or thick nylons.

✓ Use moderate makeup and very little perfume. Some companies have a "fragrance free" policy due to people who are prone to headaches from scents.

✓ Wear classic jewelry. Subtle earnings, one ring, and a nice watch are sufficient.

✓ Hair and fingernails should be well groomed. Avoid long, brightly colored nails.

For men

✓ A clean, ironed shirt, and conservative tie are a must.

✓ A simple jacket or business suit is also a good idea.

✓ Shoes should be polished and not show age or wear. Wear thin, not heavy, socks.

✓ Face should be clean-shaven; facial hair should be neatly trimmed.

✓ Hair and fingernails should be well groomed.

✓ Use light cologne or after-shave very sparingly. Consider going fragrance-free.

✓ If your hair is long, consider tying it into a ponytail and tucking it into your shirt. You can always wear it differently after you get the job. Better to err on the conservative side during the job interview.

Making a good impression—three important factors

Sometimes qualifications are *not* the overwhelming consideration when hiring an individual! If you make it to the interview process, the HR representative likely thinks you can perform 8 out of 10 things in the job description. Three primary factors are what make the difference between you and another person getting the job:

1. *Interpersonal relationships* – People hire personality (chemistry), not just skills. The most qualified candidate doesn't always get the job. Personality "fit" and personal "qualities" are very important to the interviewers.

2. *Passion for the job* – Demonstrate the enthusiasm that you know you can bring to the job. Employers believe that a candidate's gen-

> *"Life is beautiful. Dress accordingly."*
> *Sonoma*

uine interest for specific job activities often translates to successful performance.

3. *Clear communication* – Your ability to communicate clearly will permeate every aspect of the interview process.

More interview suggestions

Before the interview

Arrive five or ten minutes early. Be on time. The interviewer usually interprets being on time (or 5 to 10 minutes early, but no earlier) as evidence of your dependability and professionalism. Do a "drive by" a day or so before the interview if you are unfamiliar with the location and parking availability.

Turn off your cell phone and pager! These can be "deal breakers" if they interrupt the flow of your interview.

Use breath mints. You will likely sit close to the interviewer. Even the slightest bad breath can sabotage the best candidate!

Don't smoke cigarettes before the interview. The smell of tobacco can really put some interviewers off, especially if they do not smoke. Don't chew gum. Avoid coffee to prevent feeling nervous and coffee breath.

Have extra copies of your job profile package ready. Be prepared for the unexpected. Someone who has not previously read your cover letter or resume may interview you. They will appreciate your preparation.

Expect to complete a job application. You may be asked to complete a job application before the interview. Be sure to have your completed master job application form handy as a reference. Bring your own pen and writing pad.

Remain positive. Try to put others at ease. If you feel nervous, take a few deep breaths and hold several seconds before breathing out slowly.

Address people by name during introductions. Smile. Act friendly and professional. It is especially appropriate to use "Mr." and "Ms." until invited otherwise. In some circumstances, equal respect is acquired by using first names. Doctors may respect a reputable accountant who interviews for a position and asks the physician, "May I call you John?" First name use can set the stage for equality in the working relationship. You should determine the formality appropriate when addressing an interviewer during initial introductions and the interview process.

Subconscious body language. Men especially need to be careful to not look at a woman's breast area. Although this conduct is often subconscious, it is quite noticeable and bothersome.

> "Everything can be taken from a person but one thing; the last of the human freedoms—to choose one's attitude in any given set of circumstances to choose one's own way."
> **Victor Frankl**

During the interview

Relax. Think of the interview as a two-way conversation. The interviewer himself or herself is usually nervous about conducting job interviews. Employers are not often well-trained or experienced in interviewing candidates. They may be nervous about making a good impression on you! Remember that you are interviewing the company to learn if you would like the job as much as they are interviewing you for the position.

Introduce yourself with a firm handshake. A firm handshake will do—one that is neither limp nor bone crushing. If your hands are prone to sweating, discretely wipe your hands or wash them in the restroom before the interview.

Use your one-minute interview introduction early in the interview process. This will help establish the tone for a professional interview.

Display self-confidence. Maintain eye contact with the interviewer. If you can't look them right in the eye, look at their eyebrows or nose, but keep face-to-face contact. Answer questions as thoroughly as possible and in the shortest amount of time. Avoid using nervous chatter to fill space. Enunciate every word and speak clearly. Work to establish a rapport with the interviewer. In general, fake it until you make it. Give the presentation of external calm and confidence even if you feel nervous.

If the interviewer is reading your materials, watch the interviewer's eyes and wait for a specific comment or response to any materials before you begin talking. Then talk only about what caught their attention. A common fear in going into an interview is that you will have to brag. What may feel like "bragging" to you will not sound that way to the interviewer. In fact, you should feel as though you are boasting. What may feel like bragging to someone lacking confidence, is really just coming across with the appearance of healthy self-esteem.

Listen carefully to the interviewer. Communication is a two-way street. Be sure to listen. You will impress the interviewer if you comment now and then about what they said about the job. If you are talking too much, you will not be able to learn about the job tasks and what the interviewer considers important.

Pause and reflect before answering a difficult question. If you are unsure how to answer a question, you might reply with another question. For example, if the interviewer asks you what salary you expect, try answering by saying, "That is a good question. What is the salary range for paying your best candidate?"

Speak favorably about former co-workers and employers. Don't make any negative comments about former employment experiences. If asked, re-frame stressful experiences in positive terms, such as how you resolved problems or used the situation to create a favorable outcome.

Be prepared to write. Bring a classy pen, writing pad, and preferably a black leather briefcase. Jot down any information you may need to remember, but avoid taking conspicuous notes.

Ask the questions you have prepared in advance when it is your turn to speak. It is important to have well-thought-out questions ready. (See the section about Asking Intelligent Questions later in this chapter). Good questions are key to your interviewing success and could be the deciding factor in your selection. These questions should cover any information about the company and job position you could not find in your own research, or issues you became curious about during the interview.

Hold off on any questions that may raise red flags. Too many questions about vacation may cause the interviewer to think you are more interested in taking time off than helping the company. If you ask, "Would I have to relocate?" the interviewer may assume that you are unwilling to relocate. If you ask, "Would I have to work overtime?" the interviewer may think your habit will be to run out the door at five o'clock, no matter what. Make sure the interviewer understands why you are asking these questions. Wait to ask these types of questions until after they know you are a strong candidate for the job. Then you may ask, "What, if any, are the overtime or relocation requirements?"

Demonstrate that you want the job (but not that you desperately want it!). Display your initiative by talking about what functions you could perform to benefit the organization and by giving specific details of how you have helped past employers. You might also ask about specific details such as day-to-day functions, responsibilities, with whom you would work, and to whom you would report. However, do not act as though you have no other options for work. Employers prefer to feel as though they are the ones who lucked out by getting *you* to work for them.

Use humor cautiously. Approach your interview in a business-like manner and follow the interviewer's lead when using humor. Be pleasant and courteous but don't act like a comedian. Moderate humor used appropriately can be effective. On the other hand, the use of off-color jokes or ambiguous phrases can be easily misinterpreted and halt your progress.

Control your body language and nervous mannerisms. An interviewer wants to see how well you react under pressure. Avoid the following signs of nervousness and tension.

Do not:

> ‣ Frequently touch your mouth or hair.

> ‣ Fake a cough to think about the answer to a question.

"You will become as small as your controlling desire and as great as your dominant aspiration."
James Allen

- Swing your foot or leg and fold or cross your arms.

- Avoid eye contact or slouch.

- Pick at invisible bits of lint.

- Bite your lip or force stiff smiles.

- Touch or pick up anything on the interviewer's desk or office.

- Accept coffee or a beverage unless the interviewer is drinking one as well.

- Talk too much about past jobs or brag about what you have done. Instead, talk about the employer's needs, how you can meet them, and how your past experience relates to the job responsibilities.

- Talk about financial or personal problems.

At the end of the interview

Reiterate your qualifications. Conclude with "I really want this job," which is reportedly one of the strongest reasons why one individual gets the job over another equally qualified candidate. Ask if you can telephone in a few days to check on the status of your application. If they offer to contact you, politely ask when you can expect the call.

Conclude the interview with a firm handshake and thank the interviewer. Nothing is worse than giving or receiving a limp handshake. Better to not shake hands at all than to have to press a limp sponge. During the interview, do not clasp your hands together or they will be sweaty when it is time to shake hands at the end. The only thing worse than a limp handshake is a limp, sweaty one. Exit the interview with appreciation and confidence. Thank the interviewer(s) for the opportunity to meet and express that you enjoyed meeting them.

If you are obviously not a right match for the job, ask the interviewer if he anticipates another position for which you might qualify. Or, ask the interviewer if he or she knows another employer who may have a suitable position. Thank the interviewer for any suggestions and leave with a favorable impression in the event something comes available in the future.

Send a follow-up "thanks for the interview" note the next day (see sample letters at the end of this chapter). This can be another key factor for getting the job over a candidate who did not send a thank-you note. It will serve as a reminder of your skills and etiquette when working with other people. In the brief note, mention pertinent topics discussed during your interview. If the job contact was made through the Internet or Email, send an Email thank-you note immediately; after the interview, then mail a second letter timed to arrive the week before the hiring decision will be made. Follow up with a phone call

> *"Success is blocked by concentrating on it and planning for it—it won't come out while you're watching."*
> **Tennessee Williams**

within a week following the interview. Depending on the circumstances, you can address any concerns that the employer raised.

THE FIVE GUARANTEED INTERVIEW QUESTIONS

You can count on an employer asking you five basic questions during a job interview. The words may vary somewhat, but a question will always fall under one of the five basic "umbrella" questions. This information is intended to get you to think about what the interviewer is really asking and provide the best response when the time comes.

1. "Tell me about yourself."

This is the most common interview question asked. It would be a mistake to begin with your personal life. This question is **intended to verify competencies** for the job. Your response should focus on your skills and abilities. Do not respond by saying, "Well, I guess I should start from high school or college." This is an excellent time to offer your one-minute interview introduction using organized statements about your education, professional achievements, and professional goals.

First, briefly discuss your most recent and/or relevant experience before presenting an overview of chronological work history. Second, highlight your professional traits and describe abilities such as in your PAR story and qualification phrases. Third, ask a question about the job responsibilities. After the employer tells you about a task, always inform the employer how you can perform the task. For example, if the employer tells you the job duty includes troubleshooting, say something like, "I am glad to hear that the job requires troubleshooting because it is one of the duties I most enjoy in my day-to-day routine. I value customer satisfaction and appreciate the opportunity to resolve problems." This strategy is similar to "closing" in sales. It is like putting the stamp on an envelope for completion. Continue to ask about the job duties and always follow up by expressing what contributions you could make to the organization. Allow the interviewer to know more about you and how you can perform the duties. Also, you will want to clarify any misunderstanding you have about the job and engage in pertinent conversation. Ask, "Would you like more detail about my experience or would you like to discuss any aspects of what I have said so far?" Avoid talking about personal/family matters at any length.

2. "What are your weaknesses?"

Some employers ask this potentially difficult question to assess how you respond under pressure. The key to negative questions is to answer the question and shift the focus back to the current job. Briefly answer the question about a weakness and return to talking about the position for which you are interviewing.

When addressing a weakness, follow a PNP (positive, negative, positive) strategy. First, tell them a positive strength, slip in the negative, and end with a positive quality. For example, if you are impatient and intolerant of inept co-workers, you don't want to tell the employer your weakness is impatience and intolerance of other people. Who wants to work with that? Say, "What I know about myself is that I have high work standards and good time management for project completion (positive). What I have learned over the years is that not all of my co-workers have the same work ethic, and there have been times when I may not have been as patient as I could have been when I've had to work with them (negative). However, lately I've come to look at it as my responsibility to motivate others though role modeling and engage others in a spirit of collaboration so the project is completed in a timely manner and, hopefully, to my standards" (positive). Who wouldn't want to work with that kind of employee?

One key to answering the weakness question is being honest but don't blurt out potentially damaging weaknesses that will appear like you are a problem employee. Examples include that you are frequently late or unable to finish projects and get along with co-workers. A confession of impatience often goes along with high performance and standards. Present the positive-negative-positive model that acknowledges you are a high functioning personality type and understand that you have to be more patient with less accomplishment oriented employees. Another key is telling the interviewer what you are doing to overcome a weakness. For example, if public speaking makes you nervous, say "I used to feel nervous in public speaking responsibilities, but since I joined Toastmasters, I'm more confident and comfortable."

The employer may have had a bad experience with an employee in the past and is fishing to find out if you will repeat the same problem. You might consider avoiding the question by asking what have been any work trait problems in the past that negatively impacted the job. Be prepared to address how you would overcome such problems. You might say, "I wonder if before I answer, you could tell me what negative experience the company has had with former employees that filled the position?"

Don't ever leave the interviewer on a negative note. Tell them something you learned, how you have improved as a result of some demonstrated "weakness." The interviewer may not necessarily be looking for an answer, but for a reaction, for how you deal with a stressful question. They may be looking for whether you get along with people or not. In general, the employer seeks maturity, self-awareness about how your weakness impacts others, and how you deal with it.

Some employers have formulated an opinion about a "perceived" weakness before the interview. The "weakness" question is posed, but loaded with their

> *"Good timber does not grow with ease; the stronger the wind, the stronger the trees."*
> **J. Willard Marriott**

bias. For example, an interviewer may say something like, "Would you tell me about your weaknesses because it has been many years since you worked in a university setting?" The goal is to turn their negative perception into your strength. You might respond by saying, "That is actually my strength because I have been working with the corporations and clients that this position will serve, so I have first-hand knowledge in meeting customer satisfaction."

3. "Why do you want to work here?" or "What about our company interests you?"

Few questions in an interview are more important than these. Answer them clearly and with enthusiasm. Show the interviewer your interest in the company. Share what you learned about the job, company, and industry through your own research or experience. Talk about how your skills will benefit the company. Even if you work in sales, your answer about why you want to work there should never be "money." The interviewer will wonder if you really care about the job.

"Why do you want to work here?" is a "goals" question. **"Why here, for us?"** This is not a "tell me about yourself" question such as saying, "I can contribute in these ways." One valid answer is, "Well, I am very interested in exploring that question! I don't know for sure and I think that is why we are here—to get more information." A key factor includes telling the employer why you think the job may be a good fit. For example, "From what I know about the job description, the position would allow me to use the skills I am most passionate about and accomplished in which include [insert your qualifications e.g., facilitating career planning in others]."

4. "What are your career goals?" or "What are your future plans?"

The interviewer wants to know if your plans and the company's goals are compatible. Show that you have researched the company. Let the interviewer know that you are ambitious enough to plan ahead.

Talk about your desire to improve your performance and earn more money, respectively. Be specific about how you will meet the goals you have set for yourself. Express that you are a lifelong learner and seek to continue acquiring new skills. Consider saying, "One of my goals is to work for a company that supports my professional growth. I want to stay current in my field and stay abreast with cutting-edge methods. I value attending conferences that will teach me new techniques to enhance the company's growth. As such, I am wondering what the company provides for professional growth opportunities?"

5. "What are your salary expectations?"

Your salary expectations should be based on three factors: 1) your experience and qualifications, 2) fair market value for a similar position, and 3) the extent of the job responsibilities. Are you experienced or attempting to gain skills? You

> "The point of a goal is who you become in the process."
> **Anonymous**

can't know what the job is worth until you know more about the job responsibilities—does it require 30 hours per week or 60 hours and travel? You might consider saying something like, "In light of my extensive work experience and the proposed job responsibilities, I believe my salary expectations are within the range of comparable positions." Answering questions about salary requires you to have done your homework, including getting salary survey information. Salary information can be acquired from www.salarysurvey.com, www.acinet. org, source.com, www.wageweb.com, and www.monster.com. Some sites are free and others charge a fee. I recommend that you not answer this question until you have mastered the subject. I cover this topic in more depth in the next chapter.

PRACTICE MAKES PERFECT

Practice answers to these five basic questions and to other common ones. Likewise, prepare a list of questions to ask the employer. Most interviews follow this pattern: First you answer questions about your experience and qualifications, and then you ask questions about the job. Keep the flow of questions and answers interactive. You must be prepared to ask intelligent questions. Some employers report selecting one candidate over another based on the relevant questions the applicant asked.

By rehearsing interview questions, you'll become more familiar with your own qualifications and will be prepared to demonstrate how you can benefit an employer. Below are some other common interview questions.

"Why did you leave your last job?" The interviewer may want to know if you had any problems at your last company. If you did not have any problems, simply give the honest reason, such as "I relocated to a different city," "the company went out of business," "I was laid off," "the company was downsized/acquired," "it was a temporary job," "the position lacked opportunity for advancement," "I wanted to take a different career path," or, "I'm seeking a position better suited to my skills."

Be positive and brief when describing the reason for leaving a past position. No negativity or complaining! Do not disparage your present or previous employers.

If there were performance-related problems in leaving, you may tell the interviewer that you were not clear about the job responsibilities and unable to understand your manager's expectations. By taking responsibility, tell the interviewer you learned from this and want to learn as much as possible in the interview process about the tasks and expectations for the job. Attitude and ability to get along with other people are 80 percent of job hiring success. Attempt to sound confident, even if you don't feel it.

> *"Thoughts become things — choose the good ones."*
> ***Anonymous***

Have you ever been fired? Many really good, professional people have been fired, let go, terminated, or on the receiving end of similar words. If you were fired or asked to leave your last job and are asked about it, briefly discuss the problems and be honest. This happens to the best of employees for many reasons, including personality conflicts, politics, internal replacements, lack of current skills set, etc. Show that you can accept responsibility and learn from your mistakes. You can explain the problem you had (or still have) with an employer, but don't describe that employer in negative terms. Demonstrate that it was a learning experience that will not affect your future work.

If you had an ethical rub with a former company, you might say, "New management affected business conduct and practices which led me to explore other options." It is difficult to discuss involuntary termination, but diplomacy is the best option. State the matter in the positive: "I think we were both lucky to get each other and it was a good opportunity for what it was. I gained valuable skills and professional attributions that I can take with me to any job situation." Be brief! Change the subject back to the job at hand and be enthusiastic about the possibility of a new opportunity.

"Do you prefer to work by yourself or with others?" Be flexible in your answer, but honest. Give examples describing how you have worked in both situations. If the job requires working in an outgoing capacity with people, express that you have more of an extroverted personality and enjoy working with people. If the job requires prolonged computer work, explain that you are more introverted and prefer working independently on projects. Or, you may want to express that you are "equally effective in both roles!" If the job requires a personality type that is the opposite of you, consider whether you can adjust to the stress it may create for you before accepting the job. If you are mismatched for the job, you'll be looking for another job again soon.

"What are your hobbies?" and *"What do you do for fun?"* The interviewer may be looking for evidence of your job skills outside of your professional experience. For example, hobbies such as chess or bridge demonstrate analytical skills. Reading, music, and painting are creative hobbies. Individual sports show stamina, while group sport activities may indicate you are comfortable working as part of a team. Also, the interviewer might simply be curious whether you have a life outside of work. Employees who have creative or athletic outlets for their stress are often healthier, happier, and more productive. Participating in family events demonstrate an ability to get along with other people. *Balancing life activities can result in more productive work.*

"What have I forgotten to ask?" Use this as a chance to summarize your good characteristics, attributes, and how they may be used to benefit the organization. Convince the interviewer that you understand the job requirements and that you can succeed. "Do you have any more questions?" This is your chance

> **"You must learn to turn you inner critic into an inner coach."**
> **Anonymous**

to let the interviewer know that you want the job. Add some humor by saying, "Yes, when do I start the job? I'm ready to move in." To get the job, express your interest by clearly stating that you want the job.

A frequent question for job applicants concerns having a prior commitment that would require a temporary absence from a new job. If you are a strong candidate for the position, an employer is likely able accommodate your circumstances. The applicant should deal with this forthrightly soon after the job is offered. For example, "I have a previous commitment which requires my attendance between the date of [insert dates]. After that, I am all yours. Is that acceptable?" It is not likely an employer will forfeit the best job candidate for a reasonable request.

In addition, it is best to prepare a list of potential concerns specific to the industry, company, and position you are applying for, to get clarity on the job as well as show the interviewer that you've done your homework and then some.

READY-SET-GO INTERVIEW QUESTIONS

You might expect one or more of the following questions.

Your Qualifications

What do you offer that someone else doesn't?

What, specifically, are your qualifications that relate to the position?

What new skills or capabilities have you recently developed?

Provide an example of when you have shown initiative.

What have been your greatest accomplishments recently?

What is important to you in a job?

What motivates you in your work?

What have you been doing since your last job?

What qualities are important in co-workers (or management)?

What is an example of how you solved a problem in your last job? (Remember to use the PAR technique found in Chapter 6.)

Your Career Goals

Where do you see yourself five years from now?

How will you determine your success?

What type of position or career field are you most interested in?

> "Defeat is not the worst of failures. Not to have tried is the true failure."
> George Edward Woodberry

How will this job fit your career plans?

What are your expectations from this job?

Do you have a location preference?

Can you travel?

Your Work Experience

What skills have you acquired from past jobs?

What are examples of your responsibilities and accomplishments?

What specific skills relate to this position?

How does your previous experience relate to this position?

What did you like most/least about your last job?

Who may we contact for references?

Your Education

How has your education prepared you for this job?

Do you plan to continue your education?

Are you currently involved in new learning methods?

Inappropriate interviewer questions

It is illegal for an employer to ask discriminatory questions about your family, ethnic origin, religion, age, social activities, and credit rating. If inappropriate questions are raised, you can respond in a way that protects you against discrimination or invasion of privacy. You may choose to answer or not.

Women may be asked their marital status or whether they are planning to start a family. The way to answer is to state that you don't have any plans in that area or that you already have a family (for example, a brother, mother, aunt). If asked your maiden name in an attempt to learn about marital status or ethnic ancestry, you can say that you are curious about how your name relates to your skills for the position.

If asked about religion, indicate you are confused about the relationship between the job and your spiritual preferences. If pressed, point out that any religious beliefs you may or may not hold will not affect your ability to perform well on the job.

In an attempt to learn your age, a question may be phrased asking what year you graduated. You can deflect the question by expressing how proud you are of finishing your schooling program and did so while working at the same time.

"Change is the law of life. And those who look only to the past or present are certain to miss the future."
John F. Kennedy

If you didn't graduate, simply indicate that you enjoyed studying various subject matters. You might mention that you have taken some additional classes over time or been involved in some self-learning opportunities.

Should you be asked to reveal financial information about your credit, you can answer that your credit rating is fine. Or, if you would rather not answer at all, state, "My ability to make a contribution to this company will not be affected by my credit rating."

Employers cannot ask you about health conditions or disabilities in an attempt to find out if hiring you will increase the health benefit plan costs. They cannot ask if you have had a worker's compensation claim. A safe response is, "I am mentally and physically capable of performing the job duties described," or, "I have no disabilities or health problems that prevent me from performing the job tasks and responsibilities." For more on this subject, read Chapter 19 about completing job application forms.

ASKING INTELLIGENT QUESTIONS

Good questioning skills require some technique and advance preparation. The questions you ask indicate whether you will fit in with the work environment and company culture and be the right person for the job. You are interviewing the company as much as the company is interviewing you for a good "fit." For more information about company culture, see Chapter 23 about analyzing job offers. Questions imply interest in the position and the company as well as analytical thinking skills. Any questions about compensation, overtime, travel, relocation, and benefits require timing, tact, and diplomacy. Following are some guidelines.

Prepare at least five questions. Try to reference "the company" in your questions, rather than direct your questions at the interviewer. It removes the "personal" aspect and keeps the interviewer from feeling defensive. In other words, phrase your questions in an impersonal form. For example, rather than asking the interviewer, "How much money do *you* pay?" say, "What is the *company's* salary range for the position?" This approach applies to any questions about compensation, benefits, or other sensitive topics. Some sample questions are:

"What are the key objectives for the position?"

"What are the reasons for the need for this position?"

"What are the three uppermost challenges for the position?"

"What are the company expectations for the position?"

"What are the qualities of the most successful candidate?"

"Awake at dawn with a winged heart and give thanks for another day of loving."
Khalil Gibran

> *"Success seems to be largely a matter of hanging on after others let go."*
> **William Feather**

"What are the key accountabilities or deliverables for success for this position?"

"What are the top qualifications necessary for this position?"

"How would you describe the company or department culture?"

"What organizations present the strongest competition?"

"What market trends create the greatest impact to the company?"

"What criteria are used for performance evaluations? Is there a policy about how often they are scheduled?"

"How are employee accomplishments recognized?"

"How does the company handle differing opinions or conflict?"

"What is the managerial or leadership style?"

"What are the qualities in the most successful company employees?"

"What are the opportunities for advancement within the company?"

"How much travel is involved with the position?"

"How much responsibility does the position entail? What are the expected challenges?"

"What are the company values regarding training and skills upgrading?"

"What opportunities exist for professional and educational advancement?"

"Have there been significant factors that affect the business?"

"What significant changes, if any, have occurred in the company in the past few years?"

"Does the company have a mission statement?"

"Are there other company locations?"

"What are the products or services and who are the customers?"

"What might be some pros and cons about the position?"

"How did the position become open? Is it a new or existing job? What happened to the last person who held the position?"

"Which corporate partner would be my direct manager should I fill the position?"

"When will the company make a decision about filling the position?"

"Would you prefer that I call in the near future and follow up or wait to hear from you?"

"What are the specific day-to-day job duties?"

"What are the training opportunities?"

"What are the promotional opportunities?"

"What is the history of the position and the people who filled it?"

"Where are the duties performed?"

"To whom would I be responsible?"

"Could I meet some co-workers?"

Ask questions to clarify something the interviewer said. Ask, "You mentioned you are seeking a candidate who is flexible. Can you speak more about how that applies to the work tasks?" "You mentioned that the position requires someone to restructure and organize systems. Can you tell me how you see how that would work in practice?" Avoid asking someone to re-explain an entire subject because it gives the impression that you have problems listening or comprehending.

If salary has not come up before the end of the interview, you might ask:

"I wonder if you could tell me the anticipated salary range of the position, so that I may know if we are in the same ballpark?"

Before ending the interview, ask:

"What concerns do you have about my candidacy or background for the position?"

"What do you consider are my strengths for the position?"

Acknowledge any concerns and address how a perceived weakness may be a possible strength, or offer some ways that you can strengthen the weakness. Express your enthusiasm about the opportunity to use your strengths. Follow up with a thank-you letter that addresses both of these questions. See the sample follow-up letters at the end of this chapter.

In summary, do as much research as possible before you accept a job. Make a good decision about whether or not the job is a reasonably good fit for you. Delay the desire for immediate gratification and then delay it longer. Don't just take any job that will force you and the employer to have to go through the job search again after a short while. Think about whether the job responsibilities will make you feel useful, productive, appreciated, and satisfied. Take an analytical approach about what kind of work you are best at and most enjoy; don't just think about safety and survival.

"Don't aim for success if you want it; just do what you love and believe in, and it will come naturally."
David Frost

You may not be able to ask all of your questions, but be prepared in case you have to carry the ball during an interview. Asking penetrating questions indicates interest in the job in order to impress as well as engage the interviewer.

HANDLING THE "OVERQUALIFIED" OBJECTION

This common reason for being turned down for a job is one of the most frustrating for many people. There is a trend, however, toward more overqualified job candidates competing for jobs, especially during an economic downturn. People are expressing interest in positions that provide flexibility in salary and job responsibilities. These are high functioning, professional people who will accept decreased salaries in exchange for other benefits such as a stable or growing company, future growth opportunities, a great working environment, or the challenge of learning new skills, tasks, and so forth. You may not have to accept a decrease in salary. An overqualified friend of mine accepted a lower salary to get the job she wanted only to receive a substantial raise within four months. Employers may mistakenly screen out highly experienced candidates who don't appear to fit right away. The pros and cons of overqualified applicants were reviewed by the Society for Human Resource Management. Consider the following and be prepared to address the advantages and disadvantages during an interview.

Some of the *advantages of hiring overqualified applicants are:*

1. They can get up to speed and contribute quickly, saving training time and costs.

2. They can help others develop by mentoring employees who can later help fill future leadership needs. This can bolster succession planning.

3. They can be a hiring bargain at below-market prices, make the hiring manager look good, meet goals sooner, and potentially contribute more to the company.

There are *disadvantages.* Overqualified candidates report being dismissed out of hand by employers due to being perceived as:

1. A flight risk; the assumption that they become bored with a lesser job and quit once they find a better opportunity.

2. Too expensive. They are priced out of the budget for a job.

3. Likely to intimidate others (peers and supervisors), thereby creating upside-down relationships and tensions around authority.

Overqualified candidates don't necessarily leave a job because of their qualifications; rather, they leave because they don't like the company, people, environment, or culture.

The employer's goal is to get the best employee for their money. The interviewer must perform a careful assessment: How big a risk is this employee? How overqualified is the candidate, and is this based on too much experience or the wrong level? How much is too much? Can the position be modified to take advantage of the candidate? Lastly, what stage is the applicant in? Do they have ambitious goals or want fast growth? Or are they at a point in their career where they're looking for less responsibility, money, and high visibility?

Both parties should be aware of the advantages and disadvantages of the job responsibilities and expectations over time. If possible, perform some simulated job tasks during the interview process so both have a sense of comfort with the job.

Three predictors of success include: the ability to do the work, the ability to do the work well with others, and motivation. You need all three but the third is the most important. The employer will want an answer to the question: "Why are you looking for a new job, and why is that important to you?" The employer will look for recent accomplishments and stated interests that validate those motivations.

Does the job description match your experience? Although the job may have a lesser title than a previous post, the new company may be a better, larger, or smaller organization. It can be a huge mistake to overlook overqualified candidates if they have the right skill set and experience. Express how you can fill opportunities using your experience such as coaching, mentoring, or participating in higher-level task forces. This is a greater return on the employer's investment.

If you are applying for a job opening that asks for 10 years of professional experience, but you have 25, you can opt to omit years of experience off of your resume. This strategy can mean the difference between getting the interview or not. Scale down the years of experience to ten, perhaps, to appeal to recruiters and the lesser level of jobs available.

FEEDBACK

In the event you do not get a job offer, you want to learn what you can do to strengthen your candidacy for future similar positions, including gaining insight into weaknesses that can be overcome. In order to gain feedback about your strengths and any weaknesses, call and ask questions that can help you for future interviews. Ask what went well and what did not go well. Ask what you could do differently for future preparation. Thank the person for truthful feedback.

> *"Gratitude is not only the greatest of virtues, but the parent of all others."*
> *Cicero*

> "The most glorious of human potential is the capacity to change."
> Marianne Williamson

The "thank you for the interview" letter

You must send a letter to the employer within 48 hours of the first interview. The simple gesture of a "thank-you" letter improves your chances of receiving a second interview by up to 30 percent. The purpose of the thank-you letter is to express appreciation for the interview, thank the interviewer for their interest and time spent in conducting the interview, show interest in the job, demonstrate good manners, and bring your candidacy to the employer's attention again.

There are two types of follow-up letters (see sample letters at the end of this chapter). A simple, Hallmark-type, plain thank-you note card, handwritten, is sufficient to acknowledge appreciation for the interview and express continued interest. It stands out from everyday mailings.

A follow-up thank-you letter may be more complex and elaborates about your qualifications and can address any concerns expressed during the interview. Keep the letter to one page and communicate any overlooked information, highlight a qualification, and/or paraphrase pertinent aspects of the interview. Depending on the circumstances, a thank-you letter may provide an opportunity to include references.

Send a separate note to each key person involved in your interview. It is ideal to include a pertinent point that was discussed or a reference to a comment in the interview, whether it was personal or business.

If it is clear that an employer prefers to, and has had a previous pattern to use Email correspondence, then by all means, use that method. I have heard some employers say that they attend to their Email in a much more timely fashion than letters and cards. If this is the case for your prospective employer, then carefully type an Email using most all of the same components discussed elsewhere in this chapter. Rather than letterhead, of course, you have the opportunity to add your contact information at the end of your Email, under your name. Do not try to make the Email too fancy through the use of electronic "stationery" or graphics. You may, however, consider changing the font in your Email to something simple but more visually appealing—for example, using a dark blue Times New Roman font that is one step larger in size than your normal font. You might also bold the typeface to make it even easier to read. As a check, to make sure the Email was sent in a timely fashion, and to track your thank-you letters, consider adding your own Email address to the :BC (blind copy) area of the Email. This will result in you receiving a copy of your own Email (thereby confirming that it was successfully sent), and yet, not making it explicit that you have retained a copy.

THE "FOLLOW UP" LETTER

A follow-up letter can serve several purposes. It thanks the employer for the interview, qualifies pertinent skills, addresses any concerns, and expresses a desire to pursue the next level. See the sample follow-up and thank-you letters.

> "What we anticipate seldom occurs, what we least expect generally happens."
> *Benjamin Disraeli*

Sample "follow-up" letter

Date

Your Name
Address
City, State Zip Code
Telephone, Fax, and/or Cell numbers
Email address

Name of interviewer
Title
Company
Address
City, State Zip code

RE: Job title

Dear Ms. or Mr._____:

Thank you for the opportunity to participate in the telephone interview on (date) regarding my qualifications for the (job title) position. I am interested in discussing further how my background may fit the needs of the position.

I realize that ABC Company requires a realistic and aggressive program developer. I believe that my diverse skills sets could complement your team development.

These qualifications include:

• Comprehensive knowledge of materials and applications

• Project management and collaboration skills

• Product and material costing and testing

• State-of-the-art computer technology

• Team leadership and organizational development

You posed a question about a perceived "weakness" for my candidacy by reason of the number of years passed since I was employed in a large corporation. I would like to take this opportunity to address your concern. In addition to the years I have served in large organizations, I bring a plethora of direct experience for effective program development through maintaining close ties and collaborative working relationships with a variety of corporations. I can bring strong competencies to accomplish your business strategies and goals.

Please feel free to contact me anytime. I look forward to discussing how my skills may contribute to ABC Company. I will contact you in the near future.

Sincerely,

Your name

enc: Reference List

Thank-you note card (handwritten and legible)

Date

Name of Interviewer

Title

Dear Ms._____:

Thank you for the opportunity to meet with you on (date). I enjoyed our conversation and appreciated learning more about Premier's operations and vision for growth.

I am looking forward to the possibility of meeting with you again. Please accept my sincere interest in the (job title) position and feel free to contact me anytime. Again, thank you for the time you spent talking with me about my qualifications.

Sincerely,

Sharon E. Point

Telephone Number

Thank-you note (by Email)

To: Email address (primary recipient)

cc: Email address (carbon copy and/or send a new Email to the interview panel member)

Subject: Insert Job Title – Thank-You note

Date:

Name of Interviewer

Title

Dear (insert name):

Thank you for the opportunity to meet you during our interview on (insert date). It was a pleasure to learn about the responsibilities for the (insert job title).

Please know that I remain enthusiastic about the possibility of fulfilling the expectations for the position and believe that I can deliver the accountabilities your organization seeks. I am looking forward to hopefully meeting with you again.

 Yours truly,

(insert your name)

(insert your telephone number)

"When we are no longer able to change a sitution, we are challenged to change ourselves."
Victor Frankl

DISCUSSION QUESTIONS/EXERCISES

1. Conduct research for one to three companies that you may send a letter and resume to.

2. What would you need to know about these companies to make an interview more effective?

3. What materials or documents will you include in your well-prepared job hunter's toolbox?

4. Prepare packets of your job search materials.

5. Write your one-minute interview introduction. Rehearse it in a mirror and again with a trusted person.

6. Select two interview outfits. Are they appropriate for the type of job you are applying for? Do they need repairs and/or do you need to purchase any new items?

7. Organize what you need (notepad, pen, cue cards, briefcase, etc.) to take to the interview.

8. Write your responses to the five basic interview questions from this chapter.

9. Prepare written responses to the other questions.

10. Using your three prepared PAR success/accomplishment stories. Create a picture story for each example.

11. Are there other examples of achievements you can use to help the foundation of your resume and interview skills? Elaborate.

CHAPTER 21

Negotiating Salary and Job Offers

GETTING THE COMPENSATION YOU DESERVE

Do you feel confident and sure about salary negotiations? Many people shrink and shake their heads when asked about their salary negotiation skills. It is a real sign of your self-worth when you are willing to ask for what you think you deserve. Some indicate surprise that they can play a part in the decision-making. Others assume that an employer has a fixed salary for a job. Then there are those who are good at negotiating until it comes to themselves. Why the adage "physician heal thyself" isn't effective becomes apparent.

How do you answer questions about your past, current, or desired salary during an interview? You need to be prepared to talk about compensation in order to make the most of your potential. The key to handling conversations about salary is knowing the best responses. This chapter will prepare you to discuss salary matters without giving yourself a disadvantage in negotiations.

In truth, *you train people how to treat you*, especially during salary and job offer negotiations. The employer may gauge how you will perform on the job by how you present yourself during this stage of the interview process. You should appear comfortable, have well-thought-out responses, and address matters without hesitation.

When talking to an employer about salary and compensation, don't make it personal. Refer to "the company" or "the organization," or "is there room in the policy?" This approach keeps an impersonal buffer between you and the person representing the company.

Remember, salary, benefits, and other compensation are always negotiable! ***Your salary should be determined by three important considerations: The job responsibilities, your experience and qualifications, and the fair market value for comparable jobs, not your current or former salary.***

A new job probably carries with it a well-deserved increase over your current salary. Level the field and establish equality during your negotiations.

DEFER DISCUSSING SALARY AS LONG AS POSSIBLE

Postpone revealing any former, current, or desired salary information. Never include salary history information in your resume or cover letter. One rule is: *He/She who mentions a number first loses*, or is at a disadvantage. Avoid being the first to reveal a dollar amount. A candidate's current salary is the single most important factor an employer will use in determining what to offer, if it is to the company's benefit. Since employers almost always have a "salary range," disclosing your current or past salary may be to your disadvantage, enabling the company to offer the same salary and no more. Similarly, stating a desired salary may be less than the employer had in mind. Avoid discussing salary until you determine whether you are a suitable fit for the job. Employers can be swayed to pay a new applicant more than the range if the candidate's resume, interviewing, and communication skills are impressive.

A strategy that employers will use to gain the upper hand is to ask you what salary you will accept for the position. To increase your potential for higher earnings, you want to tie the conversation about the salary to the job responsibilities as much as possible. You can't know what the job is worth unless you have sufficient information about the expectations of the position. The more you know about the job responsibilities, the more power you have to negotiate a higher salary. Salary discussions should appeal to fairness.

"What salary are you looking for?" is a common question posed by interviewers. If asked about your salary requirement during an interview, you have a couple of options: Defer the question until you know more about the job responsibilities, or, put the ball back into the employer's court to reveal the anticipated salary range.

In general, it is a mistake to discuss another employee's salary as ammunition to increase earnings. Even if you have knowledge about an apparent discrepancy, it is better to negotiate from three strengths: Your experience and qualifications, the job requirements, and salary survey data.

Following are some typical questions and possible responses.

Question: "What salary are you looking for?"

Possible responses:

"That is a good question. I was wondering what the salary range for the position is?"

"Thank you for raising the question. I was wondering if you could discuss the company's anticipated salary range for the position."

"I assume the compensation package is within the industry standards. I am open to discussing this. Perhaps when we talk more about my qualifications and the job responsibilities, we can address this."

> *"The biggest mistake you can make in life is continually fearing that you'll make one."*
> **Anonymous**

"I would prefer to discuss salary matters after we have established that my qualifications are what you are seeking for this position, or, did you want to discuss what sort of salary the company has budgeted or anticipates for the job?"

"That is a good question and certainly we will want to discuss compensation. But before we do, I would like to learn more about the job responsibilities and discuss whether my qualifications may be a fit."

"I am interested in hearing what the company's best offer is for the position."

"I am wondering what the company expects to pay the best candidate for the position."

"I am interested in hearing what the company's best offer for the most qualified candidate would be."

After responding, it's time to be quiet and utilize the power of silence. Silence may be uncomfortable, but it is to your advantage to wait for the employer to reveal the cards in the deck first. Lastly, you might consider using humor, which can help ease tension.

"Well, I think I am worth a million dollars a year, but I was wondering what the salary range for the position is?"

ABOUT THE SALARY RANGE

Before the interviewer asks first, you might want to prompt the employer to discuss the salary. For example:

"I wonder if you could discuss the anticipated salary of the position, so that I may know if we are in the same ballpark?"

Question: "Can you tell me what the salary range for the position is?"

Answer: "Between $_____ to $_____."

When the employer reveals the salary range for the position, it is important for you to keep a good poker face. By not responding, you don't tip your hand about whether the salary is acceptable or not. If the employer prompts you to respond with a look suggestive of, "Hello, is anybody home?" or "Is that acceptable?" you might give one of these responses:

"Is that negotiable?" or, "Does the company have some flexibility with that range?"

"That is in the ballpark of what I was thinking. With my experience and the job responsibilities, it appears the high end of the range may be acceptable. Of course, we will want to talk about benefits and other compensation."

> **"We work to become, not to acquire."**
> **Elbert Hubbard**

"Is that salary open for further negotiation? In light of my experience and qualifications, it appears to me that a comparable salary should be around $_____. I wonder if the company is able to make an adjustment in the salary structure in light of my credentials and years of experience?"

Outdated salary range

If your salary range is currently outdated and does not reflect the job responsibilities, you may have been underpaid. A motivating factor when seeking an equitable salary in your next job placement includes a current salary range.

Ask the length of time the salary range has been in place. If your current or former job has held a salary range for many years, it may be outdated. The same goes for the job you are applying for. The job responsibilities may have changed and you may be expected to develop the job into more demanding goals.

Possible Questions:

"I am wondering how long that salary range has been in place because it occurs to me that it may be outdated. From my research, a more current range is $____ to $____."

"My former company did not update the salary range for the job responsibilities, which is one of the reasons I am asking what the company's current salary range is for this position."

"The reason I am asking about salary and compensation is that my last position paid below other comparable positions. In light of my additional experience and training since that job, it seems appropriate to start at the high end of the salary range."

When asked about your salary requirements, don't reveal a bottom dollar. If you say, "a minimum of $X per hour," you've sold yourself short if you discover your colleague performing the same job earns more per hour. If you say a lower range figure, the employer may accept your low bottom in lieu of paying a higher dollar amount.

For example, an experienced and long-time medical transcriber for a company earned $18.00 per hour. The company desperately needed another medical transcriber. A candidate who clearly lacked confidence and interview skills, when asked about the salary she sought, answered, "Well, I just can't work for less than $13.00 an hour." The employer paused, and finally said, "Well, I guess the company could go that high." The employer would gladly have paid $18.00 an hour or more!

The strategy is two-fold: First, hold your cards close and do not reveal former or desired salary information until after you get the employer to tell you what the company anticipates for the salary range. Second, get the employer to reveal as much information as possible about the job responsibilities. This information will provide you with the ammunition about why a higher salary is merited. You will have positioned yourself to say, "In light of the extensive job responsibilities, it occurs to me that a fair salary for the position is in the range of $X to X."

If you must discuss a figure

If you must state a figure, do so at about 15 percent higher than you would accept. Remember, salary is always negotiable. You can always come down and the employer can always come up in price. But, if you start low, it is nearly impossible to go higher. Learn what other companies are paying for similar positions in order to negotiate the value of the job.

Many people say, "What if the employer thinks I'm being greedy?" You need to shoot higher than your acceptable income goal so the employer will feel as though he/she was able to bring you down, and you'll feel like you brought the salary up. The goal is to negotiate.

You must step up to the challenge of requesting a satisfying salary. When you state your desired salary, be quiet. You are only speculating if you think you know what the interviewer may think about your salary expectations. Often, the interviewer does not have the authority to agree to your salary request and will need to ask approval from their manager. Your silence can be golden.

Question: "I really need to know what salary you are seeking."

Possible Responses:

"It is my understanding that the position in this region pays between $_____ and $_____."

"Well, I don't have enough information about the job responsibilities; however, in light of my experience and abilities, as well as what I know similar jobs pay, it occurs to me the position should command about $_____ per year.'

"In light of the extensive job responsibilities, my qualifications, and the amount other companies pay for similar positions, the position should command around $_____ per year. Of course, that does not account for benefits and other compensation."

Many people express how uncomfortable they feel about salary negotiations. One hour of discomfort may be worth thousands of dollars. It's OK to feel uncomfortable. All you have to do is appear confident.

Revealing your salary history

If you are not able to deflect a question about your salary history and are pressed to answer, include your current or former benefits and provide a broad range.

> *"All labor that uplifts humanity has dignity and importance and should be undertaken with painstaking excellence."*
> **Martin Luther King, Jr.**

Discuss your total compensation, not just your salary. Make the most of your current salary without lying, but use the truth to your advantage. The simplest way is to consider the value of your total compensation. When providing salary information, include the base salary, any bonuses or profit sharing, and benefits. The latter may add an additional 40 percent to compensation. If possible, avoid being too precise, at least during the preliminary discussions.

Employers are interested in knowing whether your work performance has merited increases in compensation, and if your salary is within the company's budget. Most interviewers are not interested in knowing your salary for every previous employer.

Question: "What is your salary history?"

Possible Responses:

"When I began my employment with [insert company name], I earned $_____ per year. Since then my job responsibilities and career have progressed. Based on my latest contributions to the company, my annual compensation including benefits are about $_____per year. Although salary is not my primary motivation, a combination of benefits and salary is negotiable."

"My last salary is in the range of $_____ to $_____ (considering benefits,) which is the range I am seeking for a new position."

"Companies are paying between $45,000 and $55,000 for graphic design work comparable to what we have discussed. I have been earning only $35,000 at Demo Graphics Company while I have been mastering CAD technology. Now that I am fully proficient, I am looking forward to comparable industry compensation."

Benefits

Make the most of your current salary without lying, but use the truth to your advantage. The simplest way is to consider the value of your total compensation. When providing salary information, include the base salary, any bonuses or profit sharing, and benefits such as such as car or mileage allowance, reimbursements, professional dues, expense accounts, deferred compensation, stock options, pension or 401(k) plans, and medical or life insurance, cell phone, entertainment, lodging, tuition, professional dues, expense accounts, deferred compensation, stock options, medical savings plans, uniforms, home-based office equipment, catered office lunches, and so forth. If possible, avoid being too precise, at least during the preliminary discussions.

If the employer is not able to raise the salary, move the conversation toward other benefits.

Possible Response:

"I understand and I appreciate your speaking with me about the matter of compensation. I remain enthusiastic about the position. While the salary is somewhat lower than I hoped, it is certainly not a deal breaker. However, is there room to expand on the benefits package?"

If the employer asks you to clarify, talk about desirable options that meet your needs.

Possible Response:

"I'd like to request other benefits in lieu of a higher salary. What is available for . . .

" . . . professional growth by way of tuition, conferences, courses, and/or seminars for skills upgrading, or certification?"

" . . . flexibility in the work schedule to accommodate continuing education classes?"

" . . . travel, lodging, temporary housing, transportation, and expenses?"

" . . . costs for renewing license and special fees?"

Tuition/continuing education

When negotiating your salary with a prospective employer, ask whether tuition is available as a benefit. The value to the employer is that the company can deduct the tuition benefits without adding increased salary and payroll tax burdens. The prospective employee receives the tuition benefit in addition to salary and does not have to pay out-of-pocket from taxable income.

The importance of continuing education to your career path cannot be overestimated. In order to keep current with changing work trends and remain valuable to an employer, continue studying best practices and acquiring relevant skills in your occupation, field, or industry. This creates a win-win situation; the employee is acquiring new skills that are invested back into the company.

Flexible work schedule ("flextime")

If the company cannot meet your salary requirements, ask for a shorter work-week. You may also want to ask for flextime in order to complete a project at home without the usual interruptions at work and commute time.

> "A ship is safe in port, but that is not what ships are built for."
> **Anonymous**

Possible Responses:

"I am certain I can complete the company's requirements and even exceed expectations in less than 40 hours per week. As such, I would be agreeable to accept the salary and benefits upon a basis of 34 hours per week."

"In lieu of a higher salary, I would request a four-day work week and am certain I can fulfill the company's requirements within that time."

"As a professional, I would like to be able to work independently from home as well as at the company office. I am sure I could accommodate the best of both environments to assure the work is completed in a timely manner." Considering the amount of time for commuting, breaks, lunch, interruptions, and how you justify it, the employer may be quite agreeable.

"As a professional, I am skillful at time management. When there are projects that require uninterrupted attention, I can serve the company best working from my home office. Is that type of professional flextime available?"

Know the salary range in the market for the job

Salary information can be obtained through a variety of resources. You should know the current labor market and salary range in your area for the position when it comes to salary discussions. In order to negotiate for the salary you deserve, you must know what other companies are paying for people with your skills in similar jobs. This information can help you negotiate compensation once the employer makes an offer. If you have been with the same employer for a lengthy period of time, your salary may not have kept up with the market. Under these circumstances it is critical to focus the discussion on the market's salary range for the position.

Salary information can be found on the Internet at www.salary.com, www.salary.com, www.salarysource.com, www.wageweb.com, www.acinet.org, www.qualityinfo.org, and www.monster.com. You can find salary surveys at the library, through professional organizations, or by calling employers. Check the classifieds to learn what comparable jobs are paying.

The state employment department usually has occupational outlook and wage information on the Internet or at the local branch. In addition, there is usually an economist who can answer market wage information. Direct employer contacts are the best and often willing to answer questions about wage information. Public and private vocational counselors often call employers to learn about wage information. If you call an employer, ask to speak to someone who can provide information about general wage data. Tell them that you are not looking for a job with their company, rather, you

> *"Worry is a misuse of your imagination."*
> **Alfred Einstein**

are wondering about the general wage range for a particular position. Some employers are willing to share the information and others are not.

You can also contact a professional organization. For example, if you want wage information for medical industry jobs, call your local county medical society/organization and ask. This is also a good way to get job description information.

An excellent way to find out about comparable salary information is to call someone in your state or county who is performing a similar job as the one you are applying for. Tell him or her the nature of your call. For example, say, "I am currently interested in employment as an administrator in a position similar to your work. I don't expect you to reveal your salary, but I was wondering if you would tell me what you believe a typical salary range is for the position in this area."

Salary Increase/Performance Review

This is often the most overlooked aspect of salary negotiations that could otherwise yield thousands of dollars a year, every year, for years to come. Ask the employer about performance reviews that coincide with salary increases. Always push for timely performance reviews, which really mean scheduled salary increases. There is usually a 90-day probationary period for most jobs and you will want a raise thereafter. Then, push for a performance review with an increase in pay at the end of six months, one year, and two years of employment.

If you are unable to raise the beginning salary and are willing to accept a lower salary to begin, performance reviews (salary increases) are especially important to you. You do not necessarily have to tie a performance review to the salary increase. Many employers do not have built-in performance reviews and overlook this entirely. Obviously, this can be to the employer's benefit. Often, managers are not experienced in performing reviews nor are they prompted by employees to conduct a review. ***You should negotiate for expected salary increases before accepting the job offer.*** If you don't address this matter up front, don't be surprised when it becomes an issue down the road. Employees often bear the burden of forcing a performance review. Don't thwart the matter to avoid the discomfort of discussing a well-deserved raise.

"Nobody can be successful unless he loves his work."
David Sarnoff

Examples:

"I expect to exceed the company's requirements in a short amount of time. As such, I would request a _____ percent salary increase at the end of 90 days. And, instead of waiting one year for a performance evaluation, I am requesting a review at the end of six months with a salary increase of _____ percent. At the end of one year, having proved myself, a salary increase of _____ percent would provide a total annual salary of $_____."

Or,

"I expect to perform admirably in the position and rather than wait two years for a performance review, will the company provide a review after month nine? If satisfactory, a 12 percent salary increase would be merited."

Benefits you desire

Write a script in advance of salary negotiations. Include all the benefits you desire including but not limited to: salary, flextime, home office equipment, cell phone, personal leave, bereavement leave, medical leave, vacation time, child care, medical insurance, travel, car, mileage expenses, profit sharing, retirement and 401K plans, medical savings plan, and tuition, to name just a few. It is acceptable to bring your notes about the subject to the negotiation table.

Employment contract and severance pay

Whatever results you get from your salary and benefit negotiations, get those results in writing. Consider having a mediator or an attorney write an employment contract that clearly specifies salary, benefits, and other compensation matters. You can write your own employment contract that you and your employer sign in agreement, but it is important to get it in writing. Samuel Goldwyn said, "A verbal agreement isn't worth the paper it's written on."

Severance pay is a benefit that ensures that, if you are laid off or "downsized" for any reason that is no fault of your own, you will have some continued salary and benefits for some reasonable period of time following your termination. This is intended to allow some "cushion" for you as you scramble to find another job and need to pay your living expenses and other obligations in the interim. You should consider a severance pay clause in your written contract. This way, you know you and your employer are both on the same page before you begin working for them. A common severance pay arrangement equates to about one month's salary for every year employed. It could save you thousands of dollars in the event there is any miscommunication down the road.

Seven principles to consider

1. Be prepared

When negotiating the salary, benefits, and other conditions of employment, the more information you have, the more control and power you possess for a successful outcome. Go to the library or local bookstore and read or skim some books about careers, salary negotiations, and job interviews. Get on the employment department website or talk with a representative to find out wage and outlook information about a specific job. There are valuable resources to help you, and research is the most important single thing you can do to ensure that you get the best deal possible.

> **"It is no use waiting for your ship to come in unless you have sent one out."**
> **Belgian Proverb**

2. Recognize limits

Negotiate the best compensation package but recognize limits. You also want to maintain a good relationship with the person with whom you are negotiating. Your success in the company may depend on that person. Both you and the employer want to feel good about the salary negotiation outcome.

3. Compromise

Employment negotiations usually involve compromises between the employer and candidate. Examine what will meet your needs and priorities. Are you comfortable with a lower salary than you hoped for if other benefits are provided? Are you comfortable with the requisite criteria to earn commissions or a bonus?

4. Understand your needs

Determine what type of company you want to work for. A new company may offer stock options, whereas an established or family-owned company might offer a higher salary. Knowing what a company can do within its organizational and budgetary constraints will enable you to determine which trade-offs are acceptable. This knowledge will also enable you to walk away from a job when a company cannot offer the type of compensation package that suits your needs.

5. Prepare a negotiation strategy

If you have skills or experience for which there is demand and a company wants to fill a position quickly, your bargaining power is strong. Ask the company how soon they want to fill the position to get a sense of their circumstances. Keep in mind that if you are a final candidate, the difference between the increase in the salary you require and the company's offer is not going to matter to the company. Six to ten thousand dollars for a good employee to the company isn't a big deal to the company, but it is to you.

If, on the other hand, you are one of several good candidates, lesser compensation may be a factor in determining who gets the job. Use your information when deciding whether to pursue a higher salary.

Negotiate the best outcome for yourself and make a request for everything that you want. Of course, be reasonable so as to not appear arrogant. Compromise means that you may not get everything you want. But by not asking for everything you want, you may sell yourself short on what you could have otherwise received.

The employer is aware that salary negotiations can be awkward and may be counting on your discomfort to increase the company's gain. Regardless of feelings of embarrassment or tension, pursue salary negotiations in a professional manner. If you need a break to stop the process, use the restroom, seek a bever-

> "When I think about work, it's mostly about having control over your destiny, as opposed to what's out there."
> **Gary Sinise**

> "The great thing in this world is not so much where we are, but in what direction we are moving."
> **Oliver Wendell Holmes**

age, or use another excuse. This helps bring new focus and effective negotiations to both parties. It may be wise to take 24 hours to "sleep on it." Tell the interviewer you want to discuss the matter with your spouse. Read Chapter 23, "Analyzing Job Offers." to help you decide whether to negotiate further if important elements of the offer are missing.

Be flexible about some of your compensation requests. If you are willing to make a few trade-offs, you may increase the value of the total package. Explore different options and creative benefit possibilities. The goal is to achieve as many of your objectives as are acceptable to the company. Withdraw requests that might be problematic to the company in return for areas where the company has more flexibility.

At the end of the negotiations, however, you must determine which elements of the employment package are critical to you. Decide if giving up an essential benefit will leave you feeling resentful and likely to be looking for another job soon.

6. Seek equity

Most employers want to be fair and reasonable, within budget constraints and organizational structure. Justify requests in terms of equitability and market analysis. Relocation may incur a higher cost of living, justifying increased compensation. Look for comparable benefits offered to select employees, such as a percentage of the company's stocks, and request consideration for the same treatment. Equitable compensation is a negotiable principle.

7. Quit negotiations when there is a "win-win"

You want to end negotiations with both parties feeling good about the salary/benefit discussion as well as knowing every opportunity has been explored. Accepting too little may impact your earning potential in the future. If you come on too strong, you can damage the relationship with the person in the negotiations. Know when to stop negotiating and make a decision to accept the offer. How you negotiate can influence, for better or worse, your success with your future earnings.

You are apt to gain more respect from an employer if you negotiate your salary with a strong sense of self-worth. Again, *you "train" people how to treat you* with your behavior, with respectful and forthright communication.

DISCUSSION QUESTIONS/EXERCISES

1. What is the salary range for similar positions (in your region) for which you are applying?

2. If you do not know, how can you acquire this information?

3. Does the job for which you are applying fall within that range?

4. Determine your salary requirements prior to interviewing. What is your minimum salary range for accepting a position?

5. Does that match salary survey data?

6. Practice answering salary-related questions with a question.

7. Practice deferring salary-related questions from the interviewer.

8. Be prepared to discuss a salary range based on your research and your salary needs.

9. Determine your benefit and compensation package needs and wants. What benefits are important to you?

10. Which are you willing to give up and which are deal breakers?

CHAPTER 22

Re-Packaging Veteran Job Seekers

With hundreds of thousands of military talent transitioning or separating from known responsibilities and active work demands, the question for many is, "How can I put my education and skills to use now?"

In writing this chapter for Veterans, the first question that I asked was, "What are the unique issues that Veterans exhibit and face in re-employment to the civilian labor market?" I sought insight from colleagues who help Veterans in career management services in the private and public sectors to help answer this question.

The first Veteran representative responded to the question by saying, "transferring military experience into civilian speak." Identifying transferable skills is a common challenge that most job seekers experience when in career transition. Similarly, the homemaker who comments, "I've only been a mom and wife for the past 11 years" discovers more accurately that this translates to "highly effective coordinator, organizer, and account manager, with strong resource management skills. Proven abilities in communicating with a variety of personality types. Adept in multi-tasking and time management. Able to work independently as well as collaborate with peers and supervisors. Talent for incorporating a positive team environment." And, this is only the tip of the iceberg when we begin shaking out the transferable skills tree.

Many veterans are likely well-qualified and skilled. A transferable skills analysis is much akin to peeling layers of an onion. Our goal is to unearth your core competencies, qualifications, enthusiasm, interests, and abilities.

What prevents Veterans from identifying their transferable skills and getting in to get some help? One response was a "Pride Factor." The vet-rep I consulted indicated that some vets think it is "weak" to go to the employment department, job council, worksource, and other federal programs designed to provide employment-related assistance. Please consider that these kindly organizations are motivated to establish your eligibility for services to ensure that grant monies keep rolling in. Their jobs exist because of Veteran participation.

If you insist on going it alone, consider exploring a few key resources. The wide array of resources available to Veterans is impressive. Three Internet sites recommended for research that include job postings, resume help, career research, and Veteran information are www.jobcentral.com/vetcentral, www.hirevetsfirst. gov, and www.military.com/Careers/Home. If you decide you would like help, schedule some time together with a Veteran representative or vocational rehabilitation counselor for career transition assistance.

Demobilization sites are established for briefings about insurance, health benefits, legal considerations, and a plethora of information. In addition, perform a Google search by keying in the words Uniformed Services Employment and Reemployment Rights Act (USERA) for information about eligibility and job entitlements.

A second issue to some Veterans is the *"I Want It Now"* syndrome common to other job seekers (and our culture). Learning how to cultivate patience to obtain a job that is the right fit can be challenging. For some who are about to lose their truck and house, the demand for a job today appears vital. Allowing a vet rep or vocational counselor to help prioritize and solve initial needs can be very helpful when there is no job today on the calendar. Recall that the average job seeker takes about four months to secure employment.

Another concern Veterans reportedly experience is self-assertiveness in the job interview in spite of self-assurance in other life management skills. Veterans don't toot their own horn because they are taught to be humble around peers. Interviewing for jobs requires a certain amount of self-promotion to prove the case for hiring one applicant over another equally qualified candidate. The need to overcome reticence and false humility or pride is perceived as an *obstacle*. Consider if self-reflection is necessary and review the techniques in the chapter about job interviewing skills. This trait is notably common among women who grew up hearing it is unattractive to boast.

Water must seek its own water table level. You may feel like you sound like a braggart, but to the interviewer, you are simply providing information so they can make a determination about hiring the most qualified or personable person for the job. Interviewers are not capable of reading minds. You must tell the potential employer about your strengths and talk about the kind of work responsibilities that you perform well.

MILITARY TO CIVILIAN TRANSITION

Transferable skills analysis is about telling employers what you can do in vocabulary that they can understand. Military jargon or acronyms must be excluded from your language and resume content—and the use of corporate speak must be included if you are applying for employment in the private sector. Employ-

> *"Everyone's a pacifist between wars. It's like being a vegetarian between meals."*
> **Colman McCarthy**

> *"The woods are lovely, dark and deep,*
> *But I have promises to keep and miles to go before I sleep,*
> *And miles to go before I sleep."*
> **Robert Frost**

ers want to know how the skills you used in the military translates to private sector jobs. If, for example your background includes "Military Vehicles Fleet Management," clarify this as "Management of over 500 fleet vehicles valued in excess of $20 Million. Accomplished 100 percent of operational objectives for two consecutive years." Can you see the difference in impact? Change your military language to civilian talk. Flush out qualifying and quantifiable skills. Use results-oriented vocabulary.

Talk the talk

Most job seekers are challenged by talking about their transferable skills analysis, qualifications, achievements, and skills in verbal and written form. Veterans who want to transfer military experience into a successful and satisfying civilian job must go through many of the same processes outlined in this book.

For help with aligning your military experience, training, and education with civilian functional competencies and needs, use the Military Skills Translator in www.hirevetsfirst.gov/militaryskills. Go to the Crosswalk Search to find matching civilian occupations that are similar to your military occupation classification. For occupations that interest you, you can view a summary report that will provide job description language and other information.

Use the OLMIS site www.qualityinfo.org. Ron Booker, vet rep, states, "We tend to buttonhole ourselves and do not realize that there are many options out there." If, for example, you want to work as a welder in a specific location, this site can help with research to accomplish your goal.

Career transition is not for everyone. Some might say, "I've always been a plumber and always going to be a plumber." They may not need to explore. Others may say, "I'll take any job or don't know what I want to do." These concerns are not so dissimilar to every job seeker. Repackaging skills sets is frequently about analyzing transferable skills and how to promote self.

Google can often help with acquiring keywords in job titles. In the example of a background of "Military Vehicles Fleet Management," use Google to enter the words, "Fleet Manager Job Description" to obtain job descriptions (and job openings) and read the civilian job speak for this position. Repeat the process for any job titles or occupations of interest. If you need to speak with someone about how to reflect your capabilities, seek out a qualified professional or local employment Veteran's representative. Resources vary from state to state, and there are re-integration teams and career transition programs designed for this purpose.

A key to your success may be letting someone get to know you. Computer research is a good strategy, but it does not replace building trust and rapport with a professional who can help unearth your skills sets and goals. We are

> *"There never was a good war or a bad peace."*
> **Benjamin Franklin**

designed to be in relationship with others. Allow someone to listen and ask questions about your military service, family, and how you are now.

Perhaps you got injured and need help explaining how that has affected you. That is a good start in the beginning. "The physical is more than the physical," says Jim Booker, Veteran's Program Coordinator, who encourages veterans to tell people about your injuries in order to overcome obstacles. Until you have exhausted your options, Veteran representatives are willing to go the distance when you can't do it alone. Jim states, "Dream! Set expectations! Latch on to something with passion!" And, as my fitness coach says, "How bad do you want it? You got to want it!"

A fictitious sample resume follows that was provided by Veterans Services.

Evan Jorgenson

EDUCATION
COLORADO STATE UNIVERSITY, Denver, CO President's List
Bachelor of Science Degree in History (2008)

COLORADO ARMY NATIONAL GUARD   2005 – Present
Reintegration Team Member/Medical Holdover, Denver, CO (2007 – Present)
Assist in the reintegration of returning service members to the State of Colorado. Connect service members to appropriate public and private sector resources. Establish two Student Veterans Resource Centers at Colorado colleges and universities. Gain support and funding through communications with legislative and school officials. Research issues unique to veterans. Create business plan.

Key Achievements
- Recognized for contributions in creating a SVRC
- Received support for the SVRC from various state Senators and Representatives

Transportation Team Leader, Camp Phoenix, Afghanistan (2006)
Served as team leader for a five-member team in a transportation platoon. Provided training, supervision, technical guidance to subordinates. Reviewed and evaluated soldier performance in military development. Participated in organizing convoys for arriving personnel and delivering supplies. Assisted in resolving problems with pay, clothing and equipment.

Key Achievements
- Successfully trained and licensed over 70 soldiers in the Armored Humvee in a combat zone.
- Promoted to the rank of Sergeant and team leader as a result of superior service.

Motor Transportation Operator, Portland and Eugene, OR, Rutland, VT
Assisted in recruiting new members into the Army National Guard. Participated in Hurricanes Katrina and Rita relief efforts. Performed training and licensing of new recruits in military vehicles. Operated wheeled vehicles and equipment. Conducted monthly inspections on a variety of vehicles. Served as radio transmission operator in a volunteer basis. Assisted with coordination of procurement and supplies.

Key Achievements
- Received Army Achievement Medal for voluntarily raising over $800 in proceeds for the unit fund and Family Support Group.
- Received Army Achievement Medal for company communications, enabling B Company to be fully operational.

COLORADO STATE UNIVERSITY   2004 – 2005
Veteran's Certification Officer Assistant, Portland, OR
Assisted more than 500 veterans in certification for monthly G.I. Bill benefits, gathering military transcripts, and providing degree requirements. Researched and gathered student information for administration. Provided student assistance, including university and graduate entrance.

Key Achievements
- Established trust and rapport for relationship building with incoming veterans.
- Exhibited motivation, dedication, and the provision of high-quality assistance to each student.

345 Van St. Colorado Springs, CO 80014 Cell 305.722.4569 evan.jorgenso@aol.com

Analyzing Job Offers

Analyzing job offers can bear a strong resemblance to looking for a marriage partner. In the beginning, both the employer (i.e., potential "mate") and candidate present themselves as attractively as possible, revealing few negative characteristics. Marriage, like a job offer, has phases of negotiating rules and roles. After the honeymoon phase is over, it is sometimes apparent there was misrepresentation—whether consciously or unconsciously. When we convince an employer (or target of our desire) that a perfect match exists, but remain unclear about expectations or challenges, things can unpleasantly unravel.

A variety of considerations and emotions come into play when deciding upon a job offer. To avoid a potentially bad experience, anticipate what these might be. Consider the questions in this chapter. If you do not know the answer, you may require more information as part of your decision-making process.

> *"I think honestly it is better to be a failure at something you love than to be a success at something you hate."*
> *George Burns*

IS THE JOB A GOOD FIT?

Do the elements that matter most for your job satisfaction exist? These include job title, your relationship to the person you report to, job responsibilities, opportunity for advancement and professional growth, base salary and incremental increases, and benefits. If the job is financially rewarding but without other psychological rewards, or conversely, psychologically rewarding but short on income, will you be happy? What personal criteria do you want it to meet? Is the commute tolerable? Will you use your preferred strengths and skills? Is it intellectually or interpersonally challenging? Does it provide leadership or opportunity to lead? Does it offer freedom and independence? Will you be able to influence change and develop programs or projects? Are important elements missing, and if so, what are they? Can you negotiate for these components?

COMPANY CULTURE

Finding the right job includes assessing organizational culture and working in an environment consistent with your beliefs, values, behaviors, and standards. Working at an organization with opposing perspectives will result in toxic feelings. Conversely, a good organizational "fit" compliments your values and instills feelings that your talents are appreciated.

> **"Sometimes you have to take the leap and build your wings on the way down."**
> **Kobi Yamada**

How you were treated during the interview process is a gauge of organizational culture. Interviewer words and behavior is a glimpse of the overall tone. Assess the phrases used and questions posed during the interview and whether a theme or tone exists. How were your responses to questions treated? Leadership and a supervisor's attitude will also directly affect the quality of your work experience. It is unlikely that a work environment will totally parallel with your values. You can, however, acquire a job in a company where the culture and your preferred values are similar.

Consider the following questions: What would inspire you to say positive comments about a company? What would inspire you to stay with a company? What would inspire you to strive to be your best with a company?"

Is the job a "transitional" (bridge) job?

Can you accept this job and still search for a better fit? Can the temporary position keep the lion off the front door and pay bills while resolving a host of unemployment-related problems? Consider what short-term and long-term goals the job will meet. Do opportunities exist within the organization for a suitable fit? How will the experience likely benefit you? Will you have any regrets if you accept the job? Are you accepting the job based on fear of not receiving another offer? Can you financially and emotionally afford to keep searching?

Salary/benefits package

Assess the total value of the job offer package, including medical insurance, retirement, anticipated raises, and so forth. Does it meet your obligations and expectations? Exceed them? Could further negotiations improve the offer? If the offer is lower than expected, can you accept the offer without feeling too disappointed or resentful?

Industry and company

Is the job in the industry you enjoy? Does the company provide services and products you value? Is the company a good fit but the industry not, or conversely, the industry is appropriate but the company is questionable? What are past trends or future projections in the company and industry? Is the company financially stable? How are employees treated in this work? Are there professional growth opportunities that match your goals? How are promotions determined? Are there training programs to keep you current and advancing in your career? What is the turnover rate and what factors contribute to this? Are the people you will work with like-minded, differently minded, or both, and is this your preference? What are the interpersonal relationships like in terms of trust, interaction, teamwork, or independent autonomy? Are you aware of any "red flags"? Will you receive adequate equipment and support to effectively perform the job? What is the dress code? Is the overall culture suitable? What about work hours? Will the job be compatible with your family and other personal aspects of your life?

Compromises are often made when deciding whether to accept a job offer. The question is: Is it good enough for right now? Accepting a job offer is not a lifetime commitment even if you desire it. Change happens, especially in today's rapid workplace turnarounds. Don't accept the wrong job because you lack information, don't like the work, think it is the only thing you are qualified to perform, or fear it is the only job offer you will ever get. The way you can make the best decision for yourself is getting as much information as possible, asking questions, and listening.

Epilogue

Recall that when this book began, you were offered the metaphor of a Global Positioning System (GPS) to represent the "orienting" benefit this book might serve for you. By completing the readings and exercises in this book, the GPS has guided your climb to the top of the career search preparation "mountain." It has guided your hike to your core values and transferable skills. The sheer exertion of assessing who you are has moved you into new territory. Trail markers (your resume, answers for tough interview questions, unveiled core competencies, master job application form, networking contacts, and salary negotiation skills) kept you on the right path as you identified the work environment that would bring you the most satisfaction.

Every step you took through the landscape of your abilities and preferences opened vistas of the financial and personal compensation that you seek in the workplace. Listing your transferable skills in strong statements that verify your past job performance is a stout walking stick that you will use on your entire trip. Your backpack is now full of wonderful tools that attract the notice of people making hiring decisions. You know who can help you locate job openings in your chosen field. You are confident and ready, with dozens of contacts already made in your community. You know how to translate your skills into qualifications for a career transition. You have mapped out what you need to do to be competitive, such as continuing education and certification.

You have done the necessary legwork and are now confident when speaking to employers on the phone and in person. Your resume is the flint that sparks an employer's interest in you as a potential employee. You can describe your "hard" and "soft" skills during an interview. Your body language reinforces your introductory "pitch" to an employer. And you know how to guide negotiations during job offers. You are at the top of the mountain. You are contemplating your choices: does the prospective job fit your likes and dislikes, your wants and needs?

Step by step, you have used the resources in this book to move forward on the path of your life/work. It is a journey that will affirm your essence and place in the world.

In closing, I hope you have the time of your life in your career pursuits and wish you all the success in the world as you explore the vistas and summits of new mountains.

Warm Wishes, Linda K. Rolie

Appendix

Internet Resources

• General Employment and Industry Information

www.qualityinfo.org – provides job listings, transferable skills identification section, and labor market information

www.jobsalaries.com

www.salarysurvey.com – Do this site map. You'll be there for hours.

www.about.com – On About.com: The Human Internet, topics include career planning, telecommuting, job searching, and information on specific careers areas.

www.iseek.org – The Internet System for Education and Employment Knowledge provides career planning, training, and an employment center.

www.myjobsearch.com – On My Job Search.com, you will find information and classifieds.

www.jobprofiles.org – Job Profiles lists interesting job profiles, information, and job facts.

www.BetterWorkplaceNow.com – lots of fun and informative articles

• Internet Job Banks / Job Search Sites

www.job-hunt.org

www.careers.org

www.employmentguide.com

www.weddles.com – a research, consulting, publishing and training firm dedicated to helping people and organizations maximize their success in recruiting, retention, job search and career self–management

www.joblocator.com – like a "meta–search" job locator—directory of other job search sites, some of which are unique

www.jobbankinfo.org – America's Job Bank

www.Monster.com

www.Indeed.com

www.6figurejobs.com – 6 Figure Jobs includes a job bank, career resources, recruiter links, and a resume bank.

www.hotjobs.yahoo.com

www.careerbuilder.com

www.execunet.com – may be fee for service and $100,00 plus jobs

www.hundredk.com

www.executivesonly.com

www.CareerShop.com

www.careermag.com

www.softwarejobs.com

• *Education and Training Sites*

www.petersons.com/ugchannel/ – Peterson's Guide—information about college programs, including admissions testing, financial aid, etc.

www.fastweb.com – Scholarship information if you're considering going back to college.

• *Career Information*

www.stats.bls.gov – Bureau of Labor Statistics—Home of the Occupational Outlook Handbook and tons of employment information

www.bls.gov/oco – Direct link to the Occupational Outlook Handbook

• *Resource Guides / Other Career Information*

www.jobstar.org/index.php

www.careerjournal.com – the *Wall Street Journal*'s career-oriented information website—chockfull of helpful articles on most every aspect of job searching.

www.quintcareers.com/index.html

• *Finding Federal Jobs*

www.federaljobs.net

www.studentjobs.gov

www.jobsfed.com

• *Interviewing*

www.fiveoclockclub.com

www.getouttoday.com/career/interview/diffcltquest.htm

• *Government Job Search / City, State, Federal, and Other Public Sector Jobs*

www.careersingovernment.com

www.jobsearch.usajob.opm.gov

• Resume Assistance

www.lindarolie.com – the website of yours truly

www.resumeplace.com – help with writing resumes for federal jobs

www.federaljobs.com – software and assistance for federal job resumes

www.eresumes.com

• Help with Researching Companies

www.hoovers.com

www.vault.com

www.corporateinformation.com – subscription service with a free trial offer

• Understanding and Implementing a Budget

www.financialplan.about.com/cs/budgeting/a/Budgeting101.htm – articles, worksheets, and tools

• Internet Technology Positions

www.computerjobs.com

www.brassring.com

• Professional Organization Websites

www.shrm.org – information about human resource issues

www.astd.org – information about training and development issues

• Flexible Work Options

www.workoptions.com – tools for negotiating a flexible work arrangement at your job

www.swt.org – shorter work time website links to related activities

• Self–Assessment Tool

www.lindarolie.com – Assessments, Myers–Briggs Type Indicator and Strong Interests

www.psychometrics.com/onlinetest

Princeton Review Career Quiz

www.princetonreview.com

Keirsey Temperament Sorter II

www.keirsey.com

Myers–Briggs Type Indicator

www.humanmetrics.com/

Motivational Appraisal of Personal Potential

www.assessment.com/

Keirsey Temperament Sorter

www.advisorteam.com/user/ktsintro.asp

• *Miscellaneous Career Related Sites*

www.stats.bls.gov/emp/ – Occupational Outlook Handbook

www.dbm.com/

www.sba.gov

www.bls.gov/bdm/home.htm – Business Employment Dynamics

Index